The
Economist

WALL STREET

OTHER TITLES FROM
THE ECONOMIST BOOKS

The Economist Desk Companion
The Economist Economics
The Economist Guide to Economic Indicators
The Economist Guide to the European Union
The Economist Numbers Guide
The Economist Style Guide
The Guide to Analysing Companies
The Guide to Business Modelling
The Guide to Financial Markets
The Guide to Management Ideas
The Dictionary of Economics
The International Dictionary of Finance
Business Ethics
E-Commerce
E-trends
Globalisation
Improving Marketing Effectiveness
Managing Complexity
Measuring Business Performance
Successful Innovation
Successful Mergers

Pocket Accounting
Pocket Director
Pocket Economist
Pocket Finance
Pocket Internet
Pocket Investor
Pocket Marketing
Pocket MBA
Pocket Money
Pocket Negotiator
Pocket Strategy

The Economist Pocket Asia
The Economist Pocket Europe in Figures
The Economist Pocket World in Figures

WALL STREET

Richard Roberts

THE ECONOMIST IN ASSOCIATION WITH
PROFILE BOOKS LTD

Published by Profile Books Ltd
58A Hatton Garden, London EC1N 8LX

Typeset in EcoType by MacGuru
info@macguru.org.uk

Printed in Great Britain by
St Edmundsbury Press, Bury St Edmunds

A CIP catalogue record for this book is available
from the British Library

ISBN 1 86197 464 7

Contents

To Sarah

1 What is Wall Street?

Like the dollar bills on which its business is based, Wall Street has two faces. On one side, it is a place – a street in lower Manhattan. On the other, the term is shorthand for an industry – the US wholesale financial-services industry. Since Wall Street, the place, is the hub of this industry, much of the time the two meanings overlap. But lower Manhattan is by no means the totality of the US wholesale financial-services industry, and so sometimes the term embraces other locations and institutions.

The US financial-services industry has two distinct parts: Main Street financial services and Money-centre financial services. Main Street financial services are retail services, that is, they meet the needs of individuals and small businesses for cheque and savings accounts, loans and mortgages, investment and insurance. Money centre activities comprise a range of wholesale financial activities, meaning that they serve the requirements of corporations, the government and other public bodies (such as states and municipalities), public agencies and the financial-services industry itself.

Wall Street, the place, is the leading US money centre and the foremost US location for the conduct of wholesale financial services. However, it is not the only money centre in North America: Boston, Chicago, Cincinnati, Los Angeles, Philadelphia, San Francisco and Toronto are also significant. But New York is without doubt the leading US money centre for international financial activities, an arena in which its peer group consists of the world's other leading international financial centres: London, Tokyo, Hong Kong, Singapore, Frankfurt and Zurich.

The Wall Street money centre

Wall Street, like other important money centres, comprises a matrix of wholesale financial sectors, financial markets, financial institutions and financial services industry firms. The principal financial sectors are:

- securities industry
- commercial banking
- asset management
- insurance.

The securities industry is the most prominent and populous Wall Street sector. Traditionally some of the activities of the securities industry were conducted by investment banks while others were undertaken by broker-dealer firms, but today the large securities industry firms conduct the full range of securities activities. Investment banking activities include the underwriting of new issues of securities (stocks and bonds) and the provision of corporate advisory services, especially regarding mergers and acquisitions. Broker-dealer activities focus on the trading of securities. Securities industry firms also undertake asset management and the development of new financial instruments.

Commercial banks receive deposits from depositors, both individuals and businesses, and use these funds, sometimes with other monies, to provide loans. Some lending is at a retail level, to individuals and small businesses, and other lending is a wholesale activity, with clients such as corporations, governments and the financial-services industry. Commercial bank employment in New York City represents close to 6% of the US total, about twice the number of jobs that might be expected in a city of its size. This suggests that at least half of the city's bankers undertake wholesale commercial-banking services, while the other half provide retail services.

Asset management is the activity of managing the funds held by institutional investors. The principal institutional investors are insurance companies, pension funds and mutual funds. These institutions receive flows of money from individuals and businesses insuring their lives and property, and from individuals saving for retirement or investing to build capital. Sometimes these funds are managed in-house by appropriately skilled investment managers, and sometimes the management is subcontracted to the asset management units of investment banks, banks, insurance companies or specialist asset-management firms. In either case, the investment managers are set performance targets. Their remuneration is usually based on the volume of assets managed.

Many US insurance companies have their headquarters in New York City or have a significant presence there, from which they service corporate clients and deal with the national and international insurance markets. As in the case of the commercial-banking sector, perhaps half of New York City's insurance industry workforce operates at the wholesale level and half serves a retail clientele.

Wall Street markets

Financial transactions are conducted in two types of financial markets: formally constituted exchanges and over-the-counter (OTC) markets. Wall Street is host to some of the world's leading financial and commodities exchanges, which employ more than 20,000 people in New York City. They are:

- New York Stock Exchange
- American Stock Exchange
- New York Board of Trade (coffee, sugar, cocoa and cotton)
- New York Mercantile Exchange (metals and energy)

Chicago is host to three exchanges that form a vital part of the US wholesale financial-services industry, specialising in trading futures and options contracts relating to a range of commodities and financial derivatives. They are:

- Chicago Board of Trade
- Chicago Mercantile Exchange
- Chicago Board Options Exchange

The Kansas City Board of Trade is an important market for trading grain futures and options and also trades stock index derivatives.

The five US regional securities exchanges also form part of the national securities industry matrix. They are:

- Boston Stock Exchange
- Chicago Stock Exchange
- Cincinnati Stock Exchange
- Pacific Stock Exchange (in San Francisco)
- Philadelphia Stock Exchange.

In the OTC financial markets, trading takes place by negotiation between the parties to the transaction. These markets have no physical market places – transactions are carried out by telephone and computer. The massive foreign-exchange market, the short-term money market and the US government debt market are OTC markets in which currencies, deposits and securities are traded between people working in the industry. To the public, the best-known OTC market is the NASDAQ (National Association of Securities Dealers

3

Automated Quotation System), on which stocks are traded electronically.

Wall Street institutions

A number of important money-centre financial institutions are located in New York. The city is home to several clearing houses and securities depositories that are crucial to the operation of the securities and banking sectors. The New York Clearing House is the oldest and largest US bank payments clearing corporation, which processes $1.4 trillion payments per day for more than 1,000 US and foreign financial firms and institutions. The Clearing House Interbank Payments System (CHIPS) is an electronic payments system that handles 95% of all dollar payments among countries, including foreign-trade payments and currency exchanges. CHIPS handles an average of 242,000 such inter-institutional transactions a day, with a value of $1.2 trillion.

The Depository Trust & Clearing Corporation (DTCC) is the largest securities depository in the world, holding in custody securities worth $20 trillion in assets for its participants and their clients. It serves as the clearing house for the settlement of trades for all US corporate and municipal securities. The DTCC processes some 200m book-entry deliveries a year valued at $77 trillion.

The Federal Reserve Bank of New York (FRBNY) is the most important of the district banks of the US central banking system. It has a special role in the operation of the Federal Reserve System, being responsible for the implementation of the monetary policy decisions of the Federal Open Market Committee through transactions in the market. It also executes foreign-exchange transactions and acts as a bank for the US Treasury, which keeps its account at the FRBNY. The Wholesale Payments Product Office oversees the strategic and day-to-day activities of the Fedwire funds-transfer and book-entry security services. The FRBNY also oversees and regulates banks, and maintains official relations with other central banks around the world.

The financial-services firms that carry out the business of Wall Street are a host of commercial banks, investment banks, securities broker-dealers, investment and insurance companies and other wholesale financial-services firms. In recent years there has been substantial consolidation in the banking and securities industries because of competitive pressures driven by deregulation, technology, the quest for economies of scale and globalisation. The result has been a significant shrinkage in the number of Wall Street banks and securities firms, and the emergence of massive conglomerates undertaking a wide spectrum of financial-services activities that were traditionally conducted by separate sectors and separate firms. However, there has also been a steady increase in the number of foreign banks with a presence in New York and the birth of new boutique financial firms.

Money-centre dynamics

Markets and firms conducting wholesale financial-services activities concentrate in the major money centres for two principal reasons. In economists' jargon, these are external economies of scale and external economies of scope.

In usual usage, economies of scale refer to efficiencies that accrue to firms as they increase the size of operations. These are internal economies of scale. External economies of scale accrue to firms when a positive relationship exists between efficiency and the size of the industry in which they operate – the industry in this context being a money centre. There are many reasons why a larger money centre provides a more advantageous operating environment than a smaller one. The quality of financial markets – that is, their liquidity and efficiency – is strongly correlated with the scale of operations. These are highly desirable features, meaning lower dealing costs and a diminished likelihood of market failure.

Furthermore, the larger number and greater range of activities of other financial firms produce a more innovative environment, which may generate new business opportunities and demand. It may also stimulate competition, perhaps promoting efficiency and probably engendering keener pricing, which will persuade clients to place their business with firms based in a larger money centre rather than a smaller one.

External economies of scope accrue to financial firms from the presence of concentrations of complementary activities in major money centres. The ready availability of the services of, for instance, commercial lawyers, accountants, specialist printers, information-technology experts and public-relations consultants enhances the competitiveness of financial firms and the attractiveness of location in a major money centre. The bigger the centre, the more extensive and more varied is the concentration of complementary activities.

The logical outcome of the existence of positive external economies of scale and scope is that all financial-services activity should concentrate in a single money centre. But centralisation also generates diseconomies, such as crowding and congestion. It may also raise costs through competitive bidding for scarce resources, such as prime locations or skilled personnel. For the delivery of some financial services, centralisation may even increase costs and diminish the quality of client relationships because of distance. For instance, for advisory financial services a smaller money centre, where local firms are closely in touch with local clients, might enjoy a competitive advantage. Moreover, in the real world, political factors, regulatory barriers and non-market incentives distort the unfettered operation of the centralising economic forces. So regional and sub-regional money centres continue to exist, and providers of retail financial services, notably commercial banks and savings banks (thrifts), are still ubiquitous.

The overriding factor for success for financial firms is information. Its quantity and quality are crucial for their competitiveness, and, other things being equal, new firms will locate in money centres with superior information flows. Moreover, centres with inferior information flows will lose financial firms, either through their failure owing to uncompetitiveness or through their migration to other centres. Superior access to up-to-date, high-quality information has traditionally been the most significant external economy provided by location in a major money centre. Today, technology provides access to abundant information almost anywhere. Yet wholesale financial-services firms continue to concentrate in money centres. This is because these centres are where they are able to recruit the scarce, highly skilled staff they need to conduct business, and because such staff are able to function most effectively and most creatively in locations where they are surrounded by like-minded people (another external economy of scale) and are plugged in to industry gossip.

Front office, back office, mid office

Financial-services firms traditionally drew a distinction between front-office activities and back-office activities. Three criteria are used to classify activities as either front office or back office: the degree to which an activity involves interaction with others outside the firm, especially clients; whether the activity is revenue-generating or funded by money generated by other activities; and the degree to which an activity is routine.

Front-office activities involve interaction with clients or counterparties outside the firm and are revenue-generating and generally non-routine. Such activities include origination of new business, selling, trading, analysis, client account handling, product development, public relations and central management.

Back-office activities, by contrast, generally involve little interaction with people outside the firm, are funded by internal financial transfers and are often routine and clerical. The processing of transactions and the compiling and supplying of data to the front office are the principal forms of financial-services back-office work, including internal audit, cheque and security transactions processing, call centres, claims processing and payment, clearing-house operations, and basic facilities and internal management support.

The mid office is a recent phenomenon, developed in response to the increasing complexity and risks of the business. Mid-office functions are information-technology (IT) management and development; risk management; regulatory compliance; human resources; legal and tax; and accounting and reporting. These are non-routine functions, but they are not revenue-generating and their focus is mostly internal rather than external. Nonetheless, they are so important to the revenue-producing side of the business that they usually accompany the front office.

Traditionally, back offices were located within or near the front office to process transactions and service the revenue generators. Technological progress in computing and telecommunications allowed greater physical separation of front and back offices, and some firms moved their back offices to locations with lower operating costs. The divorce from support operations allowed the location of revenue-generating front offices to be less constrained by cost considerations and more driven by strategic factors, such as proximity to markets, clients and specialist services.

But then other considerations began to push front and back offices closer together again. A series of financial scandals involving lax controls over dealing rooms or transactions processing, such as at Salomon Brothers in 1990 and again in 1995, at Kidder Peabody in 1994, at the New York office of Daiwa Bank in 1995 and, most chillingly, the collapse of the London-based merchant bank Barings in 1995, heightened management concern about financial controls. Another factor was the increasing importance of IT for both front-office and back-office operations, generating internal economies of scale in its provision.

In New York, the relocation of back-office activities to cheaper locations away from Manhattan Island to the boroughs, New Jersey or upstate began in the 1970s. This dispersal increased the concentration of front-office wholesale financial-services personnel in the Wall Street area. A different phenomenon has been Wall Street firms' establishment of front-office activities in New York City's midtown. Not only were

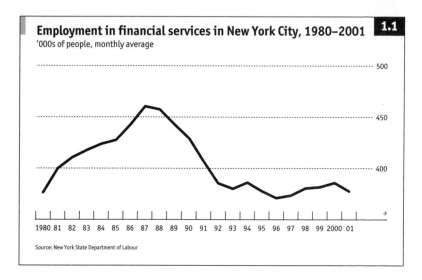

Employment in financial services in New York City, 1980–2001 `1.1`
'000s of people, monthly average

1980 81 82 83 84 85 86 87 88 89 90 91 92 93 94 95 96 97 98 99 2000 01

Source: New York State Department of Labour

rents cheaper, but in some cases proximity to clients who lived or worked in midtown was a competitive advantage; for instance, advising the millionaires of the upper East Side on their investment portfolios. Although a few miles away from lower Manhattan, such firms are still part of the New York money centre.

Wall Street jobs

At the beginning of the 1980s, 376,000 people were employed in New York City's financial-services industry. The headcount began to rise sharply from 1982, powered by strongly rising stockmarket prices, reaching a record 460,000 in 1987. The stockmarket crash of October 1987 was followed by redundancies, particularly in the securities industry. By 1992 the number of jobs in financial services in New York City had fallen to 385,000; and despite the resumption of bull-market conditions in the 1990s, aggregate employment in the industry hovered around this level until late 2001 (see Figure 1.1).

Although the total number of people working in financial services in New York City was almost identical in 1980 and 20 years later in 2001, there was considerable change in the number employed in each of the component sectors (see Figure 1.2).

Securities industry

The number of people working on Wall Street in the securities industry

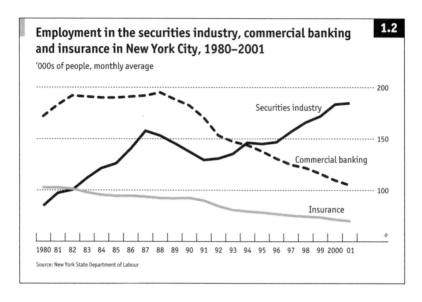

Employment in the securities industry, commercial banking and insurance in New York City, 1980–2001 `1.2`

'000s of people, monthly average

Source: New York State Department of Labour

more than doubled during the 1980s and 1990s. From 85,000 at the beginning of the 1980s, the headcount rose to 158,000 in 1987, boosted by the stockmarket bull run that began in summer 1982. The 1987 crash was followed by big job losses in the securities industry on Wall Street, the workforce falling back to 129,000 by 1991. Hiring resumed in 1992, as stock prices and activity revived, and rose almost continuously throughout the 1990s to a peak of 190,000 in August 2000.

The expansion of the securities industry in the 1980s and 1990s was a nationwide phenomenon driven by a set of powerful underlying factors. Demand for securities, particularly stocks, was boosted by the expansion of mutual-fund and pension-fund investment, which itself was a consequence of the country's economic prosperity and the coming to adulthood of the baby-boomer generation (born 1946–60). On the supply side, securitisation – that is, the replacement of traditional bank borrowing by the issue of tradable securities – and disintermediation – the replacement of bank borrowings by the issue of securities by corporations and other borrowers – increased the volume and variety of marketable financial assets. A further factor was the boom in mergers and acquisitions activity that customarily accompanies bull markets. As a result, the securities industry's share of Wall Street jobs grew from 24% of the total to 49% (see Figure 1.3).

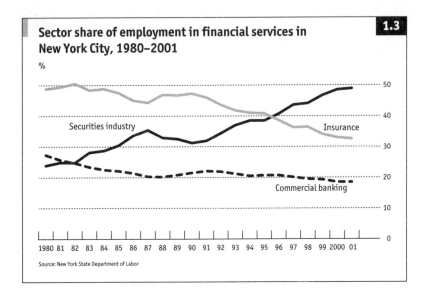

1.3

Sector share of employment in financial services in New York City, 1980–2001

%

Securities industry

Insurance

Commercial banking

1980 81 82 83 84 85 86 87 88 89 90 91 92 93 94 95 96 97 98 99 2000 01

Source: New York State Department of Labor

Banking and insurance

Employment in commercial banking and insurance declined in the 1980s and 1990s, both in absolute numbers and as a proportion of total employment in financial services in New York City. In both cases, a high proportion of the job losses were in low-skill back-office positions and the proportion of higher-paid front-office staff rose as the headcount dwindled.

In the insurance sector, employment in New York City declined gradually but relentlessly from 103,000 in 1980 to 70,000 in 2001. The reductions were a result of efforts by firms to improve profitability, including wholesale relocation of firms to less costly areas, outsourcing of lower-skill operations and the discontinuation of lines of business. The decline mostly affected the big insurance firms, but it also hit independent agents and brokers. It resulted in New York City's share of US employment in insurance falling from 6% to 3%.

Employment in commercial banking hovered around 190,000 jobs in New York City in the 1980s, but it fell rapidly in the 1990s to 105,000 by 2001. Beginning as a result of the slowing of financial-market activity after the 1987 crash, the decline continued because of the widespread consolidation and restructuring that affected the industry during the 1990s. Across America, the 12,000 commercial banks in operation in 1990 fell by a quarter to 9,000 during the decade, and the number of

Table 1.1 **Employment in finance and insurance in New York City, 2001**[a]

	Number of employees	%
Securities industry	185,000	49
Commercial banking[b]	105,000	28
Insurance	70,000	18
Other finance	18,000	5
Total	378,000	100

a Before September 11th terrorist attacks.
b Includes credit institutions.
Source: New York State Department of Labour

thrifts shrank from 2,500 to 2,000. In many cases, these amalgamations involved job losses as the new institutions sought to eliminate staff overlap or reduce supernumerary branch offices. As the head-office location of many banks, New York City suffered a disproportionate number of job losses from the consolidation process.

Another factor was the dispersion of back-office activities, such as call centres and credit-card and other processing operations, to lower-cost locations outside the city. These developments, coupled with the strong growth of population and employment in other regions of the country, resulted in a reduction in New York City's share of nationwide banking employment from 9% in the early 1990s to 6% at the end of the decade.

Since most of the job losses in the commercial banking and insurance sectors were relatively low-skill back-office positions, an outcome of the decline in the headcount was an increase in the proportion of higher-paid front-office staff in the city in these sectors. In the insurance sector, the decline in New York City's share of total US insurance industry earnings was only 15%, despite the 50% drop in employment. It was the same story in the commercial-banking sector, where the respective statistics were a 9% decline in earnings in the face of a 33% drop in employment. In the extensive restructuring and downsizing of the banking and insurance sectors, Wall Street had retained the skilled positions performing the sophisticated functions that had the most impact on earnings.

New York State Department of Labour statistics record that in summer 2001 – before the terrorist attacks of September 11th – 378,000 people worked in finance and insurance, both wholesale and retail, in New York City (see Table 1.1).

The largest sector was the securities industry which employed 185,000 people, almost half of New York City's finance and insurance industry workforce. The commercial-banking sector employed 105,000 people, more than a quarter of the total, and 70,000, almost a fifth, worked in the insurance sector. A further 18,000 people had jobs in a variety of other finance activities.

Wholesale financial services industry

To arrive at an estimate of the number of people who work in the Wall Street wholesale financial-services industry, it is necessary to deduct those who work on the retail side. Employment statistics suggest that proportionally New York City has around twice as many people working in commercial banking, insurance and "other finance" as might be expected in other cities of its size (who in other locations would mostly serve retail clients), implying that perhaps half such personnel undertake retail activities and half wholesale functions. For the securities and investment-banking sector, all personnel may be classified as working on the wholesale side. Based on these assumptions, it is estimated that the total headcount of personnel undertaking wholesale financial services on Wall Street is:

185,000 (securities and investment banking) + 55,000 (commercial banking) + 35,000 (insurance) + 10,000 (other finance) = 285,000

But then there are others who work in the sector indirectly, such as specialist law firms, accountancy firms, consultants, IT firms and other providers of services to the wholesale financial-services sector. New York State Department of Labour data show that there are around 80,000 lawyers and 325,000 people working in business services in the New York City labour force, but there are no estimates of how many of them specialise in servicing money-centre firms, thereby forming an integral part of Wall Street. However, data are available for London, another major money centre. Its wholesale financial-services sector, the City, is similar in size to Wall Street, with a combined workforce in securities, banking and insurance of 255,000. In London, the providers of such professional and specialist services to the City's securities, banking and insurance industries are estimated to number 70,000. This suggests that 75,000 such workers might be a reasonable guess for New York. Thus, on the basis of these distinctly speculative estimates and projections, it can be reckoned that the Wall Street wholesale

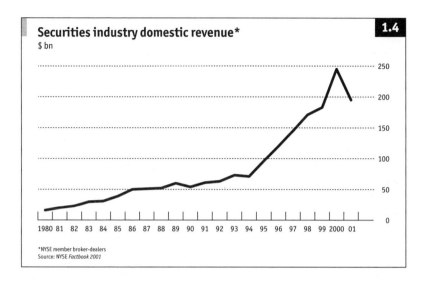

Securities industry domestic revenue*
$ bn

1.4

*NYSE member broker-dealers
Source: NYSE *Factbook 2001*

financial-services industry employs some 360,000 people (the comparable total for London is 324,000). Or rather, that was the picture before the terrorist attacks on the World Trade Centre on September 11th 2001.

Wall Street and the New York economy

The growth in securities industry employment in the 1990s reflected the sector's record prosperity. The domestic revenue of New York Stock Exchange (NYSE) member firms rose from $61 billion in 1991, when the industry's growth resumed after a pause following the 1987 crash, to a peak of $245 billion in 2000, with a new record being set virtually every year. But it fell to $195 billion in 2001 because of the downturn in the market and the September 11th attack (see Figure 1.4).

Along with record revenues came bumper profits. Between 1991 and 2000, the domestic pre-tax profits of NYSE member firms virtually quadrupled, rising from $5.8 billion to $21 billion, despite downturns in 1994 and 1998. The surge in profits was good news for staff. According to a report, *New York City's Economic & Fiscal Dependence on Wall Street*, by New York State Comptroller H. Carl McCall, average salaries for securities industry personnel increased by almost 50% between 1992 and 1999, rising from $131,152 to $195,533. In the rest of the city's economy, average salaries increased by 31% to $46,955. At the start of the 1990s, average securities industry salaries were 3.6 times greater than the combined average of other New York City salaries; by the end of the decade the multiple had risen even higher, to 4.2 times.

Although the securities industry comprised only 5% of New York City's workforce, securities industry workers received 19% of total salaries. The city administration estimates that each job in the Wall Street securities industry generates two additional city jobs, meaning that about 15% of total employment in New York City derives, either directly or indirectly, from the securities industry.

Direct beneficiaries are the suppliers of services to the securities sector, such as legal, accounting, IT, publishing, marketing, public relations and business services firms. Indirect beneficiaries, via the securities industry personnel's big pay cheques, are the city's retail, restaurant and entertainment industries. According to McCall's report, the securities sector accounted for over half of all new job growth in New York City in the 1990s when the multiplier effects in supplier industries are factored in.

Extrapolating from the securities-sector data to the entirety of New York's wholesale financial-services industry – that is, securities plus wholesale commercial banking and wholesale insurance activities – places Wall Street even more centre stage. Assuming that half of the banking and insurance sectors' New York City workforces undertake highly paid wholesale financial activities (the other half conducting retail activities), Wall Street jobs comprise 7–8% of New York City's employment. If each of these jobs supports two more, Wall Street accounts for as much as 20% of New York City employment. Moreover, Wall Street workers receive perhaps 30% of total earnings.

Wall Street's boom was the principal factor in the city's revival in the 1990s, Comptroller McCall proclaiming "the overwhelming centrality of Wall Street in the city's resurgence". It was the foremost contributor to the expansion of business and income-tax collection, generating 39% of the growth in personal income and business taxes over the decade. This expansion of the fiscal base transformed the city's finances from chronic budget deficits at the start of the decade to surpluses. The city was even indebted to Wall Street for its new mayor, Michael Bloomberg, a former investment banker who had made a fortune from his financial information empire, who took office in succession to Rudolph Giuliani in 2002.

As Wall Street became more and more crucial to New York's prosperity, the city became increasingly vulnerable to a downturn in the fortunes of the financial-services industry. As stock prices and securities industry activity fell from spring 2000, in the wake of the bursting of the technology stocks bubble and the slowing of the US economy, Wall Street's revenues, profits and remuneration levels decreased. And that was before the terrorist destruction of the Twin Towers on September 11th 2001.

September 11th and after

The terrorist attacks on the World Trade Centre killed 2,800 people in New York City. Around two-fifths of the casualties worked in the financial-services industry, financial-services firms being the principal occupants of the Twin Towers and surrounding buildings. In fact, just four firms accounted for 70% of the industry's casualties and almost one-third of the total loss of lives. Cantor Fitzgerald, a leading firm in the bond market, suffered 658 fatalities, one-third of its staff. Sandler O'Neill & Partners, a securities house, and Keefe Bruyette & Woods, an investment bank, had similar casualty rates. Fred Alger Management, an asset manager, also incurred heavy losses.

In the aftermath of the attack, fellow Wall Street firms rallied to the assistance of these firms: Jefferies Group donated a day's trading revenue to help them back on their feet; Cisco Systems, a telecommunications provider, rewired Cantor Fitzgerald's makeshift offices in New Jersey without charge; and Merrill Lynch included Sandler O'Neill and Keefe Bruyette in the distribution syndicate of a stock offering for Allied Capital. "I felt I was standing on the soup line," John Duffy, chairman of Keefe Bruyette, told the *Wall Street Journal.* "We were grateful for what we got, but we didn't want to be there."

The cost of the devastation in dollars was estimated to total as much as $95 billion over the years 2001–04, heading towards four times the record $25 billion damage caused by Hurricane Andrew in 1992. A stark report by the Comptroller for the city of New York titled *One Year Later, the fiscal impact of 9/11 on New York City,* published in September 2002, calculated the physical damage at $21.8 billion: the six buildings comprising the World Trade Centre, 13.4m sq ft of office space, were completely destroyed; nine buildings, including the adjacent World Financial Centre, totalling 15.1m sq ft, suffered serious damage and required extensive repair; 16 buildings, 10m sq ft, had significant but reparable damage; and another 400 buildings had smashed windows or damaged facades. There was also the damage to communications, power and urban transit facilities, which made it difficult to conduct business in lower Manhattan, even from buildings where the damage was superficial. And then there was the $8.7 billion "human capital" cost, accountancy-speak for the people killed, based on multiplying their average earnings of $130,000 a year by the number of years to retirement – a chilling reckoning.

The Twin Towers attacks resulted in the displacement of 138,000 people from their workplaces in lower Manhattan, of whom 100,000 worked in the financial-services industry. Around half of those displaced found new quarters in New York City, mostly in midtown. Many of the others relocated across the Hudson River to New Jersey, the principal out-of-town refuge, temporarily at least, and some headed upstate or as far afield as Connecticut. Six months after the attacks, only 17% had moved back to lower Manhattan; and there were predictions that half the relocations would prove permanent, implying a lasting loss of some 50,000 jobs to lower Manhattan's financial-services sector. New York City's share of America's securities industry jobs has been in long-term decline for years: between 1981 and 2001 its share fell from 37% to 22%. The devastation of September 11th can only have reinforced that trend.

The fatalities and relocations inflicted by the September 11th terrorist attacks accelerated the contraction of the size of the New York City securities sector that had been under way for over a year as a result of the economic slowdown, falling stockmarket prices and structural changes in the sector. Following the September 11th attacks, employment in the New York securities industry slumped from 181,000 jobs to 166,000 – a record 8.3% fall in a single month. From the all-time peak of 190,000 jobs in August 2000, the job total had fallen to 165,000 by the end of 2001, an unprecedented loss of 25,000 securities industry jobs (a 13% drop) in just 16 months. Before the attacks, it was estimated that the securities industry's profits for 2001 would fall from 2000's record $21 billion to $15 billion, but afterwards the profits forecast was revised down to $10 billion.

Given the reliance on the financial-services industry that the city, and state, of New York had developed in the 1990s, the destruction and dislocation inflicted by September 11th were heavy blows. At the first anniversary it was estimated that 146,000 job losses were attributable to the attacks, which had cost the city $17 billion in lost wages and a further $3.5 billion in lost taxes. Despite a $21.5 billion federal aid package, New York City's economy struggled to recover.

The laying waste of much of lower Manhattan by the September 11th attacks also raises the question of the future of the Wall Street area as a focus for financial-services activity. Will the diaspora of Wall Street firms prove permanent? Or will there be a remarkable renaissance of a vibrant financial sector and community in lower Manhattan?

2 How we got here

This chapter traces the historical development of Wall Street. From 1896 onwards, the narrative is accompanied by a series of charts depicting the progress of the Dow Jones Industrial Index and key historical events. For recent decades, the broad overview presented in this chapter should be read in conjunction with later chapters that focus in detail on particular aspects of Wall Street.

Origins

Wall Street – the street itself – is a windy canyon running east-to-west across lower Manhattan. The name derives from the wooden palisade erected in 1653 by Dutch settlers, the inhabitants of what was then called New Amsterdam, to protect themselves against marauding indigenous people and New Englanders. The wall proved ineffectual against both and the Dutch settlement was soon captured by the British, who renamed it New York.

At the beginning of the 19th century, New York emerged as the leading American centre for shipping and trade in commodities, overtaking its rivals, Boston and Philadelphia. One reason was its superb natural harbour. Another was the construction in the 1820s of the Erie Canal, which by linking the port to the Great Lakes made New York the gateway to the vast and rapidly developing continental hinterland.

The expansion of foreign trade and wholesaling in New York stimulated the establishment and growth of banks, to provide trade finance, and insurance firms, to cover risks for merchants and ship-owners. New York also developed an active money market, with instruments including bankers acceptances and overnight loans. These mercantile and financial undertakings concentrated in lower Manhattan close to the docks, crowding out colonial-era residential housing, which moved uptown from the early 19th century.

The US securities market came into existence in the 1780s, trading bonds issued by the newly independent state and federal governments. The market expanded vastly during the civil war of 1861–65 as a result of Union government borrowing to finance the war effort. In the subsequent decades of the late 19th century, fundraising by railroad companies, manufacturing industries, mining companies and utilities added a raft of corporate bonds and stocks and greatly expanded the scale and scope of the market. Securities firms and securities business grew rapidly: one indicator was the first 1m stock turnover day in 1886; another was the establishment of the *Wall Street Journal* in 1889.

Enter "The Dow"

By the end of the 19th century, the stockmarket had become an important feature of the US economy, with an abundance of individual stocks. Indeed, the ups and downs of stock prices had become of crucial interest not only to borrowers, investors and those working in securities markets, but also as a broad indicator of the economic health and vitality of the nation.

But keeping track of the direction of the market as a whole was problematic because of the lack of a general market yardstick. The Dow Jones Industrial Average (the Dow), a daily index of stock prices, was devised to meet this need. It was the invention of Charles H. Dow, whose firm Dow Jones & Company published the *Wall Street Journal*, and made its debut in that newspaper in May 1896. Dow added up the prices of 12 of the biggest New York Stock Exchange (NYSE) stocks and created an average by dividing the total by the number of stocks. In 1916 the number of stocks in the Dow was increased to 20 and in 1928 it became 30, as it is today. Although there is now a multitude of stock indices, the Dow Jones Industrial Average remains the most widely recognised and cited index, and, having the longest life span, is the most useful for tracking the long-term development of the stockmarket.

First billion-dollar deal

At the time of the Dow's launch, America was rapidly becoming an industrial powerhouse. Production was expanding and industries were consolidating, the years 1895–1904 witnessing the first big mergers and acquisitions boom. The amalgamations were helped, and in some cases instigated, by Wall Street investment banks, particularly J.P. Morgan and Kuhn, Loeb, the leading houses. The capstone of the merger movement was the formation of US Steel, the first billion-dollar corporation, in 1901. At that time, American GDP was $20 billion, making US Steel's $1.4 billion capitalisation equivalent to 7% of total economic output. An equivalent capitalisation today would be around $700 billion, double the size of the largest corporate amalgamation, the AOL–Time Warner merger of 2000, which at that time had a combined market value of $340 billion.

The US Steel deal was masterminded by J. Pierpont Morgan, head of J.P. Morgan and the pre-eminent Wall Street figure of the day. Morgan, or one of his partners in the firm, was on the board of 50 of America's top corporations and his authority over Wall Street has never been rivalled. He played a crucial role in organising support operations for stock prices in the panics of 1893 and 1907, saving other banks, brokers and investors from financial oblivion and enhancing his influence over Wall Street. It was estimated that he earned $5m a year – $3 billion in today's money, six times Michael Milken's remuneration at his peak.

The "Money Trust" under investigation

The US Steel deal and other prominent mega-mergers aroused public concern because of mistrust of monopolistic corporate "robber barons" and fears about the power of a small inner circle of Wall Street financiers. It did not pass unnoticed that there were more investment bankers than steel men on US Steel's board of directors. Reformist commentators and politicians began to call for antitrust action from government and for regulation of financial intermediaries and the securities market. In 1912 the House of Representatives established a Banking Committee to investigate the Wall Street "Money Trust", a term coined by Charles Lindbergh Snr, a congressman and father of the celebrated pioneering aviator. Morgan was the star witness at the Pujo hearings, named after Arsène Pujo, a Louisiana Democrat congressman. A retiring man, acutely self-conscious about his sanguinary bulbous nose that was reported to resemble a pomegranate, Morgan found the hostile cross-examination an excruciating experience. Friends linked the ordeal to his death the following year. Despite the bankers' dogged denials that they either possessed or exercised the power attributed to them, observers were unconvinced and the case for legislative regulation of Wall Street took a stride forward.

At that moment the creation of a US central bank was a topical issue. There were many arguments in favour, above all the country's need for better monetary management. Reformers also argued that the existence of a public lender of last resort would reduce the need for banks and corporations to be beholden to powerful private financiers such as Morgan. Many on Wall Street were hostile to interference in what they considered to be their private affairs, but not all. Paul Warburg, a partner of Kuhn, Loeb who was familiar with the workings of European central banks, was a leading proponent of reform. The outcome was the establishment in 1913 of the Federal Reserve System. The American

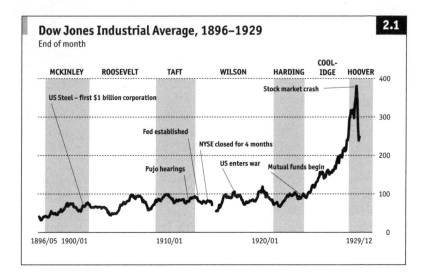

Dow Jones Industrial Average, 1896–1929

End of month

2.1

MCKINLEY · ROOSEVELT · TAFT · WILSON · HARDING · COOL-IDGE · HOOVER

US Steel – first $1 billion corporation

Stock market crash

Fed established

NYSE closed for 4 months

Pujo hearings

US enters war · Mutual funds begin

400 · 300 · 200 · 100 · 0

1896/05 · 1900/01 · 1910/01 · 1920/01 · 1929/12

central bank comprised a board in Washington and a dozen district banks covering the country. From the outset, the Federal Reserve Bank of New York (FRBNY), initially headed by Benjamin Strong, formerly president of Bankers Trust and an esteemed and trusted figure on Wall Street, played the leading role amongst the Federal Reserve regional banks.

Economic expansion and the corporate amalgamation boom propelled stock prices upwards in the years 1896–1905; the Dow more than doubled from 40 to 96 (see Figure 2.1). As the merger wave waned, stock prices calmed and the Dow drifted sideways for several years. The outbreak of war in summer 1914 led to fears that securities would be dumped on the market and prices would collapse. For this reason, the NYSE closed its doors on the outbreak of hostilities in Europe and stayed shut for four and a half months till mid-December. By then investors' nerves had rallied, and although prices were marked down there was no panic sell-off; in fact, the Dow soon rebounded, reflecting the general prosperity of the American economy. But America's entry into the war in 1917 alarmed investors and the Dow took another dip.

Liberty bonds and foreign loans

Wars cost money, lots of money. The US war effort was financed partly by taxation but mostly by borrowing – over the war years America's national debt rose from $1.2 billion to $25.5 billion. Five issues of Liberty bonds in the years 1917–19 raised a total of $21.5 billion, at least $200 billion in today's money. But the government did not use the services of Wall Street investment banks to raise the funds. Instead, the bonds were issued by the Treasury, with the FRBNY undertaking their distribution among banks and brokerage houses, which sold them to retail clients. This arrangement had two advantages: it avoided the payment of unnecessary underwriting charges to the members of the "money trust"; and it enhanced the standing and clout of the tyro New York Fed. Another beneficiary was Salomon Brothers, formed in 1910. Its energetic selling of Liberty bonds transformed it from a minor money-market broker to a major player in the government-bond market.

America's allies in the war, especially Britain and France, also tapped Wall Street for funds to finance their war efforts. J.P. Morgan acted as their agent and was well-remunerated for its work. The foreign bonds were popular with investors since these borrowers offered higher yields than Uncle Sam. During the war, foreign sovereign borrowers raised $3 billion in the US capital markets. Moreover, many overseas holdings of dollar securities were sold to US investors. The outcome was that the United States emerged from the war as the world's greatest creditor, having been the world's biggest overseas debtor at the outbreak of the conflict. Up to 1914, London had been pre-eminent in the international capital markets and sterling was the most widespread currency for international bond issues. But with the European capital markets closed to foreign borrowers during the hostilities, New York and the US dollar took over, providing a serendipitous boost to Wall Street's burgeoning business.

Post-war securities boom
The Liberty bond sales drive created the world's first mass market for securities. Before the war some 350,000 Americans owned securities, but the Liberty bonds were bought by millions. As US government-backed obligations there was no risk of default, and they paid higher interest than bank deposits. Another attractive feature was that they were exempt from federal income tax, a recent and resented imposition upon the affluent.

The return of peace brought an end to large-scale borrowing by the federal government. This created an opportunity to sell other securities to a public whose appetite for them had been whetted by the Liberty bond sales drives. Recognising a potential goldmine, money-centre commercial banks began to market securities through their branches and moved into bond underwriting. Foremost among them was National City Bank (forerunner of Citigroup), headed by Charles Mitchell, who had begun his career on the securities side. In the 1920s, Mitchell turned National City Bank, already America's biggest commercial bank, into the first integrated all-purpose financial intermediary, a "financial department store" as he conceived it. He rapidly developed its investment-banking subsidiary, National City Company, which joined the front rank of underwriters, originating or participating in bond issues totalling $11 billion, more than one-fifth of all US bond issues in the 1920s. These issues were sold to investors through National City Bank's branches and National City Company's nationwide network of offices in 51 cities.

At the end of the hostilities the victorious allies (with the exception of the United States) followed the long-established practice of presenting the defeated power, Germany, with a massive bill for reparations. Being unable to pay, Germany borrowed the funds for the first instalment through a massive bond issue – $1.1 billion in America and $1.1 billion in European markets – known as the Dawes loan (after General Charles Dawes, a Chicago banker). The 1924 Dawes loan was followed by a deluge of issues by foreign borrowers, totalling $10.2 billion between 1921 and 1929. The foreign bond issues appealed both to the investment banks, which were able to extract hefty fees for their services, and to investors, since they paid substantially higher yields than domestic government securities or corporate bonds.

Governments, municipalities and government agencies were the principal foreign borrowers in the US capital market in the 1920s. The National City Company was one of the leading underwriters of foreign bonds, originating or participating in over 150 issues for borrowers from 26 countries totalling $3.8 billion, almost two-fifths of the total. Initially, the foreign bond market was restricted to countries of sound financial standing, but before long bond issues were successfully being brought out for places of distinctly dubious creditworthiness. When the world went into recession in the early 1930s, many such borrowers, particularly the countries of Latin America and central Europe, defaulted on their debts, bitterly aggravating public disillusion with Wall Street and its works.

Stocks join the party

The bulk (around three-quarters by value) of all new securities issues in the 1920s were bonds. This fitted the portfolio preferences of investors who were mostly cautious and liked the low-risk nature of bonds. But as they became more familiar with securities, a growing number of investors, both individual and institutional, began to buy stocks, enticed by their potential for capital gains. A variety of technological developments – the automobile, radio, electrical appliances, petrochemicals – offered alluring prospects for investors, just like dotcom and other stocks in the 1990s. For the first time, millions of ordinary citizens began buying stocks in the hope of backing a winner. From spring 1924 to summer 1929 the stockmarket staged a virtually uninterrupted bull run, with the Dow rising almost fourfold. The first upswing, from spring 1924 to summer 1926, saw a steady advance that took the index from 90 to 160 before pausing for breath. But in the second upswing, which got under way in spring 1927, prices raced ahead, pushing the Dow to a peak of 380 in summer 1929.

The rise in stock prices in the years 1927 to 1929 was driven by a speculative frenzy that was encouraged by investors being required to put up margin money of only 10–20% of the price of the stocks they bought, the rest being credit from brokers with the securities as collateral. The brokers financed their credit operations by borrowing from the banks, which funded themselves in the money market. Since the interest rates paid by speculators for margin money were far higher than could be charged for other loans, banks, both domestic and foreign, were eager lenders. They became even more eager when in spring 1927 the Fed cut interest rates to assist international currency stability. Further contributing to the eightfold increase in new stock issues between 1926 and 1928 was the relaxation in 1927 of restrictions on commercial banks underwriting equity issues.

The Wall Street crash

By August 1929, relative to even the most wildly optimistic corporate earnings forecasts, stocks were massively overpriced. Indeed, some of the market's most savvy operators, such as Joseph Kennedy, father of the future president, had already sold up. The confidence of other investors was also becoming more fragile, worries about losses overshadowing dreams of gains. As the mindset of speculators shifted from greed to fear, the bubble burst. Panic selling began on Wednesday October 23rd 1929 and continued the next day, Black Thursday, when $10 billion was wiped off stock values in the first two hours of trading. At 12 noon a group of senior Wall Street figures from Morgan, Chase, National City and Bankers Trust, which controlled combined assets of $6 billion, the greatest pool of wealth in the world, convened at J.P. Morgan's building at 23 Wall Street. Armed with pledges from these firms for stock purchases totalling $240m, at 1.30pm Richard Whitney, acting president of the NYSE, strode on to the trading floor and started buying US Steel, the market's bellwether stock. Prices rallied and for a while it looked as if the bankers had pulled it off, as similar market support operations had done in the panics of 1893 and 1907. But the vast expansion of securities sales in the 1920s meant that the market was now beyond the control even of a consortium of its most powerful firms.

Panic selling resumed on Monday October 28th, when the Dow slumped 12.9%, a record until 1987. The following day, more than 16m shares were traded, another record that stood for 60 years. In these two days alone, stock prices fell almost 25%. Prices continued to decline in the following weeks, taking the Dow down to 240 by mid-November, a loss of two-fifths its peak value. Individuals who had bought on margin were ruined. Tales of suicides abounded, giving rise to gallows humour. One wisecrack was that New York hotel clerks had taken to asking: "You wanna room for sleeping or jumping?" Another was the story of two men who jumped hand-in-hand from an upper window at the Ritz – they had a joint account.

The Wall Street crash of 1929 was the harbinger of the Depression of the early 1930s, the deepest depression in American history. Between 1929 and early 1933, unemployment rose from 3.2% of the workforce to 24.9%, industrial production declined by nearly 45%, there were 85,000 business failures wiping out assets of $4.5 billion, and gross national product (GNP) fell from $150 billion to $108 billion.

The Depression

America's descent into economic depression took place in a series of four stages, each marked by a fresh financial crisis that further undermined public confidence in the financial system and the confidence of business in the economic outlook. The Wall Street crash was just the first stage of the process; indeed, by mid-1930 many were optimistic that the worst was over and that the recession would be short-lived, as in 1907 and 1920–21. Although domestic business was still thin, Wall Street was profiting from a revival of foreign bond issuance led by the Young loan of June 1930, a second massive international loan for Germany to make reparations payments, named after US negotiator Owen Young, chairman of General Electric. In 1930 total foreign bond issues in the US once again topped $1 billion.

But the fragile recovery of confidence in the domestic economy was shattered by the failure of Bank of United States (a private bank named deliberately to give the impression of public backing – note the missing "the") in December 1930. This large New York bank with 59 branches and 440,000 depositors had become insolvent because of fraud, incompetence and losses from the Wall Street crash. Although a large number of individual investors were participants in the boom before the crash, the bulk of trading was undertaken by banks and other financial institutions. Banks joined the party either by speculating with depositors' funds or by lending to speculators. When stock prices crashed, they found themselves either with depleted assets or with a slate of non-performing loans, or both. So they went bust: 10,000 US banks, about two-fifths of the total, failed in the Depression of the 1930s in the aftermath of the Wall Street crash.

The failure of Bank of United States resulted in the loss of $300m of depositors' funds, triggering panic withdrawals throughout the country that caused other banks to fail and accelerated the slide into recession. The failure of the big banks and the authorities to mount a rescue of Bank of United States and its depositors was described at the time by Joseph Broderick, New York superintendent of banks, as "the most colossal mistake in the banking history of New York". Historians do not take issue with his words.

The third stage of the downturn began in May 1931 in Vienna with the failure of Credit Anstalt, Austria's largest bank. The crisis spread rapidly to Germany, the world's biggest international borrower, which suspended external payments in July 1931. In subsequent months, the countries of central Europe defaulted on their bonds, as did the whole of Latin America (except Argentina); it was the 20th century's first international debt crisis. The defaults were disastrous for the holders of foreign bonds, including a legion of US small investors who had bought them as safe investments on the basis that countries do not go bust. Underlying the defaults was the collapse of the international economy arising from the recession, widely adopted deflationary monetary policy and the protectionist Smoot-Hawley Tariff Act passed by Congress in June 1930, which provoked retaliatory protectionist measures from other countries. In September 1931 the crisis spread to Britain, forcing sterling off the gold standard and engendering currency instability that further discouraged international trade and investment. By then the international capital market had virtually closed down – and it would stay closed for more than a decade.

Wall Street in the dock

As the economy slid into the mire, politicians started to blame Wall Street for the country's plight. President Hoover denounced short selling by Wall Street traders for aggravating the falls in stock prices, making money out of the losses of ordinary investors. At his instigation, the Senate began hearings into such Wall Street practices in February 1932. These became known as the Pecora hearings after Ferdinand Pecora, their legal counsel, and lasted on and off for two years. The Hoover administration also devised a plan to create a credit pool subscribed by the big banks to make loans to help other banks that were in trouble. But potential subscribers refused to co-operate, arguing that it threatened the integrity of the banking system. So Hoover went ahead without them, establishing a government-owned entity, the Reconstruction Finance Corporation (RFC), which set about bailing out banks with liquidity problems – a forerunner of the New Deal reforms instigated by his successor Franklin D. Roosevelt.

In the limbo months between Roosevelt's victory in the November 1932 presidential election and his assumption of office in March 1933, a fourth and final financial crisis arose as a result of the activities of the RFC. Loans to banks by the RFC were confidential, as it was feared that recipients would be regarded as unsound, prompting depositors to withdraw their funds and attracting the attentions of short sellers. But the House of Representatives decided for reasons of democratic accountability that the recipients of RFC loans should be identified and a list was published in February 1933. As predicted, this led to depositors panicking and withdrawing their money, thus triggering a wave of bank failures.

Fearful that the US banking system was collapsing, the new president immediately declared a "bank holiday", shutting every bank in the country until its books had been inspected and it had been certified sound. Having restored the faith of depositors in the banking system, the New Deal administration set about reform of the financial system with gusto. By the time of Roosevelt's inauguration the Pecora hearings had begun to reveal Wall Street practices that outraged public opinion and required a political response. The outrage related to such matters as the marketing of bonds of high-risk borrowers, especially foreign bonds, to small savers by the big commercial banks; how the banks had gambled with, and lost, depositors' funds playing the stock market; the scale of brokerage and investment banking fees; the "preferred lists" kept by J.P. Morgan and other investment bankers, through which favoured clients, including politicians, received preferential prices and allocations of new issues; and short selling. As public anger mounted, Roosevelt's New Deal administration embarked upon reforms that touched virtually every aspect of Wall Street's activities.

The New Deal

The banking and securities reform legislation comprised nine measures that established the fundamental features of the regulatory framework within which Wall Street operated for the following half century and beyond. They were as follows.

Securities Act 1933

This was the first piece of national securities legislation passed by Congress. It obliged the vendors of new securities issues to register them with the Federal Trade Commission (later the Securities and Exchange Commission), which required specific information relating to the issuer's business and the terms, purposes and intended use of the funds. A false prospectus could result in a criminal prosecution. It was plainly framed to prevent a repetition of the activities of National City Bank and the National City Company.

Banking Act 1933 (Glass-Steagall)

This measure had three main purposes.

- The separation of commercial banking (deposit taking and lending) from investment banking (securities underwriting and dealing).
- To increase the authority of the Federal Reserve Board to prevent member banks of the Federal Reserve System from engaging in speculation.
- The creation of the Federal Deposit Insurance Corporation (FDIC), which guaranteed depositors' funds up to $5,000 in the event of the failure of a bank.

The separation of investment banking and commercial banking was clearly intended to curtail the extensive influence of J.P. Morgan.

Securities Exchange Act 1934

The objective of this was to regulate securities exchanges in order to protect the purchasers of stocks and bonds against fraudulent practices. It established the Securities and Exchange Commission (SEC) to register and supervise the sale of new issues of stocks and bonds. It also authorised the Federal Reserve Board to control the purchase of securities on margin.

Banking Act 1935

This strengthened government control over the banking system through revisions to the Federal Reserve Act of 1913 by:

- requiring all banks with deposits in excess of $1m join the Federal Reserve System and have their deposits guaranteed by the FDIC;
- requiring member banks to purchase government bonds only in open-market transactions;
- changing the name of the Federal Reserve Board to the Board of Governors of the Federal Reserve System, increasing the membership of financial experts from six to seven, and increasing its power over the 12 regional federal reserve banks.

Public Utilities Holding Act 1935

This provided for the control and regulation of public utility holding companies through requiring them to register with the SEC. It was prompted by the collapse in June 1932 of the extensive public utilities empire built up by Samuel Insull.

Maloney Act 1938

Named after Senator Francis Maloney of Connecticut, Democrat, this established the National Association of Securities Dealers (NASD), which was entrusted with policing the over-the-counter markets.

Trust Indenture Act 1939

This required that debt securities offered for public sale, except certain exempted issues, be issued under a trust indenture approved by the SEC, a tightening of the provisions of the Securities Act 1933.

Investment Company Act 1940

The purpose of this was to control abuses associated with investment companies and investment advisers. Mutual funds and investment funds were required to register with the SEC and make an array of disclosures about their financial condition and policies, providing investors with full information about their activities.

Investment Advisers Act 1940
This regulated persons and firms engaged in investment advisory work by requiring their registration with the SEC.

Shake-up on Wall Street

The separation of commercial banking from investment banking by the 1933 Glass-Steagall Act was a novel measure that made the US financial-services industry different from the rest of the world, where no such separation existed (though one was later introduced in Japan under the US military occupation). The big commercial banks that had developed securities affiliates, notably National City, Chase and First National Bank of Boston, chose commercial banking, as did J.P. Morgan. The act led to a shake-up in the investment banking industry in 1934–35. Morgan Stanley and First Boston emerged as new firms formed by people from the investment-banking sides of their former employers. Investment bankers from National City Company and other securities affiliates joined and reinvigorated some existing firms, notably Blyth & Co, Brown Harriman and Edward B. Smith. Old investment-banking partnerships such as Kuhn, Loeb and Lehman Brothers continued as before, except for the loss of their deposit business.

As required under the Securities Act, the NYSE registered with the SEC in 1934, but many members were hostile to the legislation. Despite SEC pressure for reform and greater professionalism, the NYSE dragged its feet. But then came the sensational arrest of Richard Whitney, a doyen of Wall Street and NYSE president 1930–35, for embezzling $1m from the exchange. In 1938 Whitney was sentenced to five to ten years in Sing Sing state penitentiary and the NYSE hastened to adopt a new management structure, appointing a salaried administrative staff including the first full-time professional president.

"Buddy, can you spare a dime?"

The Dow touched bottom at 42 in July 1932, from which it climbed gradually to 187 in February 1937, mirroring the faltering recovery of the US economy (see Figure 2.2). Securities market activity picked up from very low levels from 1934, secondary trading volumes rose significantly, and bond issuance increased fifteenfold from 1934 to 1936. But 1937 saw the onset of another recession, with falling output and rising unemployment. Down again went the Dow and the volume of securities business. And with the outbreak of war in Europe in September 1939 prices and activity fell further.

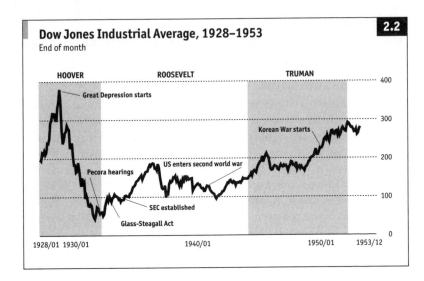

Dow Jones Industrial Average, 1928–1953
End of month

`2.2`

HOOVER ROOSEVELT TRUMAN

Great Depression starts

Korean War starts

Pecora hearings

US enters second world war

SEC established

Glass-Steagall Act

400

300

200

100

0

1928/01 1930/01 1940/01 1950/01 1953/12

The United States was drawn into the second world war by the Japanese attack on Pearl Harbor in December 1941. To finance military expenditure, seven war-bond issues were made between 1941 and 1945, which increased the US national debt from $48 billion to $260 billion. The issues were undertaken by the US Treasury, with each district Federal Reserve Bank handling the sales in its region. To meet the government's borrowing needs the Federal Reserve took steps to curb consumer credit. It also stabilised interest rates, pegging money-market and bond rates through open-market operations. This was an unprecedented interference with the markets by the authorities and bad news for Wall Street traders, whose livelihood depended on free and fluctuating markets. The outlook was just as bleak for investment bankers, because of the level of government borrowing and the reduced market for corporate securities. Moreover, funds for capital expenditure for war production were provided by two government agencies, the Reconstruction Finance Corporation and the Defence Plant Corporation. It was not only work that was in short supply on Wall Street in the war years; manpower was decreasing too, as many bankers and brokers enlisted in the armed forces. During the war the back offices of banks and securities firms became staffed by women, although most had to leave when the men returned.

The end of the war in 1945 led to a sharp drop in government borrowing. This allowed a revival of corporate issues and underwriting activity. But the authorities did not retreat from the financial markets, and interest rates remained pegged through to the end of the Korean War in 1953. Stockmarket turnover picked up from 1944 and the Dow staged a more-or-less steady recovery from a post-Pearl Harbor low of 95 to 280 at the end of the Korean War.

Harry Truman became president in April 1945 following the death of Franklin D. Roosevelt. Truman was no friend of big business or Wall Street, and under his administration the Justice Department embarked on a trust-busting spree. In October 1947, it filed an antitrust complaint against 17 leading investment banking firms and the Investment Bankers Association, their trade association, charging them with conspiring to share underwriting business among themselves through reciprocal arrangements to participate in each other's issues for clients. It was a revival of the old "money trust" accusation, but this time with the threat of fines or disposals. It threw the industry on the defensive. The complex case went on for more than six years, generating more than 100,000 pages of printed material. The trial itself opened in November 1950 before Judge Harold Medina, sitting without a jury. Eventually, in October 1953, after almost three years of depositions, testimony and argument, Medina dismissed the case, having concluded that the alleged conspiracy was a fantasy of the Justice Department. This was a significant victory for Wall Street which went some way to restoring its tarnished public reputation and marked the end of New Deal meddling in the affairs of the money markets.

1950s revival

The dismissal of the charges against the "Wall Street Seventeen" was just one of several developments that makes 1953 a turning-point in the story of Wall Street. The return of President Dwight Eisenhower, a Republican, to the White House after 20 years of Democrat "big government" meant a more market- and banker-friendly administration in Washington. The end of the Korean War in July 1953 reduced government borrowing needs and allowed the new administration to start cutting the budget deficit. This gave more scope for corporate fundraising – and the prospects of lower taxes helped stock prices. Moreover, with the end of the war the official interest-rate peg was lifted and the Federal Reserve curtailed its operations in the money market. Overall, these developments amounted to a significant lifting of the clouds and constraints under which Wall Street had been operating for the previous two decades.

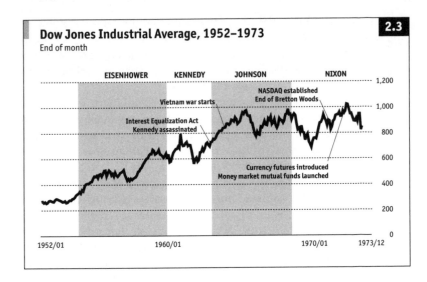

Dow Jones Industrial Average, 1952–1973
End of month

2.3

EISENHOWER   KENNEDY   JOHNSON   NIXON

NASDAQ established
End of Bretton Woods

Vietnam war starts

Interest Equalization Act
Kennedy assassinated

Currency futures introduced
Money market mutual funds launched

1952/01   1960/01   1970/01   1973/12

In the 1950s, the US economy became geared to meeting the consumption demands of the population and delivered unprecedented prosperity. Between 1940 and 1960 US GNP increased by almost 150%, from $205 billion to $500 billion. Unemployment was low at 3–5%, inflation was negligible and interest rates were low. The production of consumer goods boomed, especially automobiles but also household electrical appliances and – a recent invention – television. The post-war housing boom continued, associated with a large-scale migration of middle-class Americans to the suburbs, now made accessible by the mass production of automobiles. Consumer expenditure was propelled by easy credit and the introduction of a new form of lending by banks and stores, the credit card. The government played a part too, through a military programme that pumped billions of dollars into the economy and through civil measures, notably the Highway Act of 1956, which funded the construction of the interstate highway system thereby boosting the mobility of goods and people and promoting economic efficiency.

Era of the "Three Martini Lunch"

It was an environment in which Wall Street could not but prosper. Rising output and healthy profits were good news for stock prices, which pushed steadily upwards from late 1953 (see Figure 2.3). From 260 in September 1953, the Dow rose to 386 in December 1954, outstripping its previous peak in August 1929 for the first time. Although there was a slowdown in 1957, the Dow ended the decade 240% higher at 650, its best ten-year performance to date. Trading volume rose too, with stock transaction volume averaging 312m a year in 1945–49, 447m in 1950–54 and 667m in 1955–59. With business buoyant and protected from price competition by fixed commissions, the living was easy for Wall Street brokers, who were able to enjoy that long-gone Wall Street institution, the three-Martini lunch.

Forbidden from competing on price by NYSE rules, the leading brokerage firms developed another competitive weapon: research. Houses such as Merrill Lynch (the largest Wall Street broker by the early 1950s), E.F. Hutton, PaineWebber, Bache, and Dean Witter began to produce rigorous stocks and market analysis for clients upon which scientific investment decisions could be made. The growing prosperity of stockbrokers, and possibly the increasing professionalism of some of their number, led to a rise in their social status. Having been virtual pariahs since the crash, by the end of Eisenhower's presidency surveys placed them in the top social echelon.

Having a stockbroker became one of the symbols of middle-class status in 1950s America, along with the detached house in the suburbs with the latest year's model automobile in the drive. Rising prices drew private investors into the stockmarket in numbers not seen since the 1920s: over the decade, the number of individual investors doubled. Others participated through mutual funds; the number of funds expanded from 98 in 1950 to 161 in 1960. The public appetite for stocks was mirrored, and nurtured, by the increased attention the market received in the media, such as Walter Winchell's nationally syndicated radio broadcasts, which began offering investment advice in late 1953. He claimed that anyone who had followed his tips during 1954 would have made a profit of $250,000.

Investment banking business

Although Judge Medina had concluded that there was no conspiracy among the Wall Street Seventeen to monopolise underwriting, the conduct of that business and corporate advisory work in the 1950s and 1960s had some distinctly cartel-like organisational and operational characteristics, being dominated by a small number of investment banking firms. Through their control of the flow of new securities, the investment banks were able to exercise substantial influence over the smaller and more numerous securities firms that undertook the retail distribution of issues. This state of affairs arose principally from the Glass-Steagall Act, which had the effect of protecting investment bankers from competition for new underwriting business from their only potential rivals, commercial banks. The failure of the 1947 antitrust suit reinforced the ring-fencing of the investment bankers' enclave. In view of the anti "money trust" sentiments of the framers of the Banking Act of 1933, this was a distinctly paradoxical outcome.

The hierarchical structure of the investment-banking industry was on public display in the "tombstone" advertisements that appeared in the newspapers announcing new securities issues. Four firms, Morgan Stanley, Kuhn, Loeb, Dillon Read and First Boston, formed a special-bracket group that had pride of place at the top of the tombstone for any issue in which they were involved. This was testimony to the prestige and clout of these so-called "white shoe" houses and the calibre of their client lists. None of these firms had any retail distribution capability; they marketed the securities that they underwrote to institutional clients or through other firms.

Next down the tombstone were members of a group of 17 major-bracket firms listed in alphabetical order. These were powerful players, but with inferior client lists and less prestige than the special-bracket firms. Then came 23 sub-major firms, often known as wire houses (because of their regional and national telegraphic links), that were noted for their retail distribution capabilities. After the sub-majors, there might be further subordinate brackets of smaller brokers or regional firms, depending on the issue.

The bulk of corporate securities issues brought to market by the investment banks in the 1950s and 1960s, as in earlier years, were debt securities, either bonds or notes. Some issues were sold publicly to retail and institutional investors; others were disposed of through "private placements" with insurance companies and other large institutional investors. For public bond and note issues, the gross spread (that is, the total compensation received by the investment banks) was about 1% of the principal amount. The spread was even less for private placements, which incurred little marketing cost. But the gross spread on equity issues was more than 6%, making such issues disproportionately profitable. The hierarchical structure of the industry ensured that the special-bracket firms enjoyed the lion's share of the proceeds of equity issues. However, the spreads were big enough for the subordinate houses to do well too – well enough for most of them to accept their place in the food chain.

Nevertheless, the 1960s saw some changes in the ranking of Wall Street houses, though not in the hierarchical structuring of the underwriting industry. By the end of the decade, Merrill Lynch and Salomon Brothers had been elevated to the special bracket, and Dillon Read and Kuhn, Loeb had been demoted to major-bracket status. Merrill Lynch ("The Thundering Herd") achieved this by developing a vast, efficient and profitable securities business serving individual investors, which provided it with unrivalled retail distribution power. Salomon Brothers enhanced its power in the market by developing market-making capacity for institutional investors, allowing them to trade large blocks of securities without disrupting the market. Lower down the scale, upstart Donaldson, Lufkin & Jenrette, founded in 1959, was promoted from submajor to major-bracket status through providing institutional investors with more sophisticated research than the normal offerings produced for the retail market.

International business

After the war, with the dollar supreme as the currency for international trade, investment and commodities, New York was the foremost location of the international capital market. The volume of dollar-denominated bond issues for foreign borrowers grew steadily during the 1950s. In addition to many corporate borrowers, sovereign borrowers included Australia (13 issues), Norway (5 issues), Belgium (4 issues), New Zealand (3 issues) and Denmark (2 issues), as well as the European Coal and Steel Community (4 issues), Japan Development Bank (3 issues) and French and Italian governments entities. Between 1955 and 1962 foreign borrowers raised $4.2 billion through Wall Street bond issues that were brought to market by syndicates usually led by one of the special-bracket investment banks. It was a particularly profitable business, because of the large size of the issues and a gross spread of around 2.5% compared with 1% for domestic bond issues.

During the 1950s a market for offshore dollars developed in Europe, focused on London. This was the outcome of a variety of economic and political factors. The most important was the recurrent US balance-of-payments deficits, which created a pool of $17 billion externally held dollars by the end of the decade. Restrictions on the rate of interest paid on bank deposits in the United States led US multinationals to hold overseas dollar earnings offshore. Moreover, the higher rates available offshore attracted a flow of dollars from the United States. A further reason was Soviet anxiety that dollar balances held in New York might be seized by a hostile US administration in the event of a cold war confrontation. Thus the communist countries kept their dollar balances with banks outside the United States.

The late 1950s saw the development of banking activity conducted in offshore dollars – the Eurodollar market. (The Euro prefix derives from the original location of the market in Europe, mostly London.) The Eurodollar market operated free of the regulations and constraints that distorted bank activity of the day, meaning that banks were able to offer higher rates to depositors and cheaper rates to borrowers than were available from domestic sources and still be highly profitable. It grew rapidly, and being largely unregulated, it allowed bankers to create innovative new products that attracted yet more business. Although the market was pioneered by UK investment banks, known as merchant banks, from the early 1960s the New York money-centre banks and other US banks flocked to London, where they established branches or subsidiaries to participate in the burgeoning Eurodollar market.

Eurobonds

Initially, the Eurodollar market just conducted bank lending on a short-term basis. Then in 1963 came the first issue of dollar-denominated offshore bonds, or Eurobonds. The lead-manager of this issue was Warburgs, a London merchant bank, and the borrower was Autostrade, the Italian state highways entity. Two weeks after the Autostrade issue, President Kennedy announced the imposition of a new tax on foreign borrowing in the US capital market: the Interest Equalisation Tax (IET). The purpose of the IET, which was strengthened by subsequent restrictions, was to restrict the external flow of dollars to alleviate the deteriorating US balance-of-payments position. But by effectively closing down foreign borrowing, it pulled down the shutters on New York as an international capital market. This made the Eurobond market, based in London, the linchpin of the international capital market. Between 1963 and 1972 the volume of Eurobond new issues rose from $148m to $5.5 billion.

The main Wall Street investment banks and US money-centre commercial banks established a presence in London to participate in the booming euromarkets. For the latter, involvement in the Eurobond market in London allowed them to develop in-house expertise in underwriting and securities business that was not possible at home but might be useful if the Glass-Steagall Act were to be repealed. From the 1960s, London emerged as a second base for Wall Street money-centre banks and investment banks, and over the years their London and other overseas offshoots became of growing importance.

The swinging sixties

Overall, stock prices moved upwards during the 1960s and early 1970s, the Dow nearly doubling, rising from 650 at the start of 1960 to 1,020 at the end of 1972. But prices were much more volatile than in the 1950s, and there were some sharp downturns – in 1961–62, 1966 and 1969–70 – largely as a result of inflation and the generally higher and more variable interest rates that accompanied it. Fuelling inflation were monetary expansion and the federal fiscal deficit, which was a result of heavy government expenditure on social welfare combined with the cost of fighting the Vietnam war. The progress of the war, notably setbacks such as the Tet Offensive of 1968, had a big effect on investor confidence and stock prices. So too did other political shocks, particularly the Cuban missile crisis of 1962 and the assassination of President Kennedy in November 1963, when the market plummeted 3%.

One factor that contributed to the rise in stock prices in the 1960s was a mergers and acquisitions (M&A) boom, a phenomenon last seen 60 years earlier. The turn-of-the-century merger movement had been about increasing market share in particular industries, such as steel, oil and tobacco, to enhance monopolistic pricing power. The M&A enthusiasts in the 1960s were fashionable conglomerates, which used their highly priced stock to buy up companies with low market ratings. The theory underlying the rise of the conglomerates was that diversification into a range of activities gave protection against the cyclical nature of many activities. It was a plausible sales pitch, but in practice it proved a deeply flawed business model since these often hugely varied collections of businesses proved difficult to manage effectively. But during the bull market, analysts and investors were dazzled by the growth rate and immediate financial results, thanks to creative acquisition accounting, and scrambled for the stocks of these serial acquirers – "giantomania", as John Mitchell, attorney general in the Nixon administration, disapprovingly put it. Leading conglomerates of the 1960s and 1970s included ITT (International Telephone and Telegraph), Gulf + Western, American Can, Litton Industries and LTV (Ling-Temco-Vaught). The predations of the conglomerates boosted stock prices because acquiring companies were willing to pay a premium for control. As ever, there were fat fees for the Wall Street investment bankers, lawyers, accountants and others who advised on the deals.

The growth of stock ownership that had begun in the 1950s contin-ued in the 1960s, with the number of individuals rising from 20m to 30m. Even more participated through mutual funds – the number of funds grew from 161 in 1960 to 356 in 1970 and their net assets almost trebled. Some mutual funds adopted pushy techniques to generate sales, such as door-to-door house visits. Public enthusiasm for mutual-fund investment provided an opportunity for crooks to perpetrate huge frauds. The most notorious were Bernie Cornfeld and Robert Vesco, whose giant mutual fund Investors Overseas Services (IOS) had, at its peak, the largest financial sales organisation in the world, assets of $2.5 billion and 300,000 shareholders. Its collapse cost investors $500m. Another mega-scam was Equity Funding Corporation, based in Los Angeles – its directors looted investors to the tune of $300m. True to form, the market downturn of 1969–70 made it impossible to conceal the missing millions and brought the frauds to light.

The stormy seventies

Stock prices in the 1970s had even more of a roller-coaster ride than in the 1960s (see Figure 2.4). The devaluation of the dollar in August 1971 set in motion the forces that in 1973, against the backdrop of a third Arab–Israeli war, provoked a quadrupling of oil prices. This pushed the United States, and much of the world, into recession and triggered a severe bout of inflation. Faced by the most dire economic conditions since the 1930s, as well as the Watergate political crisis which led to the resignation of President Nixon in 1974, stock prices slumped. The Dow almost halved, plunging from 1,020 at the start of 1973 to 580 in Decem-ber 1974. The price fall was accompanied by a decline in volume, with dire consequences for securities firms; in 1973–74 NYSE firms lost $255m and job losses on Wall Street amounted to 30% of the workforce.

Securities prices staged a robust recovery in 1975–76, pushing the Dow back above 1,000. In fact, 1975 was a bumper year on Wall Street – Merrill Lynch's profits soared to a record $100m, a 30% increase com-pared with its last good year. But it was just a respite and prices and prosperity soon retreated again. The wintry conditions on Wall Street persisted through the late 1970s and into the early 1980s.

Back office "paper crunch"

The traditionally neglected back offices had their own problems. The 1960s saw such a large and rapid increase in the volume of secondary-market securities trading that there was a crisis. Average daily volumes

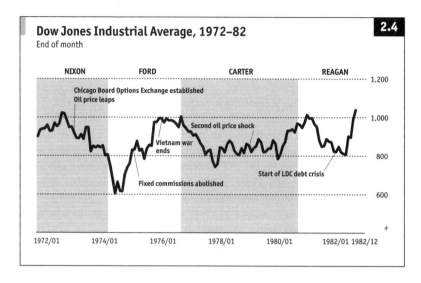

2.4

Dow Jones Industrial Average, 1972–82
End of month

NIXON   FORD   CARTER   REAGAN

Chicago Board Options Exchange established
Oil price leaps

Second oil price shock

Vietnam war ends

Fixed commissions abolished

Start of LDC debt crisis

1,200

1,000

800

600

1972/01   1974/01   1976/01   1978/01   1980/01   1982/01 1982/12

on the NYSE rose from 3m stocks per day in 1960 to 6m in 1965, 10m in 1967 and 13m in 1968. By then many brokerage firms, operating with non-automated processing equipment, were drowning under the tidal wave of paperwork generated by the transaction flows. The solution to the back-office "paper crunch" was computerisation, and from the early 1970s financial-services firms emerged as pioneers in IT and some of the IT sector's biggest customers.

The back-office chaos, coupled with a spate of client defaults stemming from the 1969–70 market reversal, led to a wave of failures among securities firms. Congress was so alarmed by the industry's problems that in 1971 it passed legislation creating the Securities Investor Protection Corporation (SIPC), a body analogous to the New Deal's FDIC insurance fund for bank depositors. The SIPC insurance fund allowed the orderly closing of troubled firms and protected investors and creditors against fraud, mishandling and broker insolvency.

Automation also offered a solution to the problem of the fragmentation of the over-the-counter (OTC) securities market. Since the early 1960s, at the instigation of the SEC, the NASD had been developing a computerised system to trade OTC securities. Trading on the NASDAQ (National Association of Securities Dealers Automated Quotation System) began in February 1971, linking the terminals of more than 500 market makers throughout the country who competed with each other to offer the best buy and sell prices. Although NASDAQ was created to automate trade in OTC unlisted stocks, it presented the NYSE with a potential rival that might threaten its position as the foremost US securities exchange.

"Mayday" 1975

Since its inception in 1792, members of the NYSE had operated under rules that required them to charge minimum fixed commission rates set by the exchange. Most NYSE firms were content for this state of affairs to continue, but the 1960s saw mounting complaints from institutional investors about having to pay the same minimum commissions for their big trades as retail investors paid for small trades. This discontent led to the growth of swap arrangements for bulk trades whereby they bypassed the exchange. Aware of these developments, in the late 1960s members of Congress began to push for the abolition of fixed commissions, holding a series of hearings about the issue. With the publication of a Senate subcommittee report in February 1972 advocating the immediate introduction of competitive rates, the writing was on the wall. In September 1973, after negotiations with the NYSE, the SEC announced the complete abolition of fixed commissions from May 1st 1975.

The "Mayday" move to negotiated commissions unleashed fierce competition among securities brokerage firms to offer discounted rates. As commission rates fell, so did the revenue of most securities firms; in 1976, the first year of negotiated rates, commissions comprised 45% of securities firms' gross revenue, compared with about 65% in the late 1960s. Between 1974 and 1978, the average commission paid by institutional investors halved, although the decline for retail investors was much less. These competitive pressures prompted some broker-dealer firms to merge to achieve economies of scale while others went out of business, resulting in a fall in the number of NYSE member firms.

The forces of competition and the growing size of trades led securities firms to seek greater capital. By the early 1970s the majority of NYSE members had incorporated, since the partnership form of business organisation limited their ability to raise capital. Initially, they became private corporations, but in March 1970 the NYSE approved public ownership of member firms, effectively ending the exchange's status as a private club.

Investors and depositors

The collapse in stock prices in 1973–74 disheartened private investors, and their number dwindled from 30m to 25m. Many investors chose to put their money in money-market mutual funds, the first of which had been launched in 1972. Alarmed by the implications of falling stock prices for pensions, Congress passed the Employees Retirement Income Security Act (ERISA) in 1974, which significantly enhanced employee protection against unscrupulous or incompetent fund managers. Although the legislature held no sway over the Dow, it was able to ensure that fund managers were legally responsible for investing pension fund monies in appropriate ways. In the mid-1970s such safe investments were mostly bonds, particularly the mortgage-backed securities issued by government agencies, such as the Government National Mortgage Association (Ginnie Mae), which originated this new class of security in 1970.

The quadrupling of the oil price in 1973 boosted oil-exporting countries' revenue, which leapt from $24 billion in 1972 to $117 billion in 1974. During 1974–80, the oil-exporting countries accumulated $383 billion in financial assets. Around half were short-term bank deposits, mostly in New York and London, and the rest consisted of securities, real estate and some bilateral sovereign loans. Petrodollar "recycling" gave a big boost to the main money-centre banks and investment banks that undertook international financial operations. Since the introduction of the Interest Equalisation Tax in 1963 (see page 36), London had been the foremost centre for the international capital market, and so it remained despite the scrapping of the tax in 1974. Wall Street banks and firms played a leading role in petrodollar recycling, but much of the business was done by their London entities. In December 1981, in an attempt to lure the international capital market back to Wall Street, the Federal Reserve sanctioned the introduction of International Banking Facilities (IBFS). These are separate accounting units through which banks can conduct international transactions without being subject to some of the restrictions that apply to domestic banking operations. But the measure met with only limited success.

Chicago derivatives revolution

The collapse of the Bretton Woods system of fixed international exchange rates in 1971 was followed by much greater currency volatility. This led to demand for financial instruments that would allow corporations and banks to hedge their exchange-rate risk or speculate on currency movements. The Chicago commodities futures and options exchanges were the world leaders in such products, and they pioneered the development of financial derivatives. In May 1972 the International

Monetary Market (IMM), an offshoot of the long-established Chicago Mercantile Exchange (CME), launched currency futures contracts, the world's first financial derivatives. The following year the Chicago Board of Trade (CBOT), the CME's arch rival, created the Chicago Board Options Exchange (CBOE) to trade options on corporate stocks. The CBOE revolutionised stock-options trading by creating standardised listed stock options as an alternative to ad hoc and unregulated OTC stock options. The growth of the new market was much helped by the pioneering paper published in 1973 by Fischer Black and Myron Scholes demonstrating for the first time how options should be valued. In 1975, the IMM launched a futures contract on Treasury bills, the first interest-rate futures contract. In New York, the American Stock Exchange responded by launching its own stock-options contracts in the mid-1970s, winning business – though not as much as the CBOE. The New York Futures Exchange, an offshoot of the NYSE, began trading financial-futures contracts in 1980, but it too was unable to catch up with the Chicago exchanges. Chicago's head start had established it as the world centre for trading financial derivatives, one of the fastest-growing activities of the wholesale financial-services industry, and continuing product development and innovation ensured that it stayed ahead.

Bitter medicine from the Fed

The Iranian revolution of 1978–79, which toppled the Shah and led to the installation of an Islamic regime, resulted in a virtual shutdown of Iranian oil production. This reduction in supply, coupled with moves by the Organisation of Petroleum Exporting Countries (OPEC) to raise the real value of its members' oil revenues which had been eroded by inflation, led to a second oil shock in 1979: the official price of "marker" crude increased from $12 to $18 a barrel, and the spot market price soared above $30 a barrel. Entrenched US inflation of around 5%, and the threat of higher levels posed by the oil-price rise and the decline of the dollar, convinced Paul Volcker, the new Federal Reserve chairman, of the need for an aggressive anti-inflationary policy stance. On Saturday October 6th 1979, the Fed announced that it was raising interest rates by one percentage point to 12%, and that in future it would target the money supply to combat inflation, a change of policy that implied steep interest-rate rises. Taken entirely unaware, Wall Street bondholders watched horrified as bond prices plunged – the "Saturday Night Massacre", as it was dubbed. There was worse to come: by December 1980 the US prime rate had reached 21.5%, although it declined thereafter.

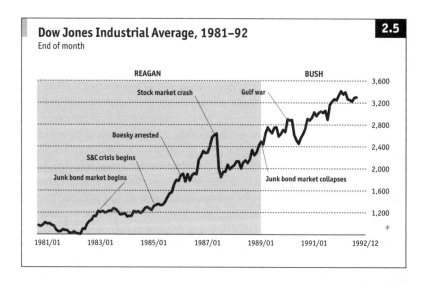

Dow Jones Industrial Average, 1981–92 `2.5`
End of month

REAGAN — BUSH

Stock market crash

Gulf war

Boesky arrested

S&C crisis begins

Junk bond market begins

Junk bond market collapses

3,600
3,200
2,800
2,400
2,000
1,600
1,200

1981/01 1983/01 1985/01 1987/01 1989/01 1991/01 1992/12

The increased energy prices and sky-high interest rates tipped the US economy into recession in 1980, and it was not until 1983 that sustained growth resumed. But in the meantime the Fed's aggressive treatment worked: by 1982 inflation had abated and interest rates were falling. Since 1977, the Dow had been hovering around 800 and in April 1980 it touched 780 (see Figure 2.4). Anticipation of the end of the recession led to a revival in the winter of 1980/81, but the upward momentum soon faltered and by summer 1982 the Dow was back at 800. But then in August 1982, despite the announcement by Mexico of its suspension of international debt payments (ushering in the 1980s less developed country [LDC] debt crisis), the trend turned and for the next five years the Dow rose almost continuously (see Figure 2.5).

Underlying the Dow's upward momentum was a dynamic domestic economy with low inflation, strong job growth and healthy corporate profits. Thrusting sectors based on new technologies, such as computers and pharmaceuticals, were expanding to take the place of declining smokestack industries. Moreover, the Reagan administration's substantial budget deficits were a source of economic stimulus. Stock prices were also boosted by the appreciation of the dollar, at least until late 1985, which led to an inflow of foreign funds to Wall Street.

Merger mania

The rise of new industries, and the decline of traditional ones, was part

43

of a widespread industrial and corporate restructuring of the US economy in the 1980s. In the decade up to 1988 there were 23,000 corporate mergers, including the swallowing up of 82 of the *Fortune* 500 companies: in 1983 the annual value of US mergers and acquisitions was $53 billion; in 1988 it was $282 billion. As in previous merger waves, the stock prices of acquisition targets were propelled upwards by the premiums that bidders were prepared to pay for control, and prices of the stocks of other corporations were boosted by the prospect of windfall gains on the part of speculators.

In the early 1980s, as a result of the rampant inflation and depressed stock prices of the 1970s, the stockmarket valuation of many corporations, particularly in traditional sectors, was below their asset or "book" value. This meant that by buying a company through the acquisition of its stocks, a purchaser acquired the underlying assets at a discount to their resale price. A number of opportunistic entrepreneurs preyed on such price anomalies, sometimes against the wishes of the incumbent management, by launching a hostile takeover bid. For a while, these "corporate raiders" (some preferred the term "vultures") – such as James Farley, James Goldsmith, Carl Icahn, Ron Perelman, T. Boone Pickens, Saul Steinberg and Gordon White – became as well known as movie stars.

The takeover battles of the 1980s were the most sensational manifestations of the corporate restructuring wave. More often it was the management itself that was most keenly aware of the discrepancy between a low stock price and the higher true value of the physical assets or performance potential of a corporation. Hence the 1980s saw a boom in leveraged buy-outs (LBOs), in which management, assisted by specialist financiers, bought a subsidiary or even an entire company from shareholders, financing the purchase with debt. Not infrequently, such buyouts were an unbundling of one of the sprawling conglomerates that had been spawned by the merger boom of the 1960s, but which by the 1980s were underperforming.

Junk bonds revolution

Much of the corporate restructuring of the 1980s was financed by high-yield debt, or "junk bonds", as such financing was known colloquially. Junk bonds are corporate bonds rated by the various ratings agencies that service Wall Street, notably Standard and Poor's and Moody's, at below "investment grade", signalling a greater default risk. As compensation for the higher risk, investors expect a higher yield than from high-grade bonds. High-risk, high-return bonds had been around for years in the form of "fallen angels", a term applied to former blue-chip bonds that had been down-graded because the issuer had fallen on hard times. Then in spring 1977 investment bank Lehman Brothers Kuhn Loeb brought out the first "original issue" junk bonds – bonds that were not and never had been investment grade. A new financial market was born.

Credit for the dynamic development of the junk bond market belongs to Michael Milken. The realisation of Milken's financial revolution had four interrelated requirements: junk-bond issuers; a leading role for his firm, Drexel Burnham Lambert; junk-bond buyers; and a secondary market maker for the bonds.

As already mentioned, the corporate restructuring process and its attendant takeover entrepreneurs and LBO technicians were potential issuers. But the US primary market was still dominated by the traditional hierarchical syndicate structure, and although Drexel was a major-bracket firm it was not in a position to engineer a revolution in the US capital market. But the longstanding syndication set-up was on the verge of disintegration. The trigger for change was a development in the Eurobond market – the advent of the "bought deal" in 1977. In a bought deal an investment bank acting alone, or maybe with a partner, commits to purchase an entire issue from an issuer at a fixed price. The speed and sureness of a bought deal appeals to issuers, since it shifts issuance risk from them to the bank. For the banks, it was a new competitive tactic for winning mandates, with the additional advantage of enabling them to retain a higher proportion of the issuance fees. The outcome was a gravitation of big corporate bond issues away from the US domestic capital market to the Eurobond market. In response in 1982, the SEC introduced a streamlined securities issuance procedure, known as shelf registration (Rule 415), whereby companies were able to register in advance details of securities so that when they needed to raise capital they could make an issue "off the shelf". The new rule had a profound impact on the relationship between investment banks and corporations. Traditionally, as an investment banker at the time described it, the ties between a bank and its principal corporate clients had been "connubial"; but since Rule 415, "we have moved from the traditional concept of marriage to one-night stands". The arrival of the bought deal on Wall Street may have been disconcerting for the established firms, but by stirring up the primary market it provided an opening for Milken.

But Milken also needed buy-side demand for high-yield bonds. He had some success in arousing interest among mutual funds and insurance companies by citing academic research, which demonstrated that the default risk on a diversified portfolio of junk bonds was only minimally higher than for high-grade bonds, and they generated substantially higher returns – in other words, they were under-priced. Another boost was the relaxation of the federal banking laws allowing banks and savings and loans institutions to buy corporate bonds to help boost their earnings in 1982. The final piece in the jigsaw puzzle was the need for a market maker for the secondary market in the bonds, since purchasers would only buy them if they could readily sell them. Drexel itself undertook this role for the numerous issues it sponsored.

As the pieces fell into place, Milken and Drexel went to town on promoting their protégés. They succeeded – by 1985 high-yield debt constituted 20% of new corporate-bond issues, providing access to the capital market for both financial entrepreneurs and a host of companies that would otherwise have been deemed uncreditworthy. Drexel undertook the lion's share of the business, and the firm's revenue soared from $1 billion in 1983 to $4 billion in 1986. Clients included the leading buy-out firm on Wall Street, Kohlberg Kravis Roberts. Its many deals included a $32 billion bid for RJR Nabisco in 1988, then the largest takeover. Milken's bonuses – $550m in 1986 alone – made him the highest-paid worker on Wall Street.

Squeeze on commercial banks

While Wall Street's investment banks and broker-dealers were prospering from rising securities prices and buoyant primary-market and secondary-market securities business, the money-centre commercial banks were struggling to cope with the impact of the LDC debt crisis on their loan books. In May 1987, Citicorp made a $3 billion provision – the largest commercial loss in history – against its LDC loans. The degree of the exposure of the money-centre banks to LDC loans was, to some extent, a reflection of adverse trends in other aspects of commercial banking during the 1970s. On the funding side, the rapidly growing money-market mutual funds, which paid higher rates than bank accounts, depleted their traditional cheap retail deposit base. So did Merrill Lynch's highly flexible Cash Management Account launched in 1977, which the banks protested was a bank account masquerading as a securities account. Simultaneously, on the lending side, the trend was for corporations to raise funds through the issuance of securities with the assistance of an investment bank – securitisation – rather than by borrowing from a commercial bank.

The erosion of the commercial banks' deposits and profitability led to appeals to the Fed to relax its interpretation of the Glass-Steagall Act to allow them to move into the booming securities business. The Fed was not unsympathetic to their predicament. In 1983, despite challenges from the securities industry, it allowed BankAmerica, at that date America's biggest commercial bank, to acquire Charles Schwab, the largest discount securities broker. Simultaneously, BankAmerica announced its entry into the insurance business by the purchase of 24.9% (the maximum permitted at the time) in HL Capital Management, with an option to buy 100% if regulations were relaxed, as later occurred. These moves, which were soon imitated by other banks, constituted the first significant steps in the process of the dismantling of the Glass-Steagall separation of commercial and investment banking and the traditional separation of banking and insurance.

Since the Glass-Steagall Act in 1933, the only securities trading undertaken by the commercial banks had been in Treasury bonds, although they also dominated trading in the foreign-exchange market. The rise of derivatives in the 1970s presented new opportunities to develop trading activities, since these new instruments were not covered by the Glass-Steagall ban. The development of the swaps market from 1982 led to a substantial expansion of the commercial banks' trading activities. Swaps trading, dealing in interest-rate and currency derivatives, is an activity in which balance-sheet size confers competitive advantage, and so large commercial banks soon emerged as the dominant players. This expansion of trading activity represented another intrusion by commercial banks into the type of activity traditionally undertaken by investment banks.

Crash of October 1987

By late 1987, stock prices had been rising for five years and conventional valuation yardsticks, such as price/earnings ratios, were looking distinctly over-stretched. The summer had seen jittery price movements in response to a variety of developments, such as Citicorp's $3 billion LDC debt write-down and the interest-rate hike that followed the arrival of Alan Greenspan, the new Fed chairman. Then in October, triggered by nothing out of the ordinary, investors suffered a collective loss of nerve and headed en masse for the exit. On October 19th 1987, the Dow plunged more than 500 points – a 20% fall, its largest one-day drop – and by early November the market had lost 30% of its value. The collapse on Wall Street triggered plunges in stockmarkets around the world, with some overseas exchanges, such as Australia, Singapore and Mexico, experiencing even greater falls than Wall Street. In the inquest after the 1987 crash, program trading (automatic computerised stock buy and sell programs, a recent innovation) emerged as the prime suspect for explaining the rapidity and depth of the collapse of stock prices and its worldwide impact. In response to this analysis, the NYSE introduced a circuit-breaker mechanism by which trading would automatically halt if prices fell too fast.

Savings and loans crisis

The crash created acute problems among savings and loans institutions, the purchasers of a considerable proportion of the $200 billion of junk bonds issued during the 1980s. Because of their high-risk nature, junk-bond prices generally shadow stock prices, which in late 1987 meant they headed sharply downwards. As a result, many savings and loans found the value of their assets much depleted. An alarming situation turned into a crisis when new accounting rules required the savings and loans to mark their assets to market prices, revealing gaping holes in many of their balance sheets. Moreover, when they tried to sell their holdings they found that there were no buyers and that the market-making facilities they had been promised functioned poorly.

As the savings and loans crisis mounted, Milken and Drexel Burnham Lambert became the butt of much criticism for selling risky and inappropriate investment products. Though true, the charges were hardly fair since the thrifts had been just as keen to buy as the bankers were to sell. Indeed, the focus on the plight of the savings and loans sector – generally regarded as the staidest of the staid – started to reveal some decidedly unstaid conduct on the part of those running thrifts. Some, most notoriously Charles Keating, head of Lincoln Savings and Loan, were found to have been using depositors' funds to finance an extravagant lifestyle. Others had assumed reckless risks in the conduct of business, calculating that if they won the gamble they would get a big bonus and if they lost the US government would rescue depositors. And so it turned out: the bill for the savings and loans bail-out of the early 1990s cost US taxpayers an estimated $500 billion.

Ivan Boesky scandal

Stockmarket downturns commonly reveal financial improprieties that are brought to light by falling prices. The 1980s boom was unusual in that a major financial scandal broke before the crash, not in its aftermath. In November 1986, Ivan Boesky, a prominent "arb" (arbitrageur), a spuriously technical label for market opportunists who specialised in speculating in the stocks of takeover targets, was arrested and charged with numerous violations of the insider-trading laws. It transpired that Boesky's legendary financial acumen amounted to an ability to spot greedy people with confidential information about takeovers who were willing to exchange it for substantial sums of money. The activities of one of Boesky's tipsters – Denis Levine, a corporate financier at Drexel Burnham Lambert – attracted the interest of the SEC, which found that the trail led to Boesky. In the world's biggest insider-trading scandal, Boesky co-operated with the authorities in a deal for a lighter sentence that led to the arrest of other avaricious Wall Streeters.

Perhaps surprisingly – after all, he hardly needed the kickbacks – one of those fingered by Boesky was Milken, who had organised junk-bond offerings that had financed some of Boesky's activities. At first Milken protested innocence, but eventually in 1990 he pleaded guilty to six counts of racketeering and fraud. Both Milken and Boesky went to jail and paid enormous fines. Drexel Burnham Lambert was also heavily fined, compounding the problems it was facing as a result of the depreciation in value of its substantial holdings of unsold junk bonds. In 1990, the firm filed for bankruptcy, closing a chapter of Wall Street history perhaps most succinctly summarised by the mantra of the so-called "master of the universe" dealmaker Gordon Gekko in the 1987 movie "Wall Street": "greed is good".

Recession and recovery

Fearing a repetition of the economic slump that had followed the 1929 crash, the Fed slashed interest rates after the 1987 crash and announced that it would provide emergency reserves to any bank that needed them. Its prompt actions helped to stave off a slump, although there was an economic slowdown and in 1990–91 the US economy went into a mild recession. The late 1980s and early 1990s were distinctly bleak years on Wall Street, the crash being followed by an abrupt contraction in the securities industry. Between December 1987 and December 1992, nearly 1,500 NASD member firms closed, a fall of 22%, and the securities industry in New York City shed 30,000 jobs.

Stock prices staged a recovery in 1988 as the dreaded depression failed to materialise, and by summer 1989 the Dow was back at 2,600.

However, prices retreated again as the recession took hold. Then in 1991 the Dow began to move gently upwards, reaching 3,800 by the end of 1994 (see Figure 2.6). A new and much more vigorous phase of the upswing got under way from 1995, with the Dow hitting 6,000 in 1996 and 8,000 in 1997, a level that once again strained conventional valuation ratios and prompted Greenspan to warn that investors were behaving with "irrational exuberance". But investors paid only momentary heed to his wise words and then went on buying, pushing the Dow to 9,000 in 1998, 10,000 in 1999 and over 11,000 early in 2000. By then the market had been rising almost continuously for nearly 18 years, and the 1987 crash had been downgraded to a mere "market break". It was Wall Street's longest bull market.

There was another market break in September 1998 when the Dow plunged from around 9,000 to 7,500. This was triggered by the news that the Federal Reserve Bank of New York had had to put together a rescue package for Long-term Capital Management (LTCM), a New York-based hedge fund. Hedge funds are large funds that use supposedly sophisticated techniques to speculate in the financial markets. Although their origins can be traced to the late 1940s, hedge funds grew rapidly in size and number in the 1980s and 1990s as vehicles for professional investors, notably banks and fund managers, to participate in risky but potentially high-return forms of financial market activity that they were unable or unwilling to undertake directly. LTCM was one of the biggest and most prestigious hedge funds, its directors including a former vice-president of the Federal Reserve, one of Wall Street's leading traders and a couple of Nobel Prize-winning economists. Nonetheless, it managed to lose most of its capital as a result of the Russian financial default and turbulence in the international financial markets in summer 1998. When the Fed stepped in it was on the point of failure and posed a "systemic risk" to the international financial system. Naturally, investors took fright – hence the price falls – but the "irrational exuberance" quickly reasserted itself as the market recovered and had soon reached new heights.

Raging bull

The bull market of the 1990s was driven by many of the same favourable factors that powered the stock rises of the 1980s, plus a couple more. In general, America was prosperous with strong growth, low unemployment and lower inflation than in the 1980s. A significant contribution to the slowing of the rate of price rises was made by the

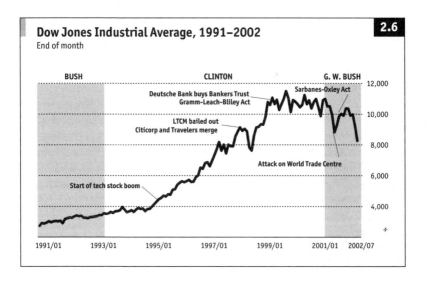

2.6

Dow Jones Industrial Average, 1991–2002
End of month

BUSH · CLINTON · G. W. BUSH

Deutsche Bank buys Bankers Trust
Gramm-Leach-Bliley Act

Sarbanes-Oxley Act

LTCM bailed out
Citicorp and Travelers merge

Attack on World Trade Centre

Start of tech stock boom

12,000
10,000
8,000
6,000
4,000

1991/01   1993/01   1995/01   1997/01   1999/01   2001/01   2002/07

low and stable price of oil on the international market after the Gulf war of 1990–91. Some analysts linked this to the rise in stock prices, arguing that the transition from an era of high inflation (the 1960s–80s) to a lower-inflation era generated a one-off rise in stock prices because of the lower interest rates that accompanied lower inflation. The appreciation of the dollar was another factor restraining inflation, one that also boosted stock prices by attracting capital flows from abroad, particularly from 1995.

Much stockmarket action focused on companies in the technology, media and telecoms (TMT) sectors. Many of these were young companies that were listed on NASDAQ rather than the NYSE. Between 1991 and 2000, the NASDAQ Composite Index rose from 500 to 5,000, a tenfold hike, whereas the Dow managed less than a fourfold increase. The most frenetic dealing of all was in the stocks of dotcom Internet companies, a mania that began with the sensational Netscape IPO (initial public offering) in August 1995 – on the opening day of trading the price of stock soared from $28 to $74 – and reached its peak in early 2000. The rocketing prices of dotcom and other TMT stocks, even of companies that had never turned in a cent of profit, were rationalised and justified by an avalanche of hype about the "new economy" and a "new economic paradigm". For sure, some of the new technologies offered the potential for productivity gains that promised increased efficiency and prosperity. But the volume of funds flowing into these sectors and the

51

proliferation of providers indicated that vast overcapacity was being created and that there would be a lot of casualties among investors when the bubble burst.

In the money

The second half of the 1990s were bumper years for Wall Street's investment banks and broker-dealer firms. As ever, rising stock prices resulted in greater investor demand and buoyant secondary-market trading. The primary market was booming too, with investors eager to back almost any half-plausible prospectus from a TMT company. There was also a boom in mergers and acquisitions, with the merger between AOL and Time Warner breaking all records.

Banks, investment banks and securities firms were closely involved in the amalgamation wave, both as professional advisers and as participants. Between 1996 and 2000 there were more than 400 acquisitions of US securities firms, a quarter of them by foreign companies. The announcement in 1998 of the formation of Citigroup through the merger of Citicorp, a commercial bank, and Travelers, a combined insurance company and investment bank that owned Salomon Smith Barney, spelt the end of the Glass-Steagall separation of commercial and investment banking. Thirteen months later, in November 1999, President Clinton duly laid it to rest by signing the Financial Modernisation Act, known as the Gramm-Leach-Bliley Act, allowing banks, securities firms and insurance companies to affiliate under a financial holding company.

The second half of the 1990s saw increased globalisation of the investment-banking industry. This involved a thrust by the Wall Street firms to boost their presence in London and elsewhere – leading, for instance, to Merrill Lynch's purchase of Mercury Asset Management in 1997 and Chase's acquisition of Flemings in 2000 – and by organic expansion. These years also witnessed a big increase in the presence of foreign banks on Wall Street through the acquisition of US firms, notably the purchase of Dillon Read and PaineWebber by UBS in 1998 and 2000 respectively, of Bankers Trust by Deutsche Bank and of Republic Bank of New York by HSBC in 1999, and Credit Suisse's acquisition of Donaldson, Lufkin & Jenrette in 2000. The other important development of that year was the merger of J.P. Morgan and Chase Manhattan to form J.P. Morgan Chase. These moves constituted a further consolidation of the industry on a global scale.

Out of the money

The dotcom bubble burst in spring 2000, letting the air out of the inflated net worth of a megabyte of new-economy paper millionaires and damaging the wealth of thousands of 1990s-style speculators known as day traders. The NASDAQ index plunged and the falls in tech stocks blighted sentiment about other sectors, finally bringing a halt to the Dow's record twentyfold increase since summer 1982. From 2000, as the US economy slowed, stock prices moved sideways, with the Dow surfing in the range 9,500–10,500. But then further developments turned a market downturn into a major crisis. First, there was the terrorist attack of September 11th 2001, which shook public confidence and sent prices plunging. Then, more insidiously, a series of scandals involving leading investment banks, top accountancy firms and prominent corporations undermined investors' faith in the stock market and financial services industry intermediaries. The harm to Wall Street's standing was substantial, but only history would reveal the full extent of the damage done.

3 Wall Street scandals

Financial scandals are as old as money itself. But they have been more prevalent and prominent in some eras than in others, recent years being an active era. This chapter looks at the contemporary crop and attempts to set them in context by presenting a general typology and a historical survey of Wall Street scandals since the 1920s, highlighting similarities to recent episodes.

What is a financial scandal? It is, according to the *Oxford English Dictionary*, a financial event that "occasions a general feeling of outrage or indignation". This definition is deliberately loose so as to cast the net widely, although the mesh is broad and the catch is confined to the biggest, most important and most notorious episodes. Many financial scandals involve infringement of the law or practitioner regulations; others are not illegal but are still regarded as abuses, hence they are scandals. "Disaster", "scam", "fiasco" are just a few of the other epithets that might also be applied to some of the scandals covered below.

Financial scandals come in many guises. Alan Peachey, a retired British banker, has compiled a dossier of *Great Financial Disasters of Our Time*, which lists 295 such episodes between 1974 and 1999 in various markets. Peachey's categorisation of types of financial disasters is the starting point for the typology of financial scandals, modified to take special account of Wall Street scandals, that follows.

Recent Wall Street scandal types

- Auditors
  - failure to detect misuse of accounting practices to mislead investors
- Fraud
- Professional conflicts of interest
  - investment-bank analysts: conflict between a bank's investment-banking operations (sell side) and advice to investors (buy side)
  - accountancy firms: conflict between role as auditor of client firm and as consultant to client firm
- Underwriting
  - preferential allocations of stock to favoured investors

- underpricing of IPOs depriving stock issuers of potential funds

Other common financial scandal types

- ◪ Bank advances
  - lack of judgment or prudence in conduct of lending
- ◪ Market ignorance
  - undertaking activities in markets outside normal sphere of operations
- ◪ Market manipulation
  - market corners, pools, etc
  - insider trading
  - short selling
  - program trading
- ◪ Rogue traders
  - inadequate management control over traders and/or back office
- ◪ Speculation
  - deliberate or inadvertent assumption of risk that goes wrong
- ◪ Unsound financial structures
  - Ponzi schemes
  - pyramid financing
  - excessive margin allowances

Each of the Wall Street scandals since the 1920s discussed below fits one, and sometimes more, of these ten types of financial scandals.

Manias, panics and crashes

Financial scandals often, though not exclusively, occur in the wake of financial bull markets. During the upswing, rising prices and easy profits lead practitioners, investors and even market watchdogs to relax their vigilance regarding the most fundamental rule of finance – that returns are positively correlated with risk (for example, junk bonds pay higher yields than Treasury bonds because the issuer is more likely to go bust than the US government). In some bull markets the final phase becomes a mania, with investors frenziedly buying and selling the favourite counter of the day in the belief that prices can only go up and that there is easy money to be made. This is true, until there is a sudden collective loss of nerve and prices crash – and whoever is left holding the counters suffers hefty losses. The losses resulting from the crash expose all sorts of dubious financial conduct that flourished during the late bull market, exposing a rash of financial scandals.

Charles Kindleberger, author of *Manias, Panics, and Crashes: A History of Financial Crises*, identifies a total of 29 speculative manias and crashes in European and American markets, from the South Sea Bubble of 1720 to the stockmarket slump of 1974–75. For the US alone there are nine: 1819, 1837, 1848, 1873, 1893, 1907, 1920–21, 1929 and 1974–75. Since the first edition of Kindleberger's book in 1978, there have been two further episodes: the merger mania of the 1980s, followed by the crash of October 1987, and the dotcom mania of the late 1990s, followed by the NASDAQ plunge of 2000–02. So there have been 11 US manias and crashes over the past two centuries, most of which have led to a spate of scandals.

Speculative manias in America have involved a variety of counters: cotton, coffee, land, silver, gold, railroad stocks, and so on. In the 20th century, some of the favourite speculative counters were technology company stocks: in the 1920s, radio and automobile companies and regional electric utilities; in the 1960s, electronics companies such as Xerox and Polaroid and conglomerates such as Litton Industries; and in the 1990s, technology, media and telecoms (TMT) companies, above all Internet companies.

During the bull markets of the 1920s and the 1990s, traditional yardsticks of stock valuation, such as net asset value, dividend yield or the price/earnings ratio, were abandoned as old-fashioned and obsolete. New measures were devised based on earnings growth or even the number of registered customers, which fitted the bill since many TMT companies had never made a profit and were destined never to do so. In both decades, the novel methods of valuation were supported by assertions that the economy had entered a new era or new paradigm. This was based on the proposition that the new technologies were opening up new vistas for growth, development and prosperity. To some extent they were, although not to the extent of rewriting the rules of economics, abolishing the business cycle, or heralding the end of history or the entry of humankind into the New Jerusalem – which became clear when the downturns arrived with a vengeance in 1929 and 2000. As Edward Chancellor, author of *Devil Take the Hindmost: A History of Financial Speculation*, has observed (citing John Templeton, a leading fund manager): "The four most expensive words in the English language are 'This time it's different'."

A bad start to the 21st century

The long bull market of the 1980s and 1990s finally peaked in early 2000. By mid-2002, the NASDAQ Composite index and the Dow were, respectively, 75% and 25% lower than their peak. The decline in stock prices in general, but particularly the collapse of a raft of dotcom and other TMT stocks, took investors by surprise – was not the natural order of things that stock prices went up, not down? Investors (both individual and institutional) and others began to ask what had gone wrong. Who was to blame for the depletion of so much wealth? Inevitably, fingers pointed at Wall Street. By September 2001 nearly 300 fraud suits had been filed in US courts against securities industry firms. There were three main classes of complaint: about misrepresentations by bank securities analysts; about the conduct and outcome of IPOs; and about conflicts of interest in relation to banks' private equity investments.

Then came a deck of corporate collapses, inflicting further damage on investors' wealth and turning misleading corporate accounting practices, executive fraud and the integrity of the audit process into burning financial and political issues. The principal scandals are listed below.

Enron

When Enron, an energy giant and once America's seventh-largest corporation, reported its third-quarter results in October 2001 it revealed a $600m loss and a $1.2 billion reduction in shareholder equity, resulting from losses from secret off-balance-sheet investment partnerships. The stock price crashed from a peak of $90 in August 2000 to less than $1, and in December 2001 Enron filed for bankruptcy. By then it had become clear that its vaunted business success and profits were no more than an accounting sham. A posse of outraged investors, staff, pensioners and politicians wanted to know why its failings had not been spotted earlier.

Arthur Andersen

Attention focused on Enron's auditors, Arthur Andersen. An obvious question was why did the auditors, who were charged with verifying the true state of the company's books, not know what was going on? Andersen's reaction was to try to cover its tracks by destroying its Enron files. In June 2002, it was found guilty of obstruction of justice, a verdict that delivered the final blow to the mortally wounded accountancy firm. It was by no means the first time that Andersen's practices had been found wanting. In 1998, it had been fined by the Securities and Exchange

Commission (SEC) for auditing deficiencies after its client Waste Management, a waste disposal firm, admitted manipulating earnings as Enron did three years later. The Andersen case raised wider questions about US corporate accounting and auditing practices.

Global Crossing
Global Crossing, founded in 1997 by a former junk-bond salesman and associate of Michael Milken, rapidly built a large international fibre-optic cable network for carrying telecoms and Internet traffic, largely through acquisitions. In January 2002, it became America's fourth-largest corporate bankrupt. The peculiar economics of bandwidth meant that firms could drum up the appearance of lively business by trading with each other, enabling them effectively to record revenue when in many cases no money changed hands. Like Enron, Global Crossing manipulated its accounts to make it appear profitable while it was actually making large losses. Both companies also spent heavily on political contributions. Again the auditor was Arthur Andersen, which also supplied management-consulting services.

Xerox
In April 2002, the SEC filed a civil suit against Xerox, a giant photocopy company, for misstating profits over a four-year period, resulting in an overstatement of $3 billion. In a negotiated settlement, Xerox agreed to pay a $10m fine and revise four years of trading statements. The penalty was the largest imposed by the SEC on a publicly traded corporation in relation to accounting lapses.

Tyco
During the 1990s, through hundreds of acquisitions, Dennis "deal-a-day" Kozlowski, Tyco's chief executive, built the company into a massive international conglomerate, valued at its peak at $62 billion. In June 2002, Kozlowski resigned, having been charged by the Manhattan district attorney with conspiracy to avoid payment of $1m-worth of sales tax on purchases of works of art. The stock price collapsed because of investors' fears that the launch of an investigation by the SEC would reveal accounting irregularities.

Adelphia
Adelphia, the sixth-largest US cable-television operator, filed for bankruptcy in June 2002. The company restated its profits for the previ-

ous two years and admitted having fewer cable subscribers than it claimed. Revelation of the company's huge personal loans to three former directors caused alarm. The Justice Department charged John Rigas, the founder, his two sons and two other managers with bank, securities and wire fraud.

WorldCom

WorldCom, a leading US long-distance call operator and host of 70% of Internet traffic, admitted the biggest accounting fraud in history in June 2002. It confessed to inflating profits by $7.2 billion by improperly booking expenses as capital expenditure. The corporation was already shrouded in scandal after the departure in April of its founder and chief executive, who borrowed millions from the firm to underwrite the inflated prices he had paid for the company's own shares. In July 2002, it achieved the dubious distinction of becoming the biggest corporate bankruptcy. Yet again, the auditor was Arthur Andersen.

Merrill Lynch and investment-bank analysts

In theory, the role of an analyst in an investment bank is to appraise the true value of securities for the benefit of the bank's brokerage operations and its buy-side investment clients, notably institutional investors. Conventionally, analysts rate stocks as "buy", "hold" or "sell". In the early 1990s, the ratio of buy to sell recommendations issued by analysts was 6-1, but by 2000 the ratio was 100-1. *Fortune* magazine reported in spring 2001 that the recommendations of the leading investment banks' research departments comprised more than 7,000 buy notes but only 57 sell notes. What accounted for the "death of the sell note"? Why had analysts turned from stock pickers into stock cheerleaders?

The origin of the corruption of the role of the securities industry analyst has been traced to the deregulation of brokerage commissions in 1975, which deprived research departments of much of their revenue and made securities industry firms more dependent on revenue from investment banking and corporate advisory services. This led to a change in the role of investment-bank analysts from dispassionate stock appraiser to go-between, linking the bank with potential clients in their specialist sector. So for clients, the issue of a sell note on their stock became out of the question. By the late 1990s, some firms were requiring analysts to run their reports past the investment bankers, or even the clients themselves, prior to publication. Credit Suisse First Boston (CSFB), for instance, conducted an internal restructuring which brought research and investment banking together into a single department, with the technology analysts reporting to the head of technology banking.

Analysts' pay came to be based not on their ability to interpret data or predict developments, but on how much investment-banking business they brought in. For example, a Merrill Lynch internal memo released to the press by Eliot Spitzer, investigating New York State attorney general, detailed how Henry Blodget, a star Internet analyst, and his team were involved in 52 investment-banking transactions between December 1999 and November 2000, earning $115m for the firm. Shortly after, Blodget's compensation package soared from $3m to $12m. A former analyst observed that when he had worked on Wall Street 20 years earlier, if he assisted the investment bankers with a new client he would receive a small thank-you at the end of the year: "But it was the frosting on the cake. Now, it is the cake."

By the late 1990s, investment-bank analysts had become salesmen – of their bank's investment-banking services to corporate clients, and of their clients' stocks, both as IPOs and in the secondary market, to investors. So it was hardly surprising that, as Spitzer's publication of Merrill Lynch's internal e-mails revealed, Blodget should be issuing research reports urging investors to buy stock in certain Internet companies while simultaneously disparaging these companies in confidential communications with colleagues as "junk", "shit" and "crap".

Spitzer's investigation into the conduct of Merrill Lynch's analysts came about in the following way, according to *Business Week.* In spring 2001, a lawyer acting for Debases Kanjilal, a Queen's (NY) paediatrician, filed a claim against Merrill Lynch claiming that Blodget had misled investors by fraudulently promoting the stock of companies with which the firm had investment-banking relationships. Specifically, Kanjilal complained that he had lost $500,000 by being advised by his Merrill broker against selling his stock in Infospace, which was then trading at $60 but subsequently slumped to $11.

Kanjilal's lawsuit attracted Spitzer's interest and he started to investigate. He required Merrill to produce tons of records, including internal e-mails. The extracts he published in April 2002 stunned investors by revealing the massive discrepancy between the public pronouncements of the firm's analysts and their private opinions. The following month Merrill agreed to pay a $100m fine – without any charge being brought forward and without admitting liability – as a settlement. It also undertook to sever all links between analysts' pay and investment-banking revenue. It was reported that Spitzer was turning his attention to Morgan Stanley, CSFB and Citigroup, and broadening his investigation of Wall Street.

Securities issues

The flood of securities issues in the late 1990s, mostly for technology companies, was a bonanza for the investment banks, which charged 7% for their services. Between the last quarter of 1998 and the first quarter of 2000, there were 1,300 new issues which raised $245 billion for the issuers, many of them profitless technology companies that later failed, and generated $10 billion in underwriting fees for the investment banks. Some observers wondered how it was that the long-entrenched 7% fee norm had not attracted the attention of the antitrust authorities, but this was not the principal source of complaint about the conduct of IPOs in the late 1990s. The burning issues were preferential allocations of stock and the under-pricing of issues.

In spring 2002, Harvey Pitt, head of the SEC, publicly expressed concern about the practice by which "valued brokerage-firm clients are given investment opportunities, but only in return for kickbacks to the brokerage firms that made the opportunity available". The kickbacks took a variety of forms, such as the conduct of unnecessary trades to generate brokerage fees, or an undertaking to support the price of the issue in the secondary market. The attention of the regulators focused particularly on CSFB, which in early 2002 paid a $100m fine to settle an investigation.

But the complaint among ordinary investors was that they never got a chance to participate in issues at ground level because all stock was being allocated to favoured clients of the investment banks. Or, even more controversially, it was being allocated to managers of the firms making the issue, as a reward for appointing the investment bank to conduct the business.

It was suggested that the latter phenomenon might help to explain why so many IPOs in the late 1990s were substantially under-priced. A doubling in price on the first day of trading was a regular feature of the dotcom boom – in 1999 more than 100 new issues saw a first-day rise in excess of 100% of the issue price, and the average was around 70%. Naturally, this was highly profitable for those lucky enough to have received an allocation of stock before the flotation. It has been calculated that had the investment banks priced the stocks issued in 1999–2000 at the first-day closing price, a further $66 billion would have been raised for the issuers, perhaps permitting some of them to avoid running out of cash and failing. That was the basis of the suit filed by bankrupt Internet toyshop eToys against Goldman Sachs.

Private equity investments
A further charge against the investment banks concerns their private equity (venture capital) investments. Investment-bank analysts identified promising, or merely plausible, young technology companies in which the firm (and not infrequently the analyst and other staff) would take an equity stake. An SEC investigation revealed that around one-third of analysts had personal stakes in the companies they covered before flotation. Sooner rather than later, the bank would organise an IPO, with the analyst extolling the attractions of the stock as an investment opportunity. Towards the end of the required six-month "lock-up" period following the issue, during which the underwriter was forbidden to sell its stock, the analyst would issue a buy note to investors, a so-called "booster shot", and when the restriction elapsed the bank and analyst would sell out and move on.

Corporate accounts
The spectacular collapse of Enron, followed by other large US corporations, raised a host of further issues. The common factor in the Enron and other debacles was the quality of financial information supplied by the companies, which, sometimes fraudulently and sometimes not, understated their liabilities and overstated their profits. The latter came as little surprise to some economists, regulators and investment managers who had been saying for several years that the aggregate data for corporate America simply did not add up – in total, the profit figures for USA Inc were impossibly high. Warren Buffett, for one, had cautioned in the late 1990s that many US corporations had to be cooking the books, although no one was sure which ones. "Accounting is being perverted," warned the head of the SEC in 1998. "We are witnessing an erosion in the quality of earnings, and therefore in the quality of financial reporting."

The principal reason senior managers would wish to massage the accounts was to boost their company's stock price. This was in accordance with the prevailing proposition that the goal of corporate governance was the maximisation of shareholder value. It was also in accordance with the maximisation of the value of senior management's own stock-option entitlements, which formed an important part of their remuneration – in 2001 stock options accounted for 58% of the pay of chief executives of US corporations. Creative accounting was one way of achieving this, such as Enron's use of off-balance-sheet partnerships to diminish its liabilities. Mergers and acquisitions were another, acquisition accounting being a well-known device for flattering companies' profits. Then there was fraud, such as charging running costs as capital expenditure, as practised by WorldCom.

Auditors

But why did no one spot these irregularities before the companies crashed? What were their auditors up to? In the case of Enron, Arthur Andersen shredded documents that might implicate the firm in negligence. Andersen and other accountants were accused of being accommodating as auditors because of a desire not to offend actual or potential clients for their lucrative consultancy services. For Andersen the consequences were dire – the demise of the firm. But Andersen was not the only culprit. A study by Bloomberg, a financial information provider, revealed that in the cases of the 673 largest bankruptcies of US public corporations over the years 1996–2002, in 54% of cases there were no warnings in the audit reports. Ann Yerger, director of research at the Council of Institutional Investors, comments: "Common sense tells you something is rotten."

What about the investment banks and all those highly paid analysts? As already discussed, most analysts are no longer in the business of analysis. In Enron's case, many analysts continued to recommend the stock right to the bitter end: 11 out of the 16 analysts who followed Enron rated it a "buy" or "strong buy" less than a month before the company filed for bankruptcy. But then since 1986 Enron had paid $323m to a variety of Wall Street firms in underwriting fees, including $69m to Goldman Sachs, $64m to CSFB and $61m to Salomon Brothers. Moreover, it was investment banks that supplied much of the financial alchemy that corporations used to disguise the truth, such as Enron's off-balance-sheet structures.

But what about the media and the host of supposedly savvy financial journalists and commentators, who are paid to be nosy and contrary? How come none of them blew a whistle loud enough to be heard before the corpses started floating to the surface? It seems that they too were caught up in the euphoria and the spirit of the times – a moral climate of what you can get away with. "The climate of the 'Clinton bubble'," writes Robert L. Bartley, editor of the *Wall Street Journal*, "was well established before anyone had heard the name Monica Lewinsky." It was a moral climate not very different to that abroad under the Harding –Coolidge administrations in the 1920s – and then too the wisdom came after the event.

Déjà vu

The wave of Wall Street scandals that broke in 2002 was not without precedent. Wall Street had been engulfed in scandal before, especially in the early 1930s. Moreover, many of the complaints about conflicts of interest and lapses of behaviour that "occasioned a general feeling of outrage or indignation" had done so before at some time since the 1920s. (In the text below, the italicised name of a recent scandal in brackets indicates some similarities with an historical episode.)

On Wall Street in the 19th and early 20th centuries stock fraud was not exceptional or even particularly reprehensible; indeed, it was part of the system. Most of the leading figures of the era of the "robber barons" and beyond – Rockefeller, Vanderbilt, Gould, Drew, Fisk, Stanford, Morgan, Kennedy – made their fortunes through shameless scams and chicanery. But around the turn of the 19th century mounting criticism of the Wall Street "money trust" indicated the beginning of a shift in public tolerance of the more outrageous financial practices. The establishment of the Federal Reserve in 1913 marked the beginning of the intrusion of public bodies into Wall Street's private affairs.

Corners and pools

The manipulation of the market by "corners" and "pools", conspiracies by market traders that sent stock prices soaring and thus drew in amateur speculators before collapsing as the insiders bailed out, was a traditional technique for making money in bull markets. Indeed, the operation of a pool in the stock of Piggly-Wiggly, a supermarket chain, in March 1923 (the stock ran up from $40 to $120 in a few weeks before plummeting) is regarded as heralding the onset of the 1920s bull market. In the final stage of the bull run, 1928–29, pools actively manipulated the price of dozens of stocks, including many of the leading stocks of the day such as American Tobacco, Chrysler, National Cash Register, Montgomery Hyde, Standard Oil of California and Union Carbide.

The stocks of radio corporations (the dotcom stocks of the day) were favourites of the pool operators, who used every possible means of hyping them, including wholesale bribery of financial journalists. Radio listening took off from 1921, boosted by the live broadcasting of President Warren Harding's inauguration; sales of radios increased from $10m in 1921 to $400m in 1929. Radio Corporation of America (RCA), the leading radio stock, soared to stratospheric heights, prompting an observer to comment that prices were so high that speculators were not only discounting the future but also the hereafter. At their peak in September 1929, RCA stocks traded at over $500; by July 1932, the price was just $3.

One of the most outrageous Wall Street pool operators of the 1920s was Albert Wiggin, chairman from 1917 to 1932 of Chase National Bank (a forerunner of J.P. Morgan Chase). During the final stages of the bull market, Wiggin organised a secret private-investment pool that profitably ramped the Chase stock price in spring and summer 1929, borrowing $8m from the bank itself to do so. When stock prices crashed in October, Wiggin was one of the Wall Street leaders whose banks subscribed to a fund to support and stabilise the market. But all the while, with a brazenness that would make a modern hedge-fund manager blush, he was aggressively shorting Chase stock, an operation that made him a personal profit of $4m. Although his activities were not criminal, the public was horrified when they were made public during the post-crash Pecora hearings in 1933. Chase withdrew Wiggin's pension and he was forced to pay $2m to settle a lawsuit by a group of stockholders. Yet he refused to admit any wrongdoing. "I think it highly desirable," he declared, "that officers of the bank should be interested in the stock of the bank." Small wonder that the public esteem for bankers and brokers plummeted in the early 1930s.

"Manufacturing" securities

Charles Mitchell, head of National City Bank (a forerunner of Citigroup), the other major Wall Street commercial bank, also emerged tainted from the post-crash inquiries. In the 1920s, under Mitchell's direction, National City's investment-banking subsidiary, National City Company (NCC), became one of Wall Street's leading securities underwriters, and Mitchell boasted of "manufacturing" securities as if they were so many Model T Fords. NCC's rapid rise was a result of its unrivalled ability to market its underwritings to retail investors through the banking side of the business. Such investors were mostly unsophisticated and unfamiliar with investment, but they were hungry for easy money and eager suckers. At first the securities NCC offered them were bonds of reasonably creditworthy domestic borrowers. But in 1927 it began to offer stocks, unscrupulously reassuring investors that they were "as safe as bonds". NCC also became the lead player in the highly lucrative foreign bond-issue boom of 1924–28, bringing out many issues that might have been regarded as speculative and some that were little better than fraudulent – for example, an issue for the Brazilian state of Minas Gerais, despite the internal report of an NCC officer that: "It would be hard to find a sadder confession of inefficiency and ineptitude than that displayed by the state officials of Minas Gerais in respect of long-term borrowing." In other words, as Blodget might have put it, NCC was knowingly peddling "crap".

NCC's conflict of interest between raising funds for clients of dubious credit status, for which it received hefty fees, and the marketing of securities to a naïve but avaricious investing public, has a resonance with the role of the investment-bank analysts in the TMT boom of the late 1990s (*Merrill Lynch and Investment Bank Analysts*). So, in the aftermath of the stockmarket crash and the widespread defaults on foreign bonds in 1931–32 (including Minas Gerais), does the opprobrium heaped upon Mitchell. In 1933, he was obliged to resign as chairman of National City Bank and the following year he was prosecuted for tax evasion (*Tyco*), although he was acquitted.

The Ponzi scheme

Another financial scoundrel of the 1920s who warrants mention is Charles Ponzi, after whom the "Ponzi scheme" is named. A Ponzi scheme is a business set-up in which interest or dividend payments exceed cash flows and are made out of capital. Of course, all Ponzi schemes come to grief sooner or later. Ponzi, a 42-year-old former vegetable dealer, forger and smuggler, launched his something-for-nothing, get-rich-quick scheme in Boston in September 1919. Offering no collateral, he promised to pay $15 for every $10 left with him for 90 days. He told lenders that his firm, the august-sounding Old Colony Foreign Exchange Company, would use the funds to buy and sell International Postal Union reply coupons, profiting from differences in currency rates (although it never really did). The scheme took off, mostly among Italian immigrants, and by June 1920 he was receiving more than $1m a week. He became a celebrity in the Italian community and a crowd followed him around. "You're the greatest Italian of them all!" cried an admirer. "No, no. Columbus and Marconi. Columbus discovered America. Marconi discovered the wireless," protested Ponzi modestly. "Yes," came the response, "but you discovered money."

Ponzi eventually ran out of money in August 1920 and the Old

Colony Foreign Exchange Company had to close its doors. A final reckoning showed that Ponzi had taken in $15m over 18 months from around 50,000 people and owed $5m. In fact, little of the money that had passed through his hands had found its way into his own possession; it had simply been redistributed to those who participated in the scheme early from those who joined late, like a chain letter. Ponzi went to jail. On his release in 1934 he was deported to Italy, where he joined the Fascist party and secured a government job. Although Ponzi lent his name to it, his scheme was not the first or last time that dividends or interest were paid out of capital – in fact, it was a recurring phenomenon of financial scandals before him and after.

Pyramid holding companies

A feature of Wall Street in the 1920s was the widespread use of debt to enhance profits through the leveraging of investors' resources. Individual speculators availed themselves of margin loans supplied by brokers (at very profitable rates of interest) which were secured against the stocks purchased. Speculators were allowed to leverage down-payments by as much as ten times, which could be miraculously lucrative when prices were rising but ruinous when they fell, as many individuals discovered to their cost in fall 1929. A New Deal reform was to place the permitted level of margin lending under the control of the Federal Reserve, protecting investors against themselves.

At the corporate level, debt was used to put together a number of enormous holding companies, particularly in the electric utility and railroad industries. The earnings of one company were used to secure a loan that was used to purchase another company, then its earnings were used to secure a loan to buy yet another company, and so on. Such "pyramiding" worked well while earnings were rising, but if they fell there might be insufficient funds to meet interest payments and the whole edifice could come crashing down. This fundamental flaw of the pyramid holding companies was compounded by the complexity of the interlocking shareholdings, which made it difficult even for insiders to keep track of how the business was faring. The opaqueness of the whole operation provided ample scope for dubious financial practices and fraud, such as the Ponzi-style payment of dividends out of borrowings to boost stock prices.

There were three spectacular failures among pyramid holding companies in the wake of the 1929 stockmarket crash. Investors were particularly outraged by these corporate collapses, having regarded them as among the safest of investments on account of their size and the supposed quality of their earnings as utilities (*Enron*).

One of them was Insull Utility Investments, an enormous combine of mid-west electric power companies as well as real estate, tyre and shoe manufacturing and other interests (*Tyco*), founded by Samuel Insull, a former secretary to Thomas Edison, an electricity pioneer. When the Insull empire imploded in April 1932, Insull fled to Greece. On his return to America he stood trial for fraud, but was acquitted. Another was the Alleghany Corporation, a railroad holding company put together by the van Sweringen brothers with loans raised by J.P. Morgan. At the end of 1932 Alleghany stock was trading at less than 1% of its 1929 peak and the brothers were bust. In both cases, the promoters were clearly out of their depth and susceptible to seemingly sophisticated "solutions" proposed by their investment-bank advisers (*Enron*).

Ivar Kreuger rose to fame and fortune by putting together a set of leveraged interlocking corporations that controlled three-quarters of the world's match production, and much else besides. Although the secretive Swedish financier's interests were mostly overseas, his financing came principally from bond issues on Wall Street. As the business collapsed, it became known that Kreuger had perpetrated massive frauds on the company by transferring funds to his personal account and other financial improprieties (*Adelphia*, *WorldCom*). In March 1932, Kreuger shot himself in a Paris hotel.

Misuse of investment trusts

Investment trusts, the number of which multiplied rapidly in the 1920s, were marketed to the investing public as a means by which ordinary investors could enjoy the benefits of professional money management and a diversified portfolio. But in practice, many operated in ways that increased risk rather than reducing it. They were run for the benefit of the investment banks that established and managed them, sometimes being used as repositories for issues the sponsoring underwriters were unable to sell. They borrowed heavily against their assets, in much the same way that individual speculators used margin money. Moreover, some of them also indulged in market manipulation to boost their stock prices, making arrangements with other trusts to buy each other's stocks (*Global Crossing*).

All investment trusts fared badly after the crash, but some fared very badly. One of the most notorious cases was Goldman Sachs Trading Corporation. Its stock price crashed from a high of $326 to $1.75. Outraged investors, including Eddie Cantor, one of the singing stars of the day, sued the firm for millions of dollars in compensation. Cantor's wisecracks about the firm, delivered nightly on stage in a Broadway theatre, made Goldman Sachs the laughing stock of New York.

Embezzlement

Richard Whitney, president of the New York Stock Exchange 1930–35, was one of the loudest cheerleaders for the 1920s bull market and a high-profile champion of the market in its post-crash adversity. As a result of his stalwart opposition, the original proposal in the Securities Exchange Act 1934 for an outright ban on short selling was watered down to the outlawing of "market manipulation". In contrast to Whitney's success and prominence as a spokesman for Wall Street, the performance of his brokerage firm was disastrous. As losses mounted, Whitney took to raiding clients' accounts and looting the funds of the New York Yacht Club and the Exchange's Gratuity Fund, a charitable endowment for the widows and orphans of deceased members, to the tune of $1m. When his activities eventually came to light in early 1938, he was expelled from the New York Stock Exchange and indicted by Thomas Dewey, an ambitious New York district attorney. Whitney was convicted and served three-and-a-half years in jail for grand larceny. Dewey subsequently became Governor of New York and Republican candidate in the presidential elections of 1944 and 1948 – a role model for Eliot Spitzer, perhaps?

The New Deal reforms and after

The 1932–34 Pecora hearings exposed a variety of scandalous practices that had been commonplace on Wall Street in the 1920s.

- Conflicts of interest. Pushing securities in which investment companies held interests; underwriting practices such as "preferred lists" for favoured clients; manipulation of investment trusts by promoters to serve their interests.
- Inadequate disclosure. The culture of secrecy and lack of disclosure of basic financial information.
- Inattention to quality. Knowingly promoting worthless securities, such as the Minas Gerais bonds.
- Insider trading. Misusing privileged information for financial gain.
- "Manufacturing" securities. The need for a stream of "product" to be peddled by a large salesforce; abuse of investment trusts,

which were used as "buyers of last resort" for slow-moving issues (i.e. as repositories for unsaleable securities).
- ◪ Selling practices. Bribery of journalists to puff securities; high-pressure salesmanship.

The New Deal legislation of the mid-1930s remedied or curbed many of these practices. The Securities Act 1933 led to an improvement in the quantity and quality of disclosure of corporate financial information. The Securities Exchange Act 1934 made market manipulation an offence, leaving the interpretation of the term to the new SEC, Wall Street's "cop on the corner". Insider trading, being a form of market manipulation, was outlawed under this act: it did not stop, but for a generation was conducted with greater caution and discretion.

The disappearance of major and even minor financial scandals in the 1940s was testament to the impact of the New Deal securities, banking and investment reforms. But it was also a reflection of the subdued condition of the wartime and post-war financial markets which provided relatively poor opportunities. Another factor was the limited capabilities of the SEC to pursue minor wrongdoers, its resources having been pared back by Congress so much that staff numbers had fallen from 1,800 in 1940 to 700 in 1954 while the workload had soared.

The bull market from 1953 saw the emergence of a new generation of crooks and con-men, though their operations were of a lower order in terms of scale and economic significance than their forerunners in the 1920s and their future counterparts of the 1980s and 2000s. A shadow fell across the American Stock Exchange towards the end of the decade with the revelation of the activities of a handful of specialists (market-makers) who abused their positions to manipulate stock prices. Another high-profile episode concerned the operation of a 1920s-style pool in the stock of American Motors whose perpetrators even used leaks to the *New York Times* to manipulate the stock price. With little effective enforcement, Wall Street's cop on the corner was becoming no more of a deterrent than a Keystone cop.

The decade of the 1960s was also free of major Wall Street scandals – the chickens came home to roost in the early 1970s. From 1961, the SEC began to pursue insider trading more vigorously resulting in an increase in prosecutions, but convictions proved elusive. The "Great Salad Oil Swindle", as the *Wall Street Journal* called it, was a well-publicised and colourful episode in 1963. Allied Crude Vegetable Oil, a commodities firm run by Tino De Angelis, a former Bronx butcher, borrowed heavily from Wall Street banks and investment firms to speculate in vegetable oil futures. The loans were secured by warehouse receipts for millions of gallons of salad oil stored in huge tanks at Bayonne, New Jersey. When De Angelis failed to meet payments the banks foreclosed on the collateral, only to find that the tanks were full of water with just enough oil floating on top to fool inspectors. The banks sustained losses of $175m and two leading brokerage firms went into liquidation. De Angelis went to jail for seven years, which he later recalled as among the happiest of his life. "There you had peace. It was tranquil," he said. "You come outside and try to make a living and all the big guys try to shoot you down."

The 1970s and 1980s

Fraud was a common feature of the four big financial scandals of the early 1970s. In none of the cases was financial irregularity spotted by auditors, provoking considerable criticism of the accounting profession (*Enron, WorldCom, auditors*). Strictly speaking, they were not Wall Street scandals, since none of the corporations that failed was based in lower Manhattan, but memories of the 1930s lived on and they revived public mistrust of financiers and Wall Street.

Investors Overseas Services

Two scandals in the early 1970s did considerable damage to the reputation of the mutual-fund business, bringing Wall Street into disrepute with savers and undermining the reputation of auditors as guardians of corporate integrity. Investors Overseas Services (IOS) was a mutual fund founded in 1956 by Bernard Cornfeld, a shrewd and ambitious salesman. It specialised in selling shares to Americans living in Europe, particularly servicemen, who wanted to participate in the rising US stockmarket. Besides having identified a substantial and poorly served market, there were other advantages to operating offshore that made the project particularly appealing. Based in Geneva, with his funds incorporated in Canada, Cornfeld was able to operate beyond the supervision of the SEC, which meant that he could charge much higher fees than onshore funds. Investors did not complain because many of them viewed his funds as attractive offshore vehicles for avoiding US tax, and his salesforce made much of IOS's strict confidentiality.

Cornfeld recruited an army of salesmen – he claimed to have 25,000 at the peak – to peddle IOS mutual funds in Europe and around the world. They were highly motivated, being paid unusually generous commissions, and pushily drummed up business on the doorstep, in the canteen or wherever. Cornfeld played an active role in publicising IOS, promoting it as "people's capitalism", the friend of the small investor. He also attracted attention on account of his ostentatious, playboy (his word, "tacky", is better) lifestyle: he liked to be photographed in the company of bikini-clad young women and appeared on the cover of *Der Stern* magazine in a velvet jacket with a cheetah at his feet.

Nevertheless, IOS grew rapidly and by the late 1960s, according to Cornfeld, its 18 funds had 1m shareholders with $2.5 billion under management, amounting to 5% of the total mutual-fund industry of the day. However, the underlying business was in poor shape because of the salesforce's high commissions and the high, multilayered management fees that financed Cornfeld's extravagant lifestyle. By the end of the 1960s, IOS was paying its "guaranteed dividends" to existing shareholders out of the proceeds of new sales – a Ponzi scheme (*WorldCom*). When the stockmarket turned down after the peak in December 1968, new sales became difficult and Cornfeld found himself with a cashflow problem.

Desperate for funds, he decided to raise money by making a stock offering to investors, turning IOS into a public company. The IPO was pulled off, partly because Cornfeld and his lieutenants persuaded staff, friends and business contacts to take advantage of this supposedly once-in-a-lifetime opportunity, many of them borrowing heavily to do so. Unfortunately, the market downturn continued, and when the predicted profits failed to materialise IOS's stock started to slide, falling from $18 to $2 and ruining many investors. In June 1970, the IOS board ousted Cornfeld.

The company was then entrusted to Robert Vesco, a 34-year-old entrepreneur with a reputation as a whizz-kid, who in a few years had built International Controls Corporation (ICC) into a conglomerate with sales of over $100m. Essentially it was a pyramid operation, based on massive borrowing and requiring more and more deals to sustain the cash flow, but this was not apparent to IOS's directors. Vesco promised to inject funds into IOS, but his real intention was to pillage its mutual funds to meet ICC's own cash needs, since it too was struggling because of the reduction in deals caused by the fall in the stockmarket.

Vesco's tenure at IOS lasted only a couple of years, but during that time he managed to skim hundreds of millions of dollars from the mutual funds. Realising that the game was up, Vesco took off to the Bahamas and later Cuba, where he ended up in jail permanently for offences unrelated to IOS. Cornfeld was also put in jail, being arrested in November 1973 when he returned to Switzerland. He was prosecuted by the Swiss but was acquitted. IOS was wound up in 1974, with investors suffering losses of $500m.

Equity Funding Corporation

In April 1973, while the tawdry Cornfeld–Vesco debacle was in full swing, another mutual-fund scandal erupted. Equity Funding Corporation was a Californian mutual fund based at Century City, Los Angeles. It was founded in 1961 to market an innovative investment product, a bundled-up combination of insurance and mutual fund saving – customers bought mutual-fund shares, the dividends of which paid the premiums on a separate life-insurance policy. It was an ingenious and attractive idea, not least to Equity Funding's salesforce, who received two up-front commissions from both the mutual-fund sale and the insurance policy. Naturally, they marketed the product keenly and sales soared. The rapidly expanding sales figures provided the basis for an IPO to raise capital in 1964, and Equity Funding became a favourite investment stock among mutual-fund managers.

Although Equity Funding was growing fast, the business was not profitable. So the senior managers (it is estimated that as many as 50–100 people became involved in the fraud) became even more innovative. They began by overstating the commissions earned on sales. Then they resorted to borrowing money without recording the liability on the books, or hiding it through complex transactions with subsidiaries. When it transpired that the company was not selling enough policies to meet its reinsurance arrangements with other insurance companies, it simply invented policies, sold them to the reinsurers and pocketed the proceeds. These phony insurance policies posed a problem, since Equity Funding's auditors would sometimes choose a random selection of policies and demand to see the files behind them. On such occasions the senior managers would convene a late-night get-together and fabricate the required documentation. When they discovered that four junior employees were embezzling funds for themselves by filing false death claims, the quartet of crooks were recruited to the "official" fraud and told to get on with the work.

The Equity Funding fraud ran from 1964 to 1973. It came to light when someone blew the whistle because he was dissatisfied with his Christmas bonus. Equity Funding went bust, investors lost $300m and a dozen senior managers went to jail. The scandal was a massive embarrassment to the mutual-fund industry and the insurance industry's regulatory agencies, but in particularly it put auditors in the dock. How had the auditors failed to spot 64,000 phony transactions with a face value of $2 billion, $25m in counterfeit bonds and $100m in missing assets over a nine-year period? The episode prompted the accountancy profession to re-emphasise the anti-fraud side of its role, although the lesson appears to have been forgotten by a new generation of auditors checking the books of Enron, Global Crossing, Adelphia and WorldCom.

Penn Central

The other pair of scandals of the early 1970s that had an impact on Wall Street were the collapse of Penn Central, at the time America's largest corporate bankruptcy, and the demise of Franklin National Bank, New York, the biggest US bank failure. Penn Central was the outcome of a merger between two ailing north-eastern railroad companies in 1968. From the outset it was bedevilled by a clash of corporate cultures and managerial feuding that produced administrative chaos. It was also burdened by massive indebtedness, a problem that got worse as senior managers went on an acquisition spree in an endeavour to turn it into a fashionable conglomerate, plus fraudulent operations in its real-estate subsidiary. In June 1970, Penn Central failed, obliging the federal government to step in to preserve vital rail services. The outcome was the creation of Conrail for freight services and Amtrak for passengers.

Franklin National Bank

The Franklin National Bank of Long Island had become America's 12th largest bank when it ran into trouble in 1971 and was sold to Michele Sindona, an Italian financier. Sindona turned out to be as much a saviour as Vesco – he was an embezzler and a gambler with Mafia ties. The foreign-exchange market had become active in the early 1970s with the collapse of the Bretton Woods system of fixed exchange rates, and Sindona decided that there was easy money to be made in foreign-exchange speculation. But instead of generating profits, these activities led to heavy losses, rendering Franklin National Bank insolvent. So Sindona fraudulently transferred the losses to the two Italian banks he controlled. Nevertheless, Franklin collapsed in June 1974 with losses of $40m, and the Italian banks soon followed. Sindona was convicted of fraud and grand larceny in America, and later in 1985 he was sentenced to life imprisonment in Italy for arranging the murder of an inspector investigating his banking empire. But he never served the sentence, being poisoned by his enemies a few days later.

Hunt brothers' silver corner

The outlawing of market manipulation by the Securities Exchange Act 1934 had put an end to robber-baron-style corners and pools in the securities market, but the act did not apply to the commodities markets. Since 1973 the Hunt family, a billionaire Texas oil dynasty, had been buying silver as a hedge against inflation and by 1979 had an enormous hoard. That year the Hunt brothers, Nelson Bunker and William Herbert, got together with some wealthy Arab speculators to form a silver pool with the intention of cornering the world market in silver, driving up the price and the value of their holdings. In a short time they accumulated more than 200m ounces of silver, equivalent to half the world's deliverable supply.

In early 1979, the price of silver was $5 an ounce, compared with $1.75 back in 1973 when the Hunts had begun to buy. By the end of the year the pool's buying spree had pushed the price to $50 an ounce. The US authorities were not amused by these cowboy shenanigans, and a combination of a change in trading rules on the metals markets in Chicago and New York and intervention by the Federal Reserve sent prices tumbling. By March 1980, the price of silver was back at $10 an ounce and the Hunt brothers were facing an estimated loss of $1 billion. They subsequently declared bankruptcy. To add to their woes, they were charged by the Commodity Futures Trading Commission with conspiracy to manipulate the silver market and convicted in August 1988.

The Hunt brothers' debacle demonstrated that crude market manipulations would not be tolerated in the US markets and were a phenomenon of the past. But away from centre stage, the episode also gave rise to a phenomenon of the future. Acting on his own initiative without official sanction, an official at Peru's Ministry of Commerce with the job of hedging the country's silver output managed to lose $80m shorting silver during the Hunt brothers' corner. The "rogue trader" entered the modern financial scene.

Drysdale Government Securities

Drysdale Government Securities, a New York dealer in the US Treasury-bond market, was hardly a household name even on Wall Street, but in May 1982 it was all over the newspapers. It had failed to make a $200m interest payment to Chase Manhattan Bank in respect of some $4.5 billion of Treasury bonds that Drysdale had borrowed from

Chase's Security Service Division. Although such securities lending was normal practice in the Treasury-bond market, it aroused wonderment on the part of onlookers. So did the scale of Chase's losses, estimated at $135m–270m. An SEC investigation subsequently revealed that earlier filings, certified by accountants Arthur Andersen (yes, them again), had hidden a $150m deficit of liabilities over assets, more than seven times the firm's $21m capital (*Enron, WorldCom*). Several Drysdale managers were indicted for fraud and went to prison. In response, the Federal Reserve Bank of New York created a new unit under a senior officer concerned solely with surveillance of the market.

Penn Square Bank
Penn Square Bank of Oklahoma City had its 15 minutes of fame in July 1982, when it was declared insolvent and closed its doors. In normal circumstances, the failure of a small regional bank, with assets of less than $500m, would not have been newsworthy outside the state, but it transpired that Penn Square's own problems were but the tip of the iceberg. The second oil-price hike of 1979 had triggered an upsurge of oil and gas activity in Oklahoma and a clamour for loans to finance expansion and exploration. With a modest capital base, Penn Square had been able to meet only a small proportion of the demand itself, so it had sold more than $2.5 billion of participations in its energy-sector loans to other US banks. With the onset of recession and a decline in energy prices in 1981, many of these loans proved non-performing and wiped out Penn Square's capital.

Penn Square was not the only casualty. Chase Manhattan suffered losses of $161m on its $275m participations in Penn Square energy-sector loans. Seattle First National Bank was forced to merge with Bank of America to forestall failure. Then in May 1984 there was a run on Continental Illinois, America's eighth largest bank, whose credit status had been undermined by its exposure to Penn Square loan participations. It was saved only by a $5 billion bail-out by the Federal Reserve System.

Ivan Boesky
Stock prices rose almost continuously between August 1982 and October 1987, a sustained bull market that rivalled that of the 1920s. The upsurge in prices was accompanied by a mergers and acquisitions boom, as corporations that the market rated highly were able to use their stock as currency to buy lower-rated companies. Financiers entered the game too, eager to take advantage of the legacy of the inflation of the 1970s that had left the stock price of many corporations valuing the company

at less than book value. These buccaneers often had to seize control from the incumbent management through a hostile takeover bid, which was fought out in the market.

The 1970s had seen the rise of "risk arbitrage" investment partnerships, which sought to profit from the large price movements typical of corporate takeovers. When a deal was announced they would buy up stock using leverage, betting that the deal would go through at the struck price. In the 1980s, they played an important role in precipitating many bids by speculatively buying the stock of potential takeover targets which became deliverable, at a significant premium to the purchase price, to a corporate raider. The raiders financed their acquisitions by borrowing, particularly through the issue of junk bonds brought out for them by Michael Milken, the junk-bond wizard of investment bank Drexel Burnham Lambert.

Ivan Boesky, who was to become the best-known risk arbitrageur (arb), set up a business betting on takeovers in 1975, backed by family money. At first Boesky did business in the normal way. But the problem was that if a deal fell through an arb could lose a lot of money, as happened in May 1982 when an announced bid for Cities Services by Gulf Oil collapsed, leaving Boesky with a $24m loss. Apparently, it was this distressing experience that led Boesky to build a covert network of investment bankers and brokers to supply him with insider tips about forthcoming deals to shorten the odds. He was by no means the only person on Wall Street doing this: a study by *Business Week* in 1985 revealed that the price of the stocks of almost three-quarters of takeover-bid targets leapt ahead of the announcement.

Two of Boesky's tipsters were Martin Siegel of Kidder Peabody and Dennis Levine of Drexel Burnham Lambert. It was Siegel who provided him with the inside information that enabled him to make $28m from the acquisition of Carnation by Nestlé in 1984. With such coups and annual investment returns of 80%, Boesky became "a legend in the financial world", in the words of the jacket blurb of his 1985 book *Merger Mania: Arbitrage – Wall Street's Best Kept Money-Making Secret*, in which he revealed the secrets of the arbitrageur's trade (with no mention of insider dealing). Columbia and New York universities appointed him an adjunct professor and he became a celebrity public speaker. This gave him opportunities to expound his self-justifying business philosophy: "Greed is all right, by the way ..." he told a gathering at a California business school in May 1986. "I think greed is healthy. You can be greedy and still feel good about yourself."

Levine, who was paid millions by Boesky for the information he supplied, felt greedy too; so he started speculating in the stocks of takeover targets on his own account, conducting his operations through the Bahamas branch of a Swiss bank. Acting on a tip-off, the SEC investigated Levine's transactions and he was arrested for insider trading. Levine then cut a deal with the authorities and squealed on Boesky and others. Boesky, in turn, ratted on his accomplices, including Siegel and Milken, the junk-bond king. Boesky served 18 months in prison and paid a $100m fine. As he left the court in 1987 he told reporters: "Greed is all right ... everybody should be a little greedy."

Michael Milken

Initially, the junk-bond issues organised by Milken were mostly used to finance leveraged buy-outs (LBO)s. The first hostile takeover backed by Milken and Drexel was the August 1984 bid by T. Boone Pickens for Gulf Oil. Thereafter they became the corporate raiders' principal backers and the deal flow grew bigger and bigger, as did the money being earned by Milken and Drexel: it is estimated that during the 1980s he accumulated a $3 billion fortune. Boesky and Milken were involved in a number of deals together, beginning in 1981 when Drexel helped Boesky raise $100m to gain control of the Beverly Hills Hotel. Thereafter their affairs became heavily intertwined, with Drexel contributing $1 billion to Boesky's risk-arbitrage fund.

In return for a lighter sentence, Boesky informed the SEC and Rudolph Giuliani, the New York district attorney, about his dealings with Milken and Drexel. The authorities were convinced that Drexel, where Levine and later Siegel also worked, was rotten to the core and determined to make an example of the firm. Under the threat of graver charges, in December 1988 Drexel pleaded guilty to six charges of malfeasance and agreed to pay a $650m fine. The following year Congress passed legislation requiring savings and loans institutions to value their holdings of junk bonds at market prices and to dispose of such securities within five years. This torpedoed the market for junk bonds and sunk Drexel, which had a junk portfolio of more than $1 billion that could not be realised. In February 1990, Drexel Burnham Lambert declared bankruptcy.

Milken initially refused to admit to any wrongdoing. Indeed, following Drexel's demise the *Wall Street Journal* wrote: "Now someone from the Justice Department needs to explain what it was that Milken allegedly did to justify the punishment being inflicted on the capital markets." But Giuliani and the SEC were convinced of his guilt. Among their supporting evidence was a payment to Milken by Boesky of $5.3m for "research", which appeared to them to be plainly a reward for insider information. Eventually in 1990, under intense pressure and rather than face a 98-count indictment, which might result in him being stripped of all his assets and incarcerated for up to 520 years, he agreed to plead guilty to six felony counts. Milken received a prison sentence of ten years (of which he served three) and a $1 billion fine. Many considered the sentence shockingly savage, and believed that Milken was paying the price of personifying Wall Street's greed.

Savings and loan debacle

The objective of the Garn-St Germain Act of 1982 had been to bolster the finances of savings and loans institutions by allowing them to diversify their assets. Laudable as this was in theory, in practice it provided a licence for unscrupulous managers to take bold punts, knowing that if they succeeded they would be rewarded with big bonuses but if the bet went wrong depositors would be bailed out by federal deposit insurance. The portfolios of the savings and loans became important repositories for the high-yield bonds brought out by Milken and Drexel. When the junk-bond market crashed in 1989, the savings and loans were left with mountains of unmarketable and worthless bonds, with US taxpayers facing a bail-out bill estimated at $500 billion – the largest banking scandal in history.

With no shortage of contenders, the rosette for the most outrageous figure of the savings and loans scandal is usually awarded to Charles Keating of Lincoln Savings and Loan of Irvine, California. Acquiring control of Lincoln in 1982, with financial assistance from Milken, Keating ran the thrift into the ground, eventually costing US taxpayers $2.3 billion in deposit insurance. Where did the money go? To bankroll a lavish lifestyle, including a private jet and a Bahamas retreat. To family members, who received $42m in salaries and payments over the five years Keating ran Lincoln. To satisfy bizarre whims, such as giving $100 a head to every child named Charles in the Bahamas. And to buying political protection, notably the notorious "Keating Five" members of the Senate, who received massive campaign contributions and repaid him by delaying regulators' moves against him. The regulators eventually ousted Keating, and in April 1992 he was convicted of securities fraud and sentenced to ten years, of which he served four.

Prudential-Bache Securities

A distraction from the unfolding savings and loans imbroglio in the early 1990s was provided by the scandal that engulfed Prudential-Bache Securities, the securities arm of Prudential, a leading US insurance company. The story started in the early 1980s, when the firm put together a set of limited partnerships to take advantage of the Reagan administration's 1981 tax reforms. Participations in the partnerships were enthusiastically marketed by Pru-Bache as investments that were as safe as bank deposits. More than 300,000 consumers, many of them elderly, retired and on fixed incomes, invested $8 billion in the limited partnerships between 1981 and 1990. Many of the partnerships invested in real estate, and there were allegations of kickbacks from developers and of managers skimming millions of dollars in bogus fees and expenses. Even before the downturn in the property market at the end of the 1980s, many of the limited partnerships had become worthless and private litigation had been initiated. The debacle cost Pru-Bache more than $1.4 billion in compensation to investors.

The 1990s

The rising stockmarket of the 1990s, when the Dow climbed from 2,580 at the start of the decade to 11,500 at the end, made millions of people wealthy. But some were impatient to get to the land of milk and honey and were prepared to cut corners to do so. The increasingly frenzied financial markets and the gold-rush mentality on Wall Street, especially from 1995, provided an environment which spawned the scandals and frauds at Enron, Tyco, WorldCom and the rest that broke after the end of the bull market in 2000. But the years of the bull market witnessed a parade of smaller-scale though not insignificant financial scandals.

Derivatives ...

In the mid-1990s there was a flurry of litigation by clients demanding compensation from investment banks for bad investment advice that had led to losses on derivatives. One of the early cases to hit the headlines was a $20m claim by Gibson Greetings Cards regarding advice from Bankers Trust. It was settled out of court, substantially in the client's favour. Bankers Trust was hit again by claims by Procter & Gamble in February 1995 over derivatives losses totalling some $200m. There were many more such episodes.

The biggest and most sensational derivatives scandal of the mid-1990s was the $1.6 billion loss sustained by Orange County, California, birthplace of former president Richard Nixon, which came to light in December 1994. Robert Citron, the county treasurer, had used Orange County's $7.5 billion investment pool, belonging to county schools, cities and the county itself, leveraged into a $20.5 billion portfolio, to bet with derivatives that interest rates would fall or stay low. Initially, the strategy did well and Citron was hailed as a financial genius in the locality, but when US rates rose unexpectedly losses soared. "Citron's problem," commented an investment banker sourly, "is that he knows about 30% of what he thinks he knows." It was the largest loss by a local government authority and led to the bankruptcy of Orange County. Citron lost his job and received a one-year jail sentence. Orange County sued its financial advisers and recovered some of the losses from them in out-of-court settlements: $420m from Merrill Lynch, $120m from KPMG Peat Marwick and $85m from CSFB.

... and desperadoes

Indictments for insider trading were served from time to time during the 1990s, but none of the cases was on the grand scale of the Boesky era. One of the more lurid episodes was the prosecution of James McDermott, former chairman of Keefe Bruyette & Woods, a boutique investment bank, for passing insider stock tips to Marylin Star, his mistress and a porn movie actress, whose pictures included "The Violation of Marylin" and "Babes on Bikes". McDermott was found guilty and sentenced to eight months in jail in August 2000. "During this trial I was called a stud stock-picker and a master of the universe," protested McDermott, a millionaire. "Those things could not be further from the truth. I'm just an average person who's tried to work hard and to give back."

Even stranger was the case of Martin Frankel, a fraudster who built up a substantial insurance business based in Greenwich, Connecticut. The business was run along distinctly unorthodox lines – investment decisions were based on astrological charts and Frankel's staff was composed of women recruited through personal ads seeking sexually submissive females. Moreover, Frankel's principal activity seems to have been orchestrating the pilfering of insurance companies' assets to finance the purchase of automobiles, real estate, gold and diamonds. Eventually, a Mississippi state insurance commissioner smelt a rat and placed Frankel's companies in his jurisdiction under state supervision. Taking a leaf out of the book of his hero, Robert Vesco, Frankel went on the run, leaving a pile of smouldering documents at his Connecticut mansion including a to-do list headed by "launder money". In September 1999, four months after his disappearance, Frankel was arrested in a luxury hotel in Hamburg, together with $8m in gems and a sexually submissive redhead. He was extradited to America to stand trial on charges of fraud and conspiracy. Asked by a reporter why he did it he replied: "To feed all the hungry people in the world. That was my goal, to make a lot of money to try to do those things."

Rogue traders

The 1980s had witnessed the triumph of traders on Wall Street, personified by the rise of John Gutfreund from a lowly municipal-bond trader to chief executive of Salomon Brothers. Trading offered a short cut to quick profits and big bonuses, but it was also a potential road to ruin. Trading and rogue traders were at the root of many of the financial scandals of the 1990s.

In May 1991, it was revealed that Salomon Brothers had cornered an auction of US Treasury notes by submitting false claims on behalf of clients. Instead of the permitted maximum of 35% of the issue to any single dealer, Salomon controlled 94% (at a cost of $10.6 billion), giving it command over the issue. The US authorities were outraged at this attempt to manipulate the US Treasury market, the bedrock of the US financial markets. Gutfreund was obliged to resign and a senior trader went to jail. In a deal negotiated with the Justice Department and the SEC in spring 1992, the firm paid a fine of $190m to the government and $100m to private litigants.

Joseph Jett joined Kidder Peabody, a venerable Wall Street investment bank owned by General Electric, as a trader in 1991. He was good at his job and rose rapidly, being appointed head of government-bond trading in 1993, when he was named the firm's "man of the year". That year he was awarded $9m in bonuses based on $150m in trading profits. But in April 1994 he was fired for allegedly perpetrating an elaborate scam involving the invention of $350m of phantom bond trades to boost his bonus and to disguise losses. Jett protested his innocence and was partially vindicated by a court ruling in 1998 that cleared him of the securities fraud charges, although he was sanctioned for lesser "books-and-records" violations and ordered to pay a $200,000 fine and return $8m of bonus money to Kidder Peabody. The long-running case generated much publicity, partly because Jett was one of the few black traders on Wall Street. GE was so exasperated with its wayward Wall Street outpost that it sold it later in the year to PaineWebber, taking a loss of $800m.

A firm of GE's size could absorb a hit of $800m, but Barings, a London merchant bank, was wiped out by the $1.4 billion trading losses racked up by Nick Leeson, a rogue trader, which came to light in February 1995. Leeson, aged 27, a trader in Barings' Singapore office, sustained the losses by trading derivatives contracts based on the Nikkei 225, betting that the Japanese market would rise when in fact it fell. He was able to lose so much because he was also responsible for the Singapore back office and was inadequately supervised by the London firm. Although not a Wall Street scandal, the episode attracted global publicity and was even made into a lacklustre movie *Rogue Trader* (1999).

Only a few months after the Barings debacle, Wall Street had a rogue-trader sensation of its own. In August 1995 it came to light that Toshihide Iguchi, a bond trader at Daiwa Bank's New York branch, had run up trading losses of $1.1 billion. Iguchi had joined Daiwa in New York in 1976 and worked on the Treasury-bond trading desk. In 1979, he had been given responsibility for the back-office processing of trades – a set-up similar to Leeson's in Singapore with similar dire consequences. In 1984, Iguchi made a $200,000 trading loss that he covered up, hoping to make the money back on other trades. But instead of winning he lost, to the tune of $400,000 per working day over 11 years. He concealed the losses by selling securities deposited by the bank's clients and hid these illegal sales by fabricating paperwork. Over the years he executed 30,000 unauthorised transactions, massively exceeded his trading limits, hid trade confirmation documents and forged statements – but nobody noticed. It was, commentated a stupefied Wall Street banker, "like not noticing there is an elephant in the living room".

Eventually, Iguchi could take the pressure no longer and sent a 30-page confession to the president of Daiwa Bank. Daiwa dithered and delayed for two months before informing the US regulators. They were furious and decided to make an example. Daiwa's entire US operations were closed down and federal prosecutors issued a criminal indictment, which was eventually settled by the payment of a $340m fine.

Yet another rogue-trader scandal erupted in February 2002 when it was revealed that John Rusnak, a foreign-exchange trader at Allfirst Financial, a Baltimore-based US subsidiary of Allied Irish Banks, had allegedly run up losses of $750m. It appeared that Rusnak had first got into trouble five years earlier by betting unsuccessfully that the yen would rise against the dollar and had then sustained further losses as he tried to make good the failed trades. He was able to cover his tracks for so long because of Allfirst's weak internal controls.

The Rusnak episode bore some similarities to the earlier Leeson and Iguchi rogue-trader debacles. All occurred in offshoots distant from the bank's main centre of operations. All went undetected for years and were only possible in the first place because of inadequate back-office controls. All led to earnest pronouncements about the importance of the back office. But the lengthy list of lapses in supervision of traders and back offices – of which Jett, Leeson, Iguchi and Rusnak are just the most sensational – suggests that Wall Street has not seen its last rogue-trader scandal.

Wall Street says sorry

"If Wall Street knows what is good for it and what is good for this country, it will very definitely clean up its act," said Felix G. Rohatyn, a respected former managing director of Lazard Freres, an investment bank, and doyen of the financial markets, to *Business Week* in May 2002 in the wake of the publication of the Merrill Lynch e-mails. "One of the precious things we have is the integrity of the financial markets. If that changes it could have dramatic repercussions on the dollar, on domestic inflation, on the economy." There were signs that the current generation of senior managers had got the message. In April 2002, David H. Komansky, Merrill Lynch's chairman and CEO, told the annual meeting of stockholders: "We have failed to live up to the high standards that are our tradition, and I want to take this opportunity to apologise to our clients, our shareholders, and our employees." "But," commented *Business Week*, "for Wall Street, just saying sorry at this stage may prove to be too little, too late."

4 Markets, markets, markets

Wall Street's financial markets are huge. In the US government debt market, the largest single-issuer market, average daily turnover is $300 billion. The daily volume of foreign-exchange trading in America is $254 billion and the daily volume of over-the-counter derivatives trading is $135 billion. At the New York Stock Exchange (NYSE), the world's leading stock exchange, the average daily value of trading is $44 billion.

Although Wall Street's financial markets and mechanisms are numerous and often technically complex, the fundamental function they perform is straightforward: the transfer of funds from individuals or institutions with surplus funds (saver-lenders) to those who require funds (borrower-spenders). This process is important economically because it channels funds from parties that do not have productive use for them to those that do (see Figure 4.1).

There are two routes by which funds can be transferred from saver-lenders to borrower-spenders.

- Indirect finance, via financial intermediaries – banks, savings institutions and investment intermediaries.
- Direct finance, via financial markets – the purchase of securities issued by borrower-spenders by saver-lenders themselves or by financial intermediaries.

There is another type of financial market in which holders of one type of financial asset exchange it (for a fee) to acquire another type of financial asset that they need or prefer to hold. The foreign-exchange market is the main example.

Financial intermediaries

This chapter focuses principally on financial markets, but because financial intermediaries are important participants in those markets, it is useful to touch upon the indirect finance route. Commercial banks, savings and loans, insurance companies, pension funds, mutual funds and other financial institutions all act as middlemen, transferring funds from lender-savers to borrower-spenders. They do so in two stages: first, by

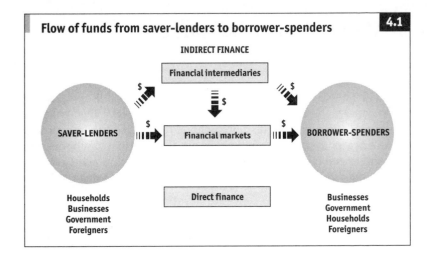

Flow of funds from saver-lenders to borrower-spenders `4.1`

INDIRECT FINANCE

Financial intermediaries

SAVER-LENDERS → Financial markets → BORROWER-SPENDERS

Direct finance

Households
Businesses
Government
Foreigners

Businesses
Government
Households
Foreigners

sourcing funds from lender-savers, incurring primary liabilities to them, such as bank deposits, premiums from insurance policies or mutual-fund shares; and second, by using these funds for the acquisition of primary assets from borrower-savers, such as loans, mortgages, stocks and bonds. The role played by intermediary institutions in indirect finance is known as financial intermediation.

There are three types of financial intermediary: depository institutions (banks), contractual savings institutions and investment intermediaries. The principal US financial intermediaries and their primary liabilities and primary assets are shown in Table 4.1

Financial intermediaries are often better placed than individual saver-lenders to bear and spread the risks of ownership of primary assets. Their substantial size enables them to diversify their asset holdings, spread risk and take advantage of economies of scale in buying and selling assets. They are able to employ expert professional staff, who are in a better position than private individuals to evaluate investment opportunities and risks. Competition among financial intermediaries ought to ensure that both saver-lenders and borrower-spenders enjoy keen prices, protecting their interests and promoting economic efficiency.

The assets of the principal US financial intermediaries at year-end 2001 are given in Table 4.2.

Table 4.1 **US financial intermediaries, primary liabilities and assets**

Type	Primary liabilities (sources of funds)	Primary assets (applications of funds)
Depository institutions		
Commercial banks	Deposits	Business and retail loans, mortgages, Treasury securities, municipal bonds
Savings and loan associations	Deposits	Mortgages
Mutual savings banks	Deposits	Mortgages
Credit unions	Deposits	Retail loans
Contractual savings institutions		
Pension funds, public retirement funds	Employer/employee contributions	Stocks, bonds
Life insurance companies	Policy premiums	Bonds, mortgages
Other insurance companies	Policy premiums	Stocks, bonds
Investment intermediaries		
Mutual funds	Shares	Stocks, bonds
Finance companies	Commercial paper, stocks, bonds	Business and retail loans
Money-market mutual funds	Shares	Money-market instruments

Source: Federal Reserve Board, Flow of Funds Accounts of the United States

Financial markets

In the direct finance route (see Figure 4.1 on page 86), borrower-spenders raise funds from saver-lenders through the sale to them (or financial intermediaries acting ultimately on their behalf) of financial securities. The buying and selling of securities takes place in the financial markets.

Financial markets carry out a variety of important functions for participants and for the economy as a whole:

- Pricing setting. Setting prices at which buyers and sellers are prepared to trade financial assets. If demand exceeds supply, prices will rise, and vice versa. When markets are functioning efficiently, buyers and sellers can be confident that the price they trade at is fair and reasonable.
- Asset valuation. Market prices provide a detached basis for

Table 4.2 **US financial intermediaries' assets, December 31st 2001**

	$bn
Depository institutions	
Commercial banks	6,875
Savings and loan associations, mutual savings banks	1,298
Credit unions	505
Contractual savings institutions	
Private pension funds	4,161
Life-insurance companies	3,305
State and local government retirement funds	2,176
Other insurance companies	881
Investment intermediaries	
Mutual funds	4,136
Money-market mutual funds	2,240
Finance companies	1,152

Source: Federal Reserve Board, Flow of Funds Accounts of the United States

determining the value of individual assets and corporations.

◪ Fund raising. For borrower-spenders, allowing corporations, governments and other borrowers to raise large sums from a large number of lenders.

◪ Income and saving. For saver-lenders, enabling them to earn a return on their funds (either directly or indirectly), to accumulate assets that will provide future income and to spread the risks of investment.

◪ Arbitrage. The transparency of market prices leads to the reduction of price discrepancies, making for greater economic efficiency.

◪ Risk management. Futures, options and other financial derivatives contracts allow purchasers to protect themselves against unfavourable developments and hold only those risks that they want to assume.

◪ Watchdog. Helps to ensure prudent financial conduct on the part of the corporations and governments in whose securities the markets deal. If they lose confidence in government policy or in a company's strategy or management, the price of its securities will be adversely affected, drawing attention to any doubts about its conduct. So the financial markets provide an important form of vigilance and discipline over the public and private sectors.

Financial securities

A financial security (also known as a financial instrument or asset) is a legal claim on a borrower's future income or assets. A financial security has an issuer that undertakes to make cash payments to the owner of the asset, who is called the investor or holder.

There are two main types of financial securities:

◪ Debt securities (bills, notes, bonds). These provide the holder with a predetermined regular cash claim deriving from the rate of interest charged (which is usually fixed, but may be variable) for a stated number of years, and then repay the principal amount upon maturity.

◪ Equity securities (stocks, equities, shares). These entitle the holder to part ownership of a business firm. They are claims to a share in the net income and assets of the firm. Owners receive a payment, known as a dividend, which depends on the corporation's profitability. They have no maturity date.

Primary and secondary financial markets

A primary market is a financial market that deals in issues of new securities, both debt and equity. These are sold to initial purchasers to raise funds for the issuer, which may be a corporation, a government or some public body. A secondary market is a financial market that deals in financial securities that have already been issued; in other words, it is a market in which second-hand securities are sold and resold.

Corporations or public bodies that wish to raise funds in the primary market engage an investment bank or securities house to advise them on the terms and timing of an offering, to make the necessary filings with the Securities and Exchange Commission (SEC) and to produce the prospectus for the offering. This document, which must be accurate and make a full disclosure of all relevant information, outlines the nature of the firm's business and the company's record and prospects. An issue of a corporation's stock for the first time is known as an initial public offering (IPO).

As agreed with the issuer, an investment bank will play the role of lead manager to the issue, advising on the various stages and organising the underwriting of it. The underwriting of an issue guarantees that the issuer gets its money regardless of whether there is demand for the securities. The risk is transferred to the underwriters, who with others involved in selling the issue will get a fee for their basic work in organising the issue as well as a commission on sales.

An active and healthy secondary market is crucial to investors and those who work in the financial markets. It is also important to issuers, since the price of their stock in the market determines the value of a corporation and signals how receptive the market would be to further fund-raising.

Secondary markets have various forms and structures. In open-outcry auction markets, such as the NYSE, trading is conducted in person on a trading floor. Alternatively, there are screen-based markets, such as the NASDAQ (National Association of Securities Dealers Automated Quotation System), in which trading is conducted among people in different locations linked by computer and telecommunications. In a call market, orders are batched together at set intervals during trading hours and a market maker conducts an auction that determines the price at which trades are made. In a continuous market, prices are quoted by market makers throughout trading hours. The NYSE employs a hybrid system in which the call method is used to determine the opening prices and a continuous trading technique is used for trades during the day.

There are a number of attributes that are desirable in a secondary market, which are generally characteristic of the major exchanges:

- Liquidity. The ease and certainty with which a trade can be executed. In an illiquid market, an investor may have difficulty selling an asset for a reasonable price, if at all. Effective market makers are a vital component of liquid markets. Larger markets generally have greater liquidity than smaller markets, and thus attract more business.
- Transparency. The availability of up-to-date and reliable information about trading and prices. The less transparent a market, the more reluctant traders are to conduct business there.
- Reliability. Mechanisms that ensure that trades are processed speedily and accurately.
- Efficiency. Competitive transaction costs, a mixture of the costs of conducting trades, regulation and taxes.
- Redress through law. Appropriate institutions, laws and procedures to enforce contracts and resolve disputes.
- Appropriate regulation and investor protection. An appropriate

balance of regulations that reassure investors and safeguard the market's reputation but do not stifle market trading volumes or innovation.

Exchanges and over-the-counter markets

Secondary-market transactions are conducted in two types of financial markets: formally constituted exchanges and over-the-counter (OTC) markets. Exchanges are membership organisations with buildings, staff and rule books. Buyers and sellers, or their brokers or agents, meet on a trading floor and execute transactions through an open-auction process. The NYSE, the American Stock Exchange and the Chicago Board of Trade are examples of organised exchanges.

In OTC markets, trading takes place by negotiation between the parties to the transaction. Dealers with a supply of securities for sale do business with anyone who wishes to buy them at their prices. Although these markets have no physical trading floors with dealers located all over the country, participants are constantly in touch with each other by computer and telephone and are aware of the prices at which other trades are being conducted. The main OTC markets are highly competitive and the prices quoted are generally as keen as in an organised exchange. Indeed, some argue that buyers get better prices because OTC markets are less costly to run than exchanges.

Although most large corporations have their stocks traded at formal exchanges, the stocks of many smaller companies – and some such as Microsoft that are not so small – are traded OTC, notably on NASDAQ, the OTC market most familiar to retail investors. Many OTC markets are confined to those working for financial-services firms and dealing among each other by computer and telephone. The US government bond market is an OTC market in which around 40 "primary dealers" are ready to buy and sell these securities. Other OTC markets include the massive foreign-exchange market, and those that trade negotiable certificates of deposit, federal funds and banker's acceptances. The swaps market is an OTC market that features tailor-made financial products.

Other factors that differentiate financial markets are the maturity of securities traded, the means of settlement and the obligation to exchange.

- ◪ Maturity of securities traded. The money market is the financial market that deals in short-term debt instruments, which have a maturity of less than a year. Debt securities with a maturity of more than a year and equities (which have no maturity date at all) are traded in the capital market.

- ◪ Means of settlement. Markets that deal on the basis of immediate settlement are known as spot or cash markets. Markets in which settlement is to be made sometime in the future are called forward or futures markets.
- ◪ Obligation to exchange. In spot and futures markets, the parties to a transaction (the counterparties) are obliged to exchange on an immediate or future basis. In the options market, the holder buys the right, but not the obligation, to buy or sell an asset within a defined period at a set price.

Participants in the financial markets

Participants in the financial markets comprise investors, mostly households (by both direct and indirect routes), borrowers, mainly corporations and government entities, and a variety of financial-services firms, including commercial banks, investment banks, broker-dealers, mutual funds, insurance companies, pension funds, retirement funds and investment companies. Big corporations, governments and government agencies, municipalities, central banks and international bodies such as the World Bank may also be important players. The importance of the different participants varies considerably from market to market and between money centres.

Investors are often divided into two types: individuals and institutional investors. According to the latest NYSE survey, 84m individuals in the United States own corporate stocks either directly or indirectly through a mutual fund, pension plan or self-directed retirement plan. Of these, 34m, 40% of the total, own stock directly, almost exactly matching the 39% of total corporate stock that Federal Reserve data show as being owned by households.

US institutional investors – insurance companies, mutual funds and pension funds – own 51% of corporate stocks (the remainder is held by foreigners, banks and other parties). This is a sevenfold increase since 1950 when institutional investors owned a mere 7% of stocks, and a substantial increase from 1990 when the proportion was 36%. Moreover, institutional investors own much higher proportions of non-stock financial assets – bonds, mortgages, loans, asset-backed securities and money-market instruments. In recent decades, institutional investors have become increasingly dominant in the financial markets.

Investors usually engage a broker to act as agent for a transaction. The broker is paid a commission for executing the trade. Brokers often offer additional services such as research, investment advice, stock custody and other services. A market maker, known as a specialist on the NYSE, is a dealer who undertakes to buy or sell specified financial securities at all times, thus making a market in them. Market makers make their turn from the spread (the difference) between the price at which they buy a security (bid price) and the price at which they sell (offer price). Market makers set prices for investors and provide liquidity to the market.

Professional investors can be divided into three types: arbitrageurs, hedgers and speculators. Arbitrageurs make money by exploiting price differentials, often fractional discrepancies, between financial markets by buying at a lower price in one market and selling at a higher price in the other market. Such opportunities are generally rare and short-lived because of modern communications technology and the activities of the arbitrageurs themselves. Hedgers aim to reduce their exposure to risk by buying or selling a financial asset to minimise or eliminate potential losses on another transaction. Speculators, however, assume risk by buying or selling financial assets in the hope of making a profit on a change in the price of an asset, in the full knowledge that they will make a loss if prices move against them. Although sometimes attacked for causing market instability, speculators provide liquidity to financial markets and on average their activities smooth price fluctuations.

The money market

The money market is a web of borrowers and investors linked to each other by telephone and computer. The principal borrowers are banks, corporations, the US government and government agencies to meet short-term funding needs. The money market is used by banks and corporations as investors to earn interest on unneeded cash, and by retail and institutional investors as an alternative to placing deposits with a bank. Money-market securities are traded actively and are mostly highly liquid. As they are fairly close to their redemption dates, they have smaller price fluctuations than long-term securities, making them reasonably safe investments.

The US money market has expanded substantially in recent decades. Its growth has been stimulated by the process of disintermediation in financial services, whereby the role of banks as intermediaries between borrowers and investors has been eroded by the ability to borrow or invest directly in the financial markets. Traditionally, savers held their

Table 4.3 **US money-market instruments, 1970–2001** (end year, $bn)

	1970	1980	1990	2001
US government agencies	51	193	435	2,141
Commercial paper	33	122	557	1,440
US Treasury bills	76	199	482	811
Certificates of deposit	45	260	479	793
Repurchase agreements	3	57	144	376
Eurodollars	2	61	103	225
Banker's acceptances	7	42	52	5

Sources: *Economic Report of the President*, February 2002; Federal Reserve Board, *Flow of Funds Accounts of the United States*

liquid assets in the form of deposits at banks, which paid at best a modest rate of interest on them. For the banks, this low-cost source of funds enabled them to provide loans to businesses or individuals. In recent decades, investors have diverted more and more of their liquid funds to money-market mutual funds that offer many of the conveniences of bank accounts but pay better rates. Borrowers, requiring money to meet temporary liquidity needs or irregular cash flows, have increasingly resorted to issuing short-term securities for sale to such funds. Thus the banks have been squeezed from both directions.

Trading in the money market is conducted via computer or telephone. When a trade is done, the parties inform the Depository Trust Company (DTC), an institution jointly owned by banks and other money-market participants, which acts as the clearing house for the US market. It clears the trade by debiting the bank that made the purchase and crediting the one that made the sale. The securities themselves remain with the DTC, existing only as electronic book entries.

Some of the principal money-market instruments (securities) and the amounts outstanding the end of selected years are listed in Table 4.3

US government agency notes
A number of federal government agencies and government-sponsored corporations are big borrowers in both the money market and the capital market. They include the Farmers Home Administration, the Federal Land Banks, the Federal Home Loan Mortgage Corporation, the Federal Housing Administration, the Federal National Mortgage Associ-

Table 4.4 **Issuance of short-term debt by US government agencies, 1990–2001**

Year	$bn
1990	581
1991	717
1992	817
1993	1,255
1994	2,098
1995	3,302
1996	4,246
1997	5,428
1998	5,757
1999	6,541
2000	8,317
2001	9,574

Source: The Bond Market Association

ation, the Government National Mortgage Association, the Student Loan Marketing Association, the Tennessee Valley Authority, an electricity utility and the Veterans Administration. The bulk of their borrowing – 90% of issuance in 2001 – is conducted in the money market, although they also issue bonds (the outstanding amounts in Table 4.3 include both short-term and long-term borrowings since the data do not differentiate). Since the early 1990s, US government agencies have become important money-market borrowers.

Although the US government does not guarantee agency securities, it is unlikely that it would allow an agency to default. Moreover, the securities are usually secured by the loans that are made with the funds raised. Should an agency encounter difficulties fulfilling its obligations, it could draw on its line of credit with the Treasury Department. Despite the low level of default risk, the interest paid by agency securities is significantly higher than Treasury securities, making them an attractive alternative for investors who want low-risk securities.

Commercial paper
Commercial paper is a short-term debt instrument issued by large corporations and banks. Mostly it has a maturity of between three and nine months. The upper limit is in order to qualify for exemption from

regulations that require registration prior to issue of securities with a maturity of over 270 days with the sec. It is usually unsecured. Around four-fifths of worldwide commercial paper is issued in America, the bulk of issues being made by the top 200 corporations.

Since the 1970s, the issuance of commercial paper has increased substantially, to the advantage of both borrowers and investors. Corporations found it cheaper to sell commercial paper than to borrow from banks, and the expansion of money-market funds enabled investors to earn higher rates than those paid by banks to depositors.

US Treasury bills

Treasury bills, familiarly known as T-bills, are short-term securities issued by the US government to meet funding requirements. They are issued in 3-month, 6-month and 12-month maturities at the end of which they are redeemed at face value. No interest payments are made, so the return to investors depends on the discount to face value at which they are purchased. They are the most actively traded of all money-market instruments and are thus most liquid. Treasury bills are mostly held by banks.

Certificates of deposit

Certificates of deposit (cds) are large-denomination negotiable time deposits sold to investors by banks. Purchasers receive interest and the principal is repaid upon maturity, but the securities can be sold in the market if funds are required before redemption. cds are an important source of funds for commercial banks. The principal investors are corporations, government agencies, charitable foundations and money-market mutual funds, which use them as a short-term repository for cash.

Repurchase agreements

Repurchase agreements, known as repos, amount to short-term loans (usually the maturity is less than two weeks) for which short-term securities owned by a borrower, in theory any security but in practice mostly Treasury bills or government agency notes, serve as collateral for the lender. A repo transaction has two stages. The first stage involves a borrower, typically a bank, selling securities it owns to an investor, while undertaking to repurchase the securities at a designated higher price at a future date. The second stage is the unwinding of the repo, when the borrower buys the securities back from the investor.

Repos are a relatively recent money-market instrument, being introduced in 1969. They are now an important source of bank funds. The most important investors are large corporations. Repos provide a useful boost to money-market liquidity by providing borrowers with additional funds at the cheapest price which can be used to buy more securities.

Repos are popular with investors because of their flexibility. Any maturity is possible: an overnight repo, which is settled the next day; a term repo, which is repaid at a future date agreed between the parties; and an open repo, which runs until one of the parties decides to terminate.

Eurodollars

Eurodollars are offshore US dollars deposited in banks, either foreign banks or the overseas branches of US banks, outside the United States (they have nothing to do with the European single currency, the euro). Eurodollar deposits are yet another source of funds for US banks, which they can borrow either from other banks or from their own foreign branches. Since the 1980s, eurodollar deposits have become a significant source of funding for US banks.

Banker's acceptances

A banker's acceptance is a promissory note, payable at a future date, issued by a company under the guarantee of a bank, which charges a fee for its endorsement. Like Treasury bills, acceptances are traded in a secondary market at a discount to their face value, the full value being paid to the holder at maturity. Investors are happy to buy and hold acceptances, even those issued by relatively small or foreign firms, because of the bank's endorsement. Banker's acceptances customarily arise from transactions in which proceeds have a time delay, such as international trade.

Bankers' acceptances have been used for the finance of international trade for centuries. They permit the vendor of a shipment of goods to receive immediate payment, and the purchaser does not have to find the funds to pay off the note at maturity allowing enough time for the goods to be sold. Banker's acceptances could also be a form of borrowing. Whereas banks were able to borrow at lower cost than other firms, banker's acceptances enabled the latter to take advantage of banks' superior credit rating. But with the growth of the commercial-paper market, corporations with good credit ratings have found it cheaper and more convenient to go directly to the market themselves. As a result, the volume and significance of banker's acceptances has greatly diminished.

Interbank loans

Banks are constantly borrowing from each other or lending on the overnight interbank market. This enables banks with surpluses to earn a return on their funds. Banks that are temporarily short of reserves borrow funds to boost their reserves to meet regulatory requirements.

In the United States, federal (fed) funds are overnight loans between banks of their deposits at the Federal Reserve. (The term is rather misleading since these are not loans made by the US federal government or the Federal Reserve, they are loans between banks.) The federal funds rate, the rate which banks charge each other for fed funds, is a closely watched economic indicator of the tightness of credit-market conditions and the stance of monetary policy: a high rate indicates that banks are short of funds; a low rate indicates that banks' credit requirements are small.

Money-market investors

Traditionally, money-market investment was a preserve of the big banks and corporations. Short-term securities were somewhat unattractive to retail investors because of the cost of acquiring knowledge of the credit status of borrowers, the transaction costs of frequent buying and selling, and the large denominations in which many short-term securities are issued.

Money-market mutual funds

Banks and big business remain important players in the money market, but from the 1980s, and particularly since the mid-1990s, there has been a phenomenal expansion of money-market mutual funds, which allow retail and institutional investors to participate by pooling their monies (see Figure 4.2). The funds are run by professional managers, simplifying investors' research costs and improving investment decisions, and investment in a portfolio of securities reduces risk.

Money-market mutual funds sell shares to investors, using the money raised to buy money-market securities. The interest earned by these assets is distributed to shareholders, the yield depending on the performance of the securities purchased. Because of lower operating costs, the funds usually offer considerably better returns than bank deposit accounts. They do so without a substantial increase in risk, since even though the funds do not have federal insurance, unlike banks in respect of their deposits, the risk of default in the securities in which money-market mutual funds invest is low. Moreover, funds are

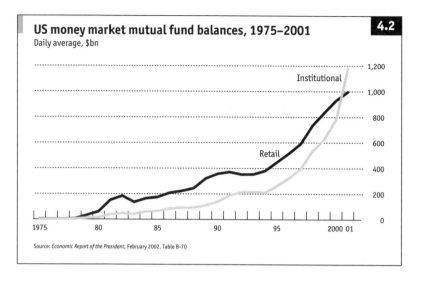

4.2

US money market mutual fund balances, 1975–2001
Daily average, $bn

Institutional

Retail

1975   80   85   90   95   2000 01

Source: *Economic Report of the President*, February 2002. Table B-70

required by regulation to invest only in securities whose safety and liquidity make them cash equivalents.

For retail investors, a convenient feature of the funds is that investors can write cheques against the value of their shareholdings, like a cheque account at a bank. Indeed, so attractive have they proved that banks and savings and loan associations have suffered substantial losses of deposits, causing them problems with liquidity and profitability.

There are two types of money-market mutual funds: retail money-market funds that serve individual investors; and institutional money-market funds that cater for corporations, government agencies, charitable foundations and other large investors. The combined assets of US money-market mutual funds total $2.2 trillion, more than one-quarter of all money-market securities in the world.

The capital markets

Capital-market securities have maturities of more than one year. They experience much greater fluctuations in price than money-market securities and are thus substantially riskier investments. The principal capital-market instruments are shown in Table 4.5.

Corporate stocks

Stocks, also called equities or shares, confer part ownership of a corporation and entitle holders to a proportionate share of dividends. Stocks

Table 4.5 **US capital-market instruments, 1970–2001** (end year, $bn)

	1970	1980	1990	2001
Corporate stocks	906	1,601	4,146	15,186
Corporate bonds	167	366	1,008	2,558
US government securities (marketable)	160	407	1,653	2,157
Municipal bonds	146	310	870	1,305
Asset-backed securities	–	–	–	1,281
Foreign bonds	–	–	–	486

Sources: *Economic Report of the President*, February 2002; Federal Reserve Board, *Flow of Funds Accounts of the United States*

are the largest class of capital-market security, with a market value at the end of 2001 of $15 trillion. About half of stocks (by value) are owned by individuals and half by institutional investors. There are several types of stock. Common stock is much the largest class. The holders of these securities benefit most when corporations prosper, but their claim on income and assets comes after all other creditors. Preferred stock pays a fixed dividend and has some characteristics of a bond. In case of liquidation, preferred stockholders rank ahead of common stockholders, but after other creditors including bondholders.

Corporate bonds

Corporate bonds are issued by large corporations that need to borrow long-term. There are various kinds of bonds, distinguished by the type of collateral upon which the bond is secured and the degree of default risk. A large firm may well have several types of bonds outstanding. Some corporate bonds – convertibles – confer an option to be converted into stocks, a feature that permits investors to enjoy a capital gain if the stock price rises, making it easier and cheaper for issuers to raise funds.

- Secured bonds. The corporation pledges specific assets as collateral. In the event of non-payment, the bond holders have the right to seize and liquidate those assets.
- Unsecured bonds. Often called debentures, these have only the general creditworthiness of the issuer as backing. Because they are not backed by specific assets, they pay higher interest than secured bonds.

Table 4.6 **Corporate-bond and municipal-bond credit ratings**

Moody's	Standard & Poor's	Guide
Aaa	AAA	Best quality
Aa	AA	High quality
A	A	Upper medium
Baa	BBB	Adequate protection
Ba	BB	Fair
B	B	Potential vulnerability
Caa	CCC	Speculative
Ca	CC	Identifiable vulnerability
C	C	Highly speculative
D	C	In payment default

Sources: Moody's; Standard & Poor's

◪ Junk bonds. Corporate bonds with a credit-rating status below "investment grade", a status that traditionally came about through a downgrading because of business or financial problems facing the corporations that issued them. Such "fallen angels" were difficult to sell because there was no properly functioning secondary market in junk bonds.

Credit-rating analysis is undertaken by a number of specialist agencies, of which Moody's and Standard and Poor's are the best known. They base their assessments on corporations' balance sheets, cash flows and activities, selling their ratings to subscribers. The higher the credit risk, the lower is the risk of payment default. Bonds with low risk of default – above Baa or BBB – are known as investment grade; bonds with ratings less than Baa or BBB are rated below investment grade.

A study of the actual default rates for different grades of bonds within the first year of issue and over a ten-year investment horizon (1970–90) reported the results shown in Table 4.7.

From the late 1970s, Michael Milken of Drexel Burnham Lambert, an investment bank, vigorously developed the issuance of junk bonds (he preferred the term "high-yield bonds"), recognising that there were borrowers whose requirements were not being met by the capital market and savers that were willing to assume higher risks for higher rewards. He cited academic research that showed that the additional risk on a

Table 4.7 **Default rates for corporate bonds, 1970–90**

Grade of bond	Default rate in first year of issue (%)	Default rate for ten-year horizon (%)
Aaa	0.00	0.37
Aa	0.04	0.65
A	0.01	0.99
Baa	0.17	3.78
Ba	1.80	11.29
B	8.08	24.17

Source: J.S. Fons and A.E. Kimball, "Corporate Bond Defaults and Default Rates 1979–1990", *Journal of Fixed Income Securities*, 1991

diversified portfolio of junk bonds was small. Drexel itself assumed the role of market maker for the bonds it brought out, providing liquidity for investors.

During the 1980s, 1,800 corporations issued junk bonds. Many were used to finance leveraged buy-outs, and others financed corporate takeover bids. In 1989, with Milken and Drexel caught up in the Boesky insider-trading scandal, the junk bond secondary market collapsed. This led to 250 corporate bond defaults in 1989–91. In 1990 Drexel filed for bankruptcy because of losses on its junk-bond holdings.

The market for high-yield bonds revived vigorously from the mid-1990s. In the mid-1980s average issuance was around $30 billion an year, but by the end of the 1990s it was $150 billion. The junk-bond market is now mostly used by medium-sized corporations to obtain capital-market financing that would otherwise not be available because of a non-investment grade credit rating.

US Treasury notes and bonds
The debt securities issued by the US government – Treasury notes, with a maturity of 1–10 years, and Treasury bonds, with a maturity of 10–30 years – are the largest single category and the most widely traded and liquid category of securities in the world. The default risk on US government securities is zero, since the federal government could always simply print dollars to pay off the debt. US Treasury securities are the standard against which all other bonds are measured as regards credit quality. Treasury notes and bonds are sold on the government's behalf by the Federal Reserve at auction to the so-called primary dealers, a

Table 4.8 **Ownership of US public debt securities, 2001**

	$bn	%
Foreign and international	1,200	40.5
US monetary authorities	534	18.0
Mutual funds	378	12.8
Pension funds	315	10.6
Banks	260	8.8
Individuals	92	3.1
Insurance companies	88	3.0
Other	50	1.8
State and local governments	43	1.4
Total	2,960	100.0

Source: Bond Market Association

group of around 40 firms through which the Fed conducts open-market operations (its selling and buying of Treasury securities). The sales are conducted to a regular schedule: every month for 2-year and 5-year Treasury notes; and every quarter for 3-year, 7-year and 10-year Treasury notes and 30-year Treasury bonds.

The safety and liquidity of US Treasury securities makes them an attractive element of many investment portfolios. The pattern of ownership of US public debt securities (Treasury bills, notes and bonds) is shown in Table 4.8.

Foreign investors are the largest category of holders of US government securities, owning two-fifths of the total. Next come the Federal Reserve and US government accounts, and US mutual and pension funds, accounting for around a further one-fifth each. The rest are owned by banks, individuals and a variety of other investors.

Municipal bonds
Bonds issued by levels of government below the federal government – municipal, county and state – are known as municipal bonds. The proceeds of these borrowings are used to finance utilities, highways, schools and other public undertakings. Most municipal bonds have the advantage for investors that interest earned is exempt from federal taxation, and often state and local taxes as well. This allows local government to borrow at lower interest rates.

There are two types of municipal bonds: revenue bonds and general obligation bonds:

- ◪ Revenue bonds. These are backed by the revenues that are generated by the project financed by the bonds. For instance, cities and counties may use revenues from water or sewage systems to guarantee payments on bonds issued to finance these works. They comprise the bulk of municipal bond issues.
- ◪ General obligation bonds (GOS). These do not have particular assets or revenue streams pledged as security, but are guaranteed by the full taxing power of the issuer and are generally considered less risky than revenue bonds.

Occasionally, there are defaults on municipal bonds because of problems with a particular project or malaise in the local economy. Indeed, in 1975 New York City, one of the largest borrowers in the municipal-bond market, almost defaulted. Its economy had been undermined by the movement of people and businesses to the suburbs which had eroded the city's tax base. New York State and a group of Wall Street bankers got together and formed a special agency, the Municipal Assistance Corporation (MAC), to issue bonds (known as "Big MAC" bonds) backed by the state, the proceeds of which went to the city. Led by Felix Rohatyn of Lazard Freres and with widespread support from Wall Street firms, which had plenty of reasons for wishing to prevent a default (commercial banks were large investors in municipal securities and investment banks made markets in them), the MAC eventually succeeded in achieving the city's financial rehabilitation.

Asset-backed securities

An asset-backed security is a type of bond. But instead of being supported by income from an issuing body, such as a government entity or a corporation, the income stream that services it derives from specific underlying assets. Mortgage-backed securities, supported by income from residential mortgages, constitute the original and principal form of asset-backed security. But there is also a rapidly growing group of asset-backed securities based on income streams from other types of assets that are mostly created by day-to-day credit transactions, such as a mortgage loan to a homebuyer, an automobile loan to a car purchaser, or the issue of a credit card. Traditionally, such loans formed part of a bank's assets and the interest payments received from them formed part of its income. But these assets can also be packaged into securities and sold to other parties, a process called securitisation.

Securitisation is conducted by a specialist intermediary, such as an investment bank. Typically, a trust is established to buy and own the assets being securitised, which are usually of a single type, using funds raised by the sale of asset-backed securities to investors. These investors receive the income stream from the assets. The trust is terminated when all the underlying assets (such as mortgage loans) have been paid off.

The securitisation of assets is attractive to banks and other financial firms for a variety of reasons. It saves them capital that would otherwise be tied up supporting the assets and the cost of deposit-liabilities insurance premiums. It allows them to focus on the generation of origination and servicing fees. It enables issuers of the underlying asset to alter their risk profile, transferring or sharing risk with investors. It also establishes a market price for some types of assets that are difficult to trade because they are difficult to value – asset-backed securities are generally much more readily tradable than the underlying assets themselves.

Mortgaged-backed securities provide investors with a stream of interest payments from a large number of individual mortgage loans that are packaged together as a security. The secondary market in mortgages originated with an initiative of the US government: the establishment of the Federal National Mortgage Association (known as Fannie Mae), in 1938. The purpose of this body was to purchase mortgages from originator lenders, mostly local banks or savings and loan associations, thereby stimulating the housing market by enabling the originators to make more loans to homebuyers.

From the outset, Fannie Mae pursued policies designed to promote the growth of the secondary market in mortgages. Standard criteria were established for new mortgages that the originators were required to follow if they wished to be able to sell them to Fannie Mae – for example, as regards property valuations, the credit credentials of borrowers, and the collection of payments from borrowers. The standardisation of these aspects led to the eventual packaging of the mortgages into mortgage-backed securities, the first of which was issued in 1970.

There are now several bodies that promote the development of secondary markets for mortgage-backed securities, operating under the sponsorship of the US government. The mortgage-backed securities they issue are known generically as agency securities. The market for agency securities grew rapidly and soon became one of the largest financial markets – by 2002 the average daily trading volume was $133 billion.

Table 4.9 **Outstanding volume of agency mortgage-backed securities, March 31st 2002**

	$bn
Fannie Maes (Federal National Mortgage Association)	1,355
Freddie Macs(Federal Home Loan Mortgage Corporation)	1,013
Ginnie Maes (Government National Mortgage Association)	590
Total	2,958

Source: Bond Market Association

The outstanding volume of the principal agency mortgaged-backed securities is shown in Table 4.9.

Mortgaged-backed securities pioneered the way for the securitisation of other types of assets. Starting in the 1980s, the volume of non-mortgage asset-backed securities increased rapidly. In 1995 the total outstanding was $316 billion; by 2002 it had quadrupled to $1,331 billion (although this was still less than half the outstanding volume of mortgage-backed agency securities).

The extension of securitisation to non-mortgage assets was led by the commercial banks, the institutions that owned the bulk of such assets. It allowed them to focus on the role of intermediary between borrowers and lenders, earning fees for their specialist services and freeing up capital for more profitable uses. Credit-card companies have also been big users of securitisation. The principle has been extended to a variety of exotic income streams, including the anticipated revenue generated by a slate of movies produced by Walt Disney and future revenue from the issued recordings of David Bowie, a rock singer (so-called Bowie Bonds).

The international capital market

In addition to the US domestic capital market, there is a substantial and growing international capital market. Before the early 1960s, the international capital market was located in New York and the US dollar was the principal currency of issue. But the introduction in 1963 of a tax designed to discourage foreign borrowing in the US capital market to reduce the US balance-of-payments deficit led to the decline of the foreign-bond market in New York and the growth of the eurobond market in other financial centres, principally London. With the removal of the discriminatory controls in the 1970s, the New York

Table 4.10 **Outstanding volume of non-mortgage asset-backed securities, March 31st 2002**

	$bn	%
Credit-card securities	370	28
Automobile loans	202	15
Home equity loans	196	15
Student loans	63	5
Equipment leases	71	5
Manufactured housing securities	43	3
Other	386	29
Total	1,331	100

Source: Bond Market Association

foreign-bond market revived, although activity trailed far behind the eurobond market.

Despite being focused offshore, the eurobond market has many ties with the Wall Street capital market: the US dollar is the foremost currency of issue; US entities are much the largest users of the market, accounting for 47% of the total volume of issuance in 2001; and many of the leading euromarket intermediaries are Wall Street investment banks and commercial banks, although usually they operate in the market through their London or other offshore offices.

The foreign-exchange market

Much the largest and most liquid market in the world, with a global daily turnover of around $1.2 trillion, the foreign-exchange market is where the currencies of different countries are traded for each other. It is where financial claims between countries, arising from trade (imports and exports) and international investment, are settled. There is also a large volume of speculative activity in the market, with speculators seeking to profit from successfully predicting changes in currency values.

A currency's value is measured by its exchange rate against other currencies. The relative values of different currencies are determined in the foreign-exchange market, which has a crucial impact upon a country's foreign trade, its interest and inflation rates, and the pattern of international capital flows. A country's exchange rate is a fundamental economic price, and the foreign-exchange market affects all other financial markets.

The foreign-exchange market is a 24-hour market. At every hour, day and night, trading is taking place somewhere in the world, following the sun from east to west. The business day opens in the Asia-Pacific financial centres, first Wellington and Sydney, followed by Tokyo, Hong Kong and Singapore. A few hours later, trading begins in Bahrain and elsewhere in the Middle East. Then the markets open in Europe, overlapping briefly with Tokyo. When it is early afternoon in Europe, trading gets under way in New York and other US centres. By the time it is late afternoon in the United States, the next day has arrived in the Asia-Pacific region and the markets are opening there. Daily activity has a regular cycle, peaking when the European markets overlap with the Asian markets, and again when it is afternoon in London and morning in New York.

The main participants in the foreign-exchange market have arrangements for monitoring markets and trading on a 24-hour basis. Some keep their New York or other trading desks open round the clock; others pass the book from one office to the next.

US dollar

The US dollar is much the most widely traded currency. According to a survey of the market conducted by the Bank for International Settlements in 2001, the dollar was one of the two currencies involved in 93% of global foreign-exchange transactions. The widespread trading of the dollar reflects its prime role in international trade and finance as:

- the investment currency in many capital markets;
- a reserve currency held by many central banks;
- the transaction currency in most international commodities markets;
- the invoice currency for many contracts; and
- the intervention currency used by monetary authorities to influence their own exchange rate.

The dollar is also the principal vehicle currency in the foreign-exchange market, where it is market practice to trade pairs of currencies against a common third currency as a vehicle, rather than directly against each other.

The foreign-exchange market is an over-the-counter (OTC) market, with a modest exchange-traded segment. In the OTC market, which accounts for over 90% of activity, transactions are done using computer or telephone links between participants in different locations. In America, the OTC market is largely unregulated (as a market, not the participating banks themselves). Commercial banks do not need authorisation from a regulator to deal in foreign exchange, which is considered an express banking power, nor do securities or brokerage firms. Transactions are carried out on whatever terms are acceptable to the counterparties, subject to law.

Although there are no official regulations about OTC foreign-exchange trading in America, there is an advisory document, *Guidelines for Foreign Exchange Trading*, which is regularly updated. It is produced by the Foreign Exchange Committee, an independent body composed of representatives of market participants under the sponsorship of the Federal Reserve Bank of New York (FRBNY). Its purpose is to foster the healthy functioning and development of the foreign-exchange market in America by explaining market practices and offering best-practice recommendations.

Foreign-exchange instruments
In America, five foreign-exchange instruments are traded in the OTC market and two more are traded in exchanges. Among the OTC instruments, spot, outright forwards and foreign-exchange swaps – the three traditional (pre-1970) instruments – constitute around 90% of total foreign-exchange market activity. The other OTC instruments, currency swaps and currency options, which were part of the wave of 1970s financial-derivative instruments, account for around 8% of activity. The exchange-traded foreign-exchange products, currency futures and currency options, make up less than 5% of activity.

- Spot. A straightforward purchase or sale of currency for settlement not more than two business days after the deal is contracted. The spot rate is the current market exchange rate, the benchmark price.
- Outright forward. A currency transaction to be settled at an agreed time in the future of more than two business days. Outright forwards are used for a variety of purposes, such as covering a known future expenditure, hedging, speculation, or a myriad commercial, financial or investment purposes.
- Foreign-exchange swap. A simultaneous exchange of two

currencies on a specific date at a rate agreed at the time of the contract, and a reverse exchange of the same two currencies at a date further in the future at a rate agreed at the time of the contract. Foreign-exchange swaps are used by market participants to shift temporarily into or out of a currency, without incurring the exchange-rate risk of an exposure in the currency that is temporarily held.

- Currency swap. A contract that commits two counterparties to exchange streams of interest payments in different currencies for an agreed period of time and to exchange principal amounts in the respective currencies at an agreed exchange rate at maturity.
- Currency option. A contract that gives the right to buy (call option) or sell (put) a currency at a specified exchange rate during a specified period. The right to execute is exercised only if the purchaser wishes to do so, in contrast to a forward contract, which obliges the parties to execute at maturity, and a futures contract, in which the parties are obligated to execute but the obligation is usually liquidated before maturity.

Exchange-traded currency instruments

In addition to the currency instruments traded in the OTC market, currency futures and options are traded on some US exchanges: the Chicago Mercantile Exchange; the Philadelphia Stock Exchange; the New York Board of Trade; and the Mid-America Commodity Exchange. As with all exchange trading, dealing is in standardised products and is conducted in public in centralised locations. Hours, trading practices and other matters are regulated by the exchange. There are margin payments, daily marking of prices to market values and cash settlements through a central clearing house.

Participants in the US foreign-exchange market

There are four main participants in the US foreign-exchange market.

- Foreign-exchange dealers. Traditionally, currency trading was dominated by the large commercial banks located in New York and other money centres. Being in constant touch with each other for buying and selling, they constituted an "interbank" foreign-exchange market. This network has now expanded to include some investment banks and non-bank institutions, becoming an "interdealer" market. Functioning as intermediaries and market makers, these players act for corporate customers and transact business as correspondents for other commercial banks throughout the country. They also buy and sell foreign exchange for their own accounts. Consolidation in the securities industry has led to an increase in the market share of the largest US foreign-exchange dealers, with the market share of the leading firms rising from 52% in 1998 to 66% in 2001. In 2001, the FRBNY specified the US foreign-exchange interdealer market as comprising 79 dealers – 68 banks and 11 non-banks. It includes a number of US branches and subsidiaries of major foreign banks – from Japan, the UK, Germany, France, Switzerland and elsewhere – that conduct a significant share of US foreign-exchange activity.

◾ Non-dealer customers. Around half the foreign-exchange trading activity in the OTC market consists of interdealer transactions, that is trading by the members of the interdealer group among themselves and with dealers abroad. The other half involves customers who undertake foreign-exchange transactions as part of the payments process to execute some commercial, investment, hedging or speculative activity. Financial firms (non-dealers) make up about three-fifths of non-dealer customers and non-financial non-dealer customers around two-fifths.

◾ Central banks. All central banks undertake operations in their country's foreign-exchange market to some extent. Occasionally, the United States has intervened heavily to influence the price of the US dollar, although recently activity has been minimal. But the foreign-exchange desk of the FRBNY is in the market daily, buying and selling currencies, usually in modest amounts, for its "customers" – other central banks, US agencies and international institutions. Such business helps it keep in touch with the market.

◾ Brokers. A broker is an intermediary who acts as an agent for one or both parties to a transaction (whereas a dealer acts as a principal, perhaps committing the firm's capital by taking one side of a trade for the firm's own account). Brokers handle about one-quarter of all transactions in the US OTC foreign-exchange market.

Growth of foreign-exchange trading

Since the 1970s, both global and US foreign-exchange trading turnover has increased massively; between the late 1970s and 2001 global average daily turnover grew more than 40 times. The growth of daily

Table 4.11 **Average daily foreign-exchange turnover in the US, 1989–2001**

	$bn
1989	115
1992	167
1995	244
1998	351
2001	254

Source: Federal Reserve Bank of New York, *Central bank survey of foreign exchange and derivatives market activity in April 2001*, Table 5

trading turnover in the United States from 1989 to 2001 is shown in Table 4.11.

Underlying the substantial expansion of both global and US foreign-exchange trading is the move in the early 1970s from fixed to flexible exchange rates. This was reinforced by widespread financial-market deregulation and expansion of the institutionalisation and internationalisation of savings and investment. The greater liberalisation of international trade was another driver, as has been the massive expansion of international capital transactions. Aiding and abetting these developments have been the advances in communications technology, making possible instantaneous real-time transmission of market information and the rapid and reliable execution of financial transactions.

Between 1998 and 2001, the volume of foreign-exchange trading turnover in the United States declined for the first time in three decades, a development also observed in the global total. The Bank for International Settlements, which conducts the triennial surveys of global foreign-exchange and derivatives trading, explains the falls as a result of a combination of technical factors: the introduction of the euro; the growing share of electronic booking in the spot interbank market; and consolidation in the banking industry. Given the powerful underlying forces promoting foreign-exchange trading in the global economy, the next survey will almost certainly see a move upwards.

Derivatives

Derivatives is the generic term for a host of financial instruments derived from conventional dealings in underlying commodities, securities and currencies. There are dozens of different varieties but only three basic types: futures, options and swaps.

- ◢ Futures. Contracts that commit both parties to the deal to a transaction in a financial product on a future date at a pre-arranged price. They are negotiable instruments that can be traded in futures markets.
- ◢ Options. Contracts giving the holder the right to buy or sell a financial instrument at an agreed price within a specified time period. There is no obligation to execute the transaction.
- ◢ Swaps. Transactions in which two parties undertake to exchange streams of payments. Swaps are used to change an existing market exposure on account of a loan, security, currency or interest rate to a different exposure.

Futures

Commodities markets where merchants trade physical goods – food-stuffs, metals, minerals or whatever – have existed for thousands of years. Futures contracts developed as adjuncts to physical commodities deals to protect merchants against commodity-price fluctuations over time. A futures contract, an agreement between two parties to exchange a specified amount of an asset at a fixed future date at a predetermined time, fulfils this function. In the 19th century, commodities exchanges introduced standardised futures contracts, allowing a market to develop in them which soon came to overshadow physical markets.

There are two motives for participation in the futures market: hedging and speculation. Hedging is the use of futures to insure against adverse price movements, that is to reduce risk. Speculation is the deliberate assumption of risk in order to profit from price movements.

The trading of futures contracts is conducted on organised exchanges. There are around 35 large futures exchanges in the world and many smaller ones.

There are two principal types of futures contracts:

- ◢ Commodity futures. The original form of futures contract based on physical commodities, such as wheat, oil, cotton and coffee.
- ◢ Financial futures. Futures contracts that provide a means of managing financial risk. The volume of financial futures traded greatly exceeds that of commodity futures.

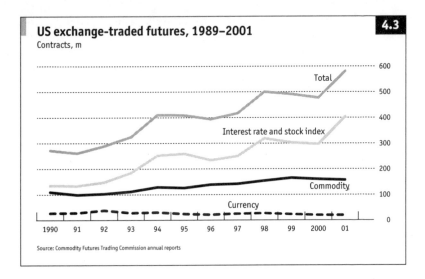

US exchange-traded futures, 1989–2001
Contracts, m

`4.3`

Total

Interest rate and stock index

Commodity

Currency

1990 91 92 93 94 95 96 97 98 99 2000 01

600
500
400
300
200
100
0

Source: Commodity Futures Trading Commission annual reports

Financial futures

Financial instability increased substantially from the early 1970s, following the abandonment of fixed exchange rates and the subsequent deregulation of interest rates. The increased volatility in financial markets led to demand for new financial instruments to hedge these risks. In response, in 1972 the Chicago Mercantile Exchange introduced interest-rate futures, the first financial-futures contract, since when both the range of products and trading volumes have multiplied many times. The principal financial-instrument futures contracts are as follows.

- ▰ Currency futures. These are the oldest type of financial future, introduced in 1972. Since 1995 the volume of contracts traded has declined, because of the advent of the euro and the increased use of OTC contracts for currency hedging.
- ▰ Interest rate futures. These permit financial institutions and investors to hedge changes in interest rates. The first contract was launched by the Chicago Board of Trade in 1975. Around 90% of all financial-futures trading consists of trading in interest-rate futures.
- ▰ Stock-index futures. These allow fund managers to hedge the ups and downs of stock indices. Demand has grown as index tracker funds have become widespread.

Exchange traded options

Options trading began in 1973 when the Chicago Board of Trade, a futures exchange, received regulatory consent to form a separate entity to trade them, the Chicago Board of Options Exchange. Today many of the world's futures exchanges also trade options, as do many stock exchanges, which trade options on stocks quoted on them and options on their stock indices. In the United States, options are traded on the American Stock Exchange, the Pacific Exchange and the Philadelphia Stock Exchange.

Exchange-traded options contracts are based on the price of some underlying instrument and are of standardised sizes and expiry dates. They are used to hedge a variety of risks or to speculate. The most widely traded types are the following.

- Equity options. These entitle the holder to buy or sell batches of stocks of individual corporations.
- Index options. These are based on indices of stock prices, commodity prices, bond prices or whatever.
- Interest rate options. These are based either on an interest rate or on the price of a government bond.
- Commodity options. These are traded on a large number of commodities, based either on the underlying commodity price or on the relevant futures market price.
- Currency options. These are based on the exchange rate between two currencies.

Over-the-counter derivatives

Over-the-counter (OTC) derivative transactions are conducted directly between two counterparties. One of the parties is usually a dealer, generally a bank, and the other is a client, such as a corporation or government agency. Bespoke OTC products may be better suited to such clients' requirements than standardised exchange instruments.

The OTC derivatives market began in the late 1980s and has expanded rapidly: in 1995 the global daily turnover was $270 billion; in 2001 it was $764 billion. The principal types of OTC derivatives are as follows.

- Forwards. Contracts that set a price for something to be delivered in the future. OTC forward contracts are similar to futures but are tailored to meet the requirements of clients.

- Interest-rate swaps. Agreements to exchange periodic payments related to interest payment obligations. The swap may be fixed for floating, or floating for floating, based on different indices.
- Currency swaps. Contracts that commit two counterparties to exchange streams of interest payments in different currencies for an agreed period and to exchange principal amounts in the respective currencies at an agreed exchange rate at maturity.
- Interest-rate options. Contracts that convey the right to pay or receive a specific interest rate on a predetermined principal for a set period.

Turnover in trading in OTC derivatives in the United States has grown rapidly in recent years: in 1995 average daily turnover was $52 billion; in 1998 $91 billion; and in 2001 $135 billion. Growth has been especially dynamic in interest-rate swaps, the biggest single instrument. Daily turnover has risen from $31 billion in 1998 to $82 billion in 2001. Dealing in OTC derivatives is concentrated among large financial institutions. The FRBNY identifies the market as comprising 54 major dealers, who conduct 71% of trading turnover in the interdealer market among themselves.

Market forces

Wall Street's financial markets have grown rapidly in recent decades and there is every likelihood that they will continue to do so propelled forward by a familiar set of forces.

- Technology. Technology has created new financial instruments and even new markets, while revolutionising existing ones. Financial services' cost structures and operating practices have been transformed by computers and communications technology, and the industry will continue to be profoundly affected by IT innovations.
- Liberalisation. In recent years, there has been a dismantling of traditional barriers between markets and traditional demarcations between market participants, such as commercial banks, investment banks, insurance companies and non-financial firms generating new competition in markets as firms enter new businesses.
- Consolidation. Liberalisation has led to mergers between firms both to diversify their range of activities and to increase their

scale of operations. This has occurred within Wall Street and internationally, as Wall Street firms expand globally and foreign banks, such as Deutsche Bank and UBS, establish a substantial footprint on Wall Street.

- Integration. Wholesale financial-services firms are also getting bigger through horizontal integration – taking over rivals in the same sector to achieve greater market share and economies of scale in the provision of services and products. Much of the industry is still fragmented, and there is plenty of scope for this process to go further.

- Amalgamation. Financial exchanges in the United States have been amalgamating for a generation, striving for economies of scale and the resources to develop better IT. Internationally, many alliances have been forged, which will eventually lead to mergers and the emergence of worldwide exchanges.

- Disintermediation. The process by which borrowers use the markets (direct finance) instead of financial intermediaries (indirect finance) to meet their financing requirements is well established and will continue.

- Securitisation. The securitisation of assets will continue, and it will be extended to create both more and new varieties of asset-backed securities.

- Globalisation. Financial firms and financial markets are increasingly global in reach and interconnections. Investors are also taking a global outlook. As host to some of the world's foremost markets, Wall Street stands to benefit from these trends.

- Deregulation. The deregulation of financial services has been under way for three decades, significant milestones being the end of fixed exchange rates in 1971, the abolition of fixed commission rates in 1975 and the repeal of the Glass-Steagall Act in 1999. The market forces released by such deregulation are continuing to have an effect.

- Reregulation. The political reaction to recent corporate failures and Wall Street scandals is leading towards some reregulation of the financial-services industry. Such moves may inhibit the expansion of the markets for a while, but probably not for long.

5 The securities industry

The securities industry lies at the heart of Wall Street, so much so that the terms are quite often used interchangeably. The securities industry is engaged in primary market activity – the issuance of new securities to raise funds for borrowers (underwriting) – and secondary market activity – the trading of existing securities. Foremost among related activities are advisory work, especially mergers and acquisitions, and asset-management services.

Traditionally, securities industry activities were undertaken by two different types of financial firms. Underwriting and advisory work was done by investment banks, and secondary-market trading was the business of securities brokers and dealers (broker-dealers). The term investment bank was always something of a misnomer, since such banks never did much deposit taking, which is the basic business of banking. Moreover, since the Banking Act 1933 (Glass-Steagall), which imposed a legal separation of the activities of securities underwriting and deposit taking, it has been illegal to do so. But there was no legal impediment to investment banks and broker-dealer firms encroaching on each other's business, and from the 1960s they increasingly did so. Today, the big securities industry firms, of which some originated as investment banks and some as broker-dealers, are engaged in the whole range of securities activities.

The convergence of the two sides of the industry is mirrored in the development of its trade association, the Securities Industry Association (SIA). In 1912, under political attack from opponents of the Wall Street "money trust", some 350 investment-banking firms met at New York's Waldorf Astoria Hotel and formed the Investment Bankers Association of America (IBA) to protect their position. Following their example, in 1913 the broker-dealers established the Association of Stock Exchange Firms (ASEF) to represent their interests. In 1972, the IBA and ASEF merged to form the SIA. Today the SIA has more than 600 members on whose behalf it promotes professional best practice, undertakes research, acts as a forum for discussion and lobbies on behalf of the whole industry.

Virtually every firm undertaking securities activities is a member of the National Association of Securities Dealers (NASD), the self-regulatory organisation of the over-the-counter (OTC) securities market, which has around 5,500 member firms. All the main firms are also members of the New York Stock Exchange (NYSE).

Beginning in the 1980s, the commercial banks – proper banks that receive deposits from the public and lend to borrowers – gradually encroached on the business of the securities industry firms. Step by step, the Glass-Steagall separation of securities underwriting and deposit taking was eroded, a process that culminated in the Financial Services Modernisation Act 1999 (Gramm-Leach-Bliley), which swept away Glass-Steagall by allowing banks, securities firms and insurance companies to affiliate under a financial holding company. This dismantling of the regulatory barriers in the financial-services industry led to many banks buying securities firms and the formation of some giant financial conglomerates, notably Citigroup and J.P. Morgan Chase.

The industry may have converged, but its principal activities – securities underwriting, securities trading and securities-related business activities – remain distinct.

Securities underwriting and investment banking (primary market activity)

The process of organising a stock or bond issue on behalf of a borrower is known as underwriting (although the underwriting itself is only one of several stages of the operation). Underwriting is also sometimes referred to as investment banking, because traditionally raising funds for clients in the capital market was the specialist activity of investment banks. Many corporations, and sometimes other bodies such as government agencies or municipalities, use securities industry firms as advisers on strategy. If implementation involves raising external finance, they seek professional advice from securities industry firms on the type of security to issue (stock or some form of debt – bonds, notes or bills), market conditions and the timing of the issue, and the issue price.

Registration of securities

Securities industry firms assist issuers with the filing of a registration statement for the securities with the Securities and Exchange Commission (SEC). All securities issues that are for sale to the public (except those for less than $1.5m or with a maturity of less than 270 days) have to be registered with the SEC through the filing of a registration statement. The statement has to provide comprehensive details about the issuer's financial condition, its business, assets and management and the use to which the funds will be put.

The SEC conducts a review of the registration statement to check that the required disclosures have been made, but it does not check the information supplied – the filing of inaccurate information renders an issuer liable to prosecution. Unless there is an objection from the SEC, the registration statement becomes effective after 20 days and the securities can be sold. While the SEC conducts its review, the securities industry firm makes arrangements for the securities certificates to be printed. For a stock issue it arranges a listing on a stock exchange, and for bonds it secures a credit rating from a credit-rating company, acquires a statement attesting the legality of the issue from a bond counsel and selects a trustee.

Pricing of issues

Then comes the underwriting itself – the purchase of the securities by the securities industry firm at an agreed price. The pricing of a "seasoned issue", when a corporation already has similar securities in the market, is straightforward since the existing securities provide a reference point. But the pricing of an initial public offering (IPO), when a company issues stock for the first time, is much more problematic and there may be a big divergence of view. The pricing of issues is inherently problematic since the issuer and the underwriter have different priorities. It is in the interest of the issuer for the securities to be sold at the highest price, or at least at a price that raises the amount of money the issuer is looking for. However, the higher the price, the more difficult it will be for the underwriter to market the securities to final investors and the greater is the risk that the underwriter will be left holding unsold, overpriced securities.

The sale of the securities to the underwriter guarantees that the issuer receives the agreed proceeds, transferring the issue risk from the issuer to the securities industry firm. It is then up to the underwriter to sell the securities to final investors at a price that is sufficiently attractive to ensure their sale and that yields a profit to the underwriter. To spread the risk, other securities industry firms may be invited to share the underwriting, a syndicate of firms buying the issue and selling it to investors through their brokerage arms. The members of the syndicate are rewarded for their services by an array of fees, commissions and spreads.

Ideally, the issue will be fully subscribed by final purchasers who have placed prior orders on the basis of a pre-circulated prospectus for the issue, a document which forms an integral part of the registration statement but need not include every detail of the filing. The worst outcome for an underwriter is for the issue to be undersubscribed, since to sell the securities it will be necessary to lower the price, resulting in a reduced profit or even a loss. But a substantially oversubscribed issue is bad news too, since it means that the issue was underpriced and there will be an aggrieved issuer who may resort to litigation.

Shelf registration

A change in SEC registration rules (Rule 415) in 1982 led to the traditional type of syndicated underwriting procedure outlined above being supplemented by the shelf registration form. Under this streamlined procedure corporations may register an intention to sell securities up to two years in advance. The securities remain "on the shelf" until market conditions are favourable, when they are quickly sold through a securities industry firm. Shelf registration allows issuers to invite competitive bids from potential underwriters, which led to downward pressure on the underwriters' "gross spread" (overall revenues). Securities industry firms responded by offering to do a "bought deal", purchasing the whole issue outright rather than sharing the risk – and potential profits – among a syndicate of underwriters. Bought deals are risky undertakings that only those with large reserves of capital can contemplate. They have been one factor behind the trend towards bigger firms and mergers between securities firms and commercial banks or insurance companies.

Another form of underwriting is a standby underwriting in which a syndicate undertakes to buy any balance of stocks or bonds unsubscribed in a corporate offering of subscription rights to stockholders. Sometimes an issue is sold on the basis that the firm selling it undertakes to use its best efforts to sell as much of the offering as possible at a price chosen by the issuer, in return for a commission on sales achieved. This leaves the risk that the issue will not live up to expectations with the issuer, but reduces the profit the securities industry firm could earn if it took on an underwriting risk.

Private placements

An alternative to a public offering of a securities issue is a private placement, in which the securities are sold to one or more large institutional investors by negotiation. This avoids the time-consuming and costly process of a public offering and allows deals to be done that in addition to being less troublesome save the buyer money without reducing the monies the seller would have received from a public offering. One of the economies of a private placement is that it is unnecessary to file a registration statement with the SEC (subject to a few conditions), since institutional investors are deemed to be capable of looking after themselves. A disadvantage for buyers is lack of liquidity in the securities, although this is mitigated to some extent by the buying and selling of privately placed securities amongst institutional investors.

Securities trading (secondary market activity)

Securities industry firms operate in the secondary market in two basic capacities: brokers and principals (dealers). As brokers they earn commissions on purchases or sales of securities for clients. The large diversified securities industry firms principally service wholesale institutional clients, notably insurance companies, mutual funds and pension funds. They also provide "agency" brokerage services to private and corporate clients, the bank acting as an intermediary to match buyers and sellers of securities without taking ownership of the securities being brokered.

For retail clients there are two levels of brokerage service: full service and discount. Full-service brokers provide customers with research analysis and investment advice, their commission rates recovering the cost of these benefits. Discount brokers simply execute customers' orders, but charge lower commissions than full-service brokers. The Internet is an increasingly popular means of accessing execution-only services; the number of online brokerage accounts grew from 7m to 19m between 1998 and 2001 and is still expanding.

Operating as principals rather than just as agents for customers, securities industry firms make money in two ways: by market making and by proprietary trading. Market makers, also known as dealers (and as specialists on the NYSE and the American Stock Exchange) are prepared to buy and sell specified securities at all times, thus making a market in them. Market makers make money from the difference (spread) between the buying and selling price. They fulfil a crucial role in providing liquidity to the secondary market, ensuring that securities can always be realised for cash.

Proprietary trading is when a bank trades for itself rather than for its customers and on its own initiative, assuming all the risk and taking all of the profit or loss. Such trading exploits the bank's skills in identifying opportunities that may yield above-average returns – and by the results of such trading will those skills be judged. The scale of proprietary trading grew substantially in the 1980s and 1990s in response to the squeeze on commissions and spreads. It was a response to market volatility and the need to generate revenue when client-driven business fell off. Dedicated proprietary trading desks conduct business in parallel with brokers buying and selling on behalf of clients on a commission basis. On the derivatives side, a separate proprietary trading desk may create and sell OTC derivatives not to specific clients but to the market.

Traditionally, some investment banks traded commodities as well as securities. Even in the 1980s Salomon Brothers, which had a particularly strong trading culture, diversified by buying Philipp Brothers, a leading commodities trading and processing corporation. However, in recent decades commodities trading has not been a significant source of revenue for NYSE member firms and has even been loss-making in some years.

Securities-related business activities

Investment banks and leading broker-dealer firms have long provided advice to companies. So-called "white shoe" (see page 34) investment banks, such as Morgan Stanley and Lehman Brothers, had longstanding relationships with many major US corporations, advising them on strategy and financial structure. Such advice on, for example, capital structure, public offerings, acquisitions or dividend policy, was provided free on the understanding that when the corporation made a securities issue the bank would be appointed to act as lead underwriter.

This relationship-based model of corporate finance activity began to break down in the 1970s. In those turbulent and difficult years, corporations became more open to talking to other securities industry firms, particularly those that proposed and could provide less conventional and more innovative financing solutions. Thus firms that were, for instance, pioneering the use of derivatives for client needs, were able to get a hearing. As they began to win corporate business, they hired more staff on the corporate advisory side. This gave them greater capability to compete in the booming market for mergers and acquisitions, leveraged buy-outs and advisory services in the 1980s and 1990s.

Securities firms have also benefited from the growing volume of funds requiring professional asset management, and they have become involved in project finance, real estate and venture capital operations. The outcome is that since the 1980s securities-related business has been the largest source of revenue for securities industry firms.

The volume and value of every securities industry activity has increased substantially in recent years. Between 1990 and 2001, annual total US corporate debt and equity issuance grew from $312 billion to $2,535 billion, average daily stock trading volume on the NYSE rose from

Table 5.1 **Sources of gross revenues of securities industry firms, 1972-2001[a] (%)**

	1972	1987	1997	2001
Principal activities				
Securities-related business[b]	6	30	45	48
Brokerage commissions	53	18	15	14
Proprietary trading and investments	15	25	16	13
Underwriting	13	10	9	8
Other revenue				
Mutual fund sales	2	3	4	3
Commodities revenue	2	3	–	2
Interest on customers' loans	9	6	7	7
Unrelated to securities business	–	5	5	5

a NYSE member firms.
b Fees for investment advice and counsel, service charges and custodian fees and miscellaneous other income.
Source: NYSE, *Factbook*

157m stocks to 1,240m, and the value of US mergers and acquisitions activity from $205 billion to $812 billion. The volume of securities industry business is affected by the ups and downs of the financial markets. For example, mergers and acquisitions reached a cyclical peak in 1999 with a value of $3.4 trillion but then fell sharply as corporate amalgamations slumped as the economy slowed. However, the experience of the last three decades is that downturns are brief, and then expansion resumes and activity reaches new highs.

Securities industry revenues

The evolution of the pattern of securities industry firms' revenue from the early 1970s to the early 2000s is shown in Table 5.1. In order of importance in 2001, the principal sources were as follows.

- Securities-related business. From the least important of the principal activities in the early 1970s to the biggest in 2001 – 48%.
- Brokerage commissions. From the bedrock of the business in the early 1970s to a significant contribution – 14%.
- Proprietary trading, market making and investment. A steady contribution – 13%.
- Underwriting. A gradual decline – 8%.

The big story of the last three decades has been the eightfold increase in securities-related revenue, meaning mergers and acquisitions, advisory work, derivatives, and asset management. Table 5.1 also shows that total trading revenue (joint revenue from brokerage commissions, and proprietary trading and market making) has fallen from over two-thirds of revenues in the early 1970s to around a quarter of total revenue. The principal reason was abolition of fixed brokerage commission rates on May 1st 1975, which led to sharp falls in institutional rates. However, although the proportion of revenue generated by commissions fell steeply, the absolute amount earned from commissions grew several times over these decades.

Underwriting generates less than one-tenth of the gross revenue of securities industry firms. But this underestimates its importance to them for three reasons. First, because equity underwriting and the underwriting of high-yield debt (though not investment grade debt or eurobonds) are among the industry's most profitable activities. Second, because it is often just one dimension of a relationship with a client that may generate fees for other services, such as mergers and acquisitions. Third, it has a high visibility.

Industry structure

The US securities industry consists of six categories of services providers.

- International financial conglomerates. Huge firms active in virtually every type of wholesale financial activity (commercial banking, securities activities, securities-related business and often insurance) and some retail activities too. America's leading financial conglomerates are Citigroup and J.P. Morgan Chase, whose European counterparts are Deutsche Bank, UBS, Credit Suisse First Boston, HSBC, ABN Amro and Dresdner Bank.
- International wholesale securities industry firms. The so-called "bulge-bracket" firms, Goldman Sachs, Merrill Lynch and Morgan Stanley, and some others, notably Bear Stearns, Lehman Brothers and Lazard Freres.
- Domestic investment banking boutiques. Specialists in US mergers and acquisitions activity and debt and equity issuance.
- Domestic wholesale broker-dealers. Specialist securities-services providers to institutional investors and securities industry firms.

Table 5.2 **US mergers and acquisitions, 2001**

Adviser	Value of deals ($bn)	Market share (%)	Number of deals
Goldman Sachs	407	50	167
Merrill Lynch	286	35	112
Morgan Stanley	284	35	136
Credit Suisse First Boston	272	33	201
J.P. Morgan	234	28	148
Citigroup/Salomon Smith Barney	144	17	113
Deutsche Bank	117	14	65
Lehman Brothers	90	11	90
UBS Warburg	75	9	63
Bear Sterns	75	9	60

Source: *Financial Times*, February 22nd 2002

Table 5.3 **US debt and equity issuance, 2001**

Adviser	Value of deals ($bn)	Market share (%)	Number of deals
Citigroup/Salomon Smith Barney	413	13	1,605
Merrill Lynch	371	12	2,857
Credit Suisse First Boston	283	9	1,606
J.P. Morgan	252	8	1,200
Goldman Sachs	252	8	883
Lehman Brothers	236	8	1,092
Morgan Stanley	200	6	1,532
UBS Warburg	188	6	759
Bank of America Securities	163	5	1,123
Deutsche Bank	140	4	620

Source: *Financial Times*, February 22nd 2002

- ◪ Retail broker-dealers. Around 5,000 firms throughout the country providing brokerage services to retail investors.
- ◪ Other providers. In recent years, accountancy firms, management consultants and commercial banks have undertaken activities that have traditionally been the preserve of securities industry firms.

The leading securities industry firms in US mergers and acquisitions are given in Table 5.2, and the leading firms in US debt and equity issuance are given in Table 5.3. Nine firms appear in both tables.

Consolidation

Since the 1960s, in common with many other sectors, the securities industry has been consolidating. Between 1973 and 2000, the proportion of industry capital accounted for by the top 25 broker-dealer firms rose from 48% to 77%. The growth in the market share of the leading firms was the outcome of two factors: corporate consolidation through mergers and acquisitions, and increases in firms' capital. The need for greater capital was driven by the following.

- Primary market developments: the increasing scale of capital raising by underwriting clients, and new capital-intensive primary market techniques, notably the bought deal.
- Secondary market expansion: the increased size of the market as a whole and of individual securities transactions.
- Expansion of proprietary business activities: when a firm commits its own capital to deals rather than acting as an agent or simply as an adviser.
- Growing competition: in some activities from new entrants, such as accountancy firms, management consultants and commercial banks.
- Technology: the increasing cost of investment in state-of-the-art information technology to remain competitive.
- Deregulation: the erosion of the Glass-Steagall separation between banking and securities underwriting led to the entry of commercial banks into activities hitherto confined to securities firms, and ultimately to the acquisition of securities firms by banks. The closing years of the 20th century saw some 300 acquisitions of broker-dealers by US banks, insurance companies and other acquirers.
- Globalisation: a two-way process involving both the global expansion of the major US securities industry firms, and a growing presence of foreign-owned firms in the US marketplace.

In some cases, the quest for capital led firms to bring in well-capitalised partners involved in banking, insurance or non-financial activities, notably Sears, General Electric and American Express. The outcome was the development of a so-called "barbell" industry structure: a set of huge, global, multifunction, mega-firms; a few mid-sized firms in the middle; and a large number of small broker-dealer and investment-banking boutique firms.

The end of Glass-Steagall

The Banking Act 1933 (Glass-Steagall) banned commercial banks from undertaking securities activities, forbade securities firms from taking deposits and restricted insurance companies to insurance-related products. The strict separation of securities, banking and insurance was reinforced by further legislative measures in 1956 and 1970.

The erosion of the demarcations began in the 1970s with the development of new products by the securities industry, which drained business and profits away from the banks and into the securities industry. On the one hand, banks' deposits were depleted by the expansion of money-market mutual funds, which were launched in 1972. On the other hand, their lending business was hit by the growth of commercial paper, junk bonds and the securitisation of mortgage, credit-card and auto loans.

In the early 1980s, the Federal Reserve and the Office of the Comptroller of the Currency began to relax their interpretation of the Glass-Steagall legislation regarding banks' conduct of securities and insurance activities. This was in response to the banks' plight and their pleas to be allowed to develop securities activities in order to redress the securities firms' encroachment into their domain. The turning point came in 1983, when, on the same day, the Fed gave consent for BankAmerica to purchase Charles Schwab, the largest US discount brokerage firm, and to establish a foothold in the insurance business.

The next milestone was in 1987, when the Fed authorised J.P. Morgan, Citicorp and Bankers Trust to engage in underwriting with a limit that it should not exceed 5% of their revenue. The limit was subsequently raised until it became meaningless.

The denouement came in 1998, with the announcement of the merger of Citicorp, a leading commercial bank, with Travelers Group, a major insurance company and owner of Salomon Smith Barney, a prominent securities industry firm. This was illegal under existing legislation, a problem remedied by the Financial Services Modernisation Act (Gramm-Leach-Bliley), which came into effect in November 1999. Henceforth banks, securities industry firms and insurance companies were free to amalgamate under a financial holding company and to undertake whatever financial services they wished.

Table 5.4 **Worldwide mergers and acquisitions, 2001**

Adviser	Value of deals ($bn)	Market share (%)	Number of deals
Goldman Sachs	594	34	343
Merrill Lynch	475	27	258
Morgan Stanley	445	26	308
Credit Suisse First Boston	387	22	451
J.P. Morgan	383	22	399
Citigroup/Salomon Smith Barney	262	15	338
Deutsche Bank	221	12	257
UBS Warburg	211	12	233
Lehman Brothers	125	7	151
Dresdner Kleinwort Wasserstein	120	7	86

Source: *Financial Times*

Globalisation and profitability

The major US money-centre banks and Wall Street investment banks began to establish a significant presence in the world's principal financial centres from the late 1960s. One motive was to service multinational clients, which were rapidly expanding overseas. Another was to participate in the burgeoning euromarkets. London, the foremost euromarket centre, was the principal focus of their overseas expansion in the 1970s and 1980s. In the mid-1990s, there was a renewed overseas push by US securities industry firms. One reason was to develop global securities trading capabilities, which had become possible through improved communications technology and for which there was demand because of the internationalisation of institutional investment portfolios.

Another reason was to exploit their expertise in securities-related business services, especially mergers and acquisitions, internationally. In the 1990s, US securities industry firms rapidly established a leading presence in global mergers and acquisitions activity, supplanting all but a few European universal banks at the top of the league tables (see Table 5.4). They focused especially on Europe, as the formation of the European single market offered massive potential for cross-border merger and acquisition work.

While US securities industry firms were making a powerful push into Europe, some European banks were establishing a substantial presence on Wall Street through the acquisition of medium-sized US securities industry firms. In 1999, Deutsche Bank bought Bankers Trust Alex. Brown for $9.1 billion and HSBC paid $7.1 billion for Republic National Bank of New York. The following year, Credit Suisse, which already had a big US presence through its ownership of First Boston, purchased Donaldson, Lufkin & Jenrette for $17.7 billion and UBS paid $16.5 billion for PaineWebber. But these were just the headline-making deals in a process that involved the acquisition of more than 100 US broker-dealer firms by foreign banks between 1997 and 2000.

The influx of foreign banks as well as domestic banks and insurance companies into the US securities industry led to the commitment of additional capital to an already crowded and highly competitive marketplace. The effect was to put even more pressure on the industry's margins, which had been declining for 20 years as a result of fierce competition, poor cost control and high capital requirements.

Many of the industry's traditional core products had become "commoditised", generating low returns. A study of industry margins in 2002 revealed that a few high-margin businesses, notably mergers and acquisitions, IPOs, derivatives activities, and the underwriting of high-yield and equity issues were supporting the rest of the product portfolio. Naturally, it was the high-margin businesses that individual firms were targeting for expansion, raising the prospect of further erosion of margins in future. Estimates of the industry's medium-term return on equity were 20% for the leading half-dozen "super bulge-bracket" firms and 15% for other firms, producing a projected securities industry average of 17–18%.

6 Banking

Banks are financial intermediaries whose business is to take funds from depositors and make loans to borrowers. The difference between the interest paid to depositors and the interest charged to borrowers, the spread, constitutes the bank's gross revenue. Like other financial-services sectors, the banking industry is broadly divided into banks that focus on big corporate customers (wholesale) and those that service local businesses and retail depositors. A common traditional pattern of the business of banking has been to take deposits from retail savers and make loans to businesses.

Money-centre banking
Money-centre banks, especially the New York city banks, focus on corporate lending. A generation ago there was a broad choice of corporate specialist banks in New York, but the number has fallen sharply in recent years through amalgamations and acquisitions. There are now three main indigenous New York city corporate banks: Citigroup, J.P. Morgan Chase and the Bank of New York. Since 1999 Bankers Trust, the other leading New York corporate bank, has been owned by Deutsche Bank.

Citigroup is a huge financial conglomerate in which banking is one of a spectrum of financial services, including insurance and securities industry activities. It was created in 1998 through the $73 billion megamerger between Citicorp and Travelers, an insurance company and owner of Salomon Smith Barney, a leading securities industry firm. The largest bank in the world, Citigroup has total assets of $1,051 billion.

J.P. Morgan Chase is the outcome of a $36 billion pooling-of-interest merger in 2000 between Chase Manhattan Bank and J.P. Morgan, both leading corporate banks. Chase Manhattan Bank had already in 1996 merged with Chemical Bank, another big New York corporate bank, which itself had absorbed Manufacturers Hanover in 1991. J.P. Morgan Chase is now the second largest bank in the United States and third largest in the world, with total assets of $693 billion.

The Bank of New York is New York's oldest bank, formed in 1784. Its history reads like the story of Wall Street: its stock was the first security traded on the newly formed New York Stock Exchange (NYSE) in 1792; it helped finance the construction of the Erie Canal in the 1820s; and it was a founder member of the New York Clearing House in 1853. The creation of a bank holding company in 1969 allowed expansion beyond New York City, and it now has 350 branches in the Metropolitan area and elsewhere. In 1966, the Bank of New York opened an office in London, the beginning of a global network. It is now one of the largest US financial holding companies, with total assets of $77 billion.

An international outlook has long been a distinguishing feature of the New York money-centre banks. In the 1960s, they were pioneers in the establishment of US banking operations in the burgeoning euromarket in London. Citibank, a component part of Citigroup, began to establish a foreign branch network more than a century ago and today has the most extensive worldwide presence of any bank, with operations in more than 100 countries. Chase too has large and long-standing overseas operations.

The development of the foreign operations of US banks has been aided by two bespoke measures.

- The Edge Act 1919. Passed by Congress at the prompting of the Federal Reserve to enable US banks to compete more effectively for international trade finance business against the British banks that dominated this activity. The Act sanctioned the formation of specialist subsidiaries, called Edge Act corporations, to conduct international banking operations that are exempt from certain US banking regulations. For example, they are able to branch across state lines, having branches in different states to conduct business with different regions of the world.
- International banking facilities (IBFs). Established in 1981 as a belated attempt to capture for New York and other US financial centres some of the international banking business that since the 1960s had been conducted offshore in the euromarkets, particularly out of London, Luxembourg, Switzerland and the Caribbean. IBFs are segregated bookkeeping arrangements that allow American onshore banks to accept offshore deposits from foreigners, without being subject to the usual reserve requirements or interest payment restrictions. IBFs have been moderately successful in achieving the objectives for which they were created.

As a leading international money centre, Wall Street is host to a large number of foreign banks. At the beginning of 2001, foreign banks operated or controlled 348 branches and 111 agencies in the United States, the majority situated in New York. Most of them operate at a wholesale level, their assets mainly comprising commercial and industrial loans. Foreign banks also own 79 American commercial banks. Foreign-owned banking institutions play an important role in the American financial system, holding around 20% of total commercial-bank assets.

Retail banking

With around 10,000 banks, the United States has many more than any other country. This abundance of banks, many of which are small local undertakings, is a historical legacy of restrictions on the establishment of branches across state lines (and also within the same state), which has inhibited consolidation. Another factor contributing to fragmentation has been the dual banking system: about 3,000 banks are chartered under federal banking legistlation while the rest are chartered under the banking legislation of individual states.

The formation of bank holding companies enabled banks to side-step some of the restrictions on them and to expand geographically and to a limited extent into new lines of activity. Since the 1960s, such holding companies have been set up by all the large US banks and now account for more than 90% of total deposits. Following the recent deregulation of the financial-services industry, they are now known as financial holding companies.

Despite continuing fragmentation, there has been considerable consolidation in the US banking system since the mid-1980s, when there were 14,000 individual banks. This was the outcome of state-by-state relaxation of laws governing interstate banking in the early 1980s, which led to a spate of regional bank amalgamations. Then in 1994, the Riegle-Neal Interstate Banking and Branching Efficiency Act swept away many remaining impediments to bank consolidation. The act permitted bank holding companies to acquire banks in any other state, overriding any state law restrictions, and allowed the creation of interstate branch banks. The outcome was an upsurge of merger and acquisition activity and the emergence of so-called super-regional banks – bank holding companies that operate not from the major money centres but from regional headquarters.

A list of ten leading US banks, ranked by assets (see Table 6.1), includes three New York money-centre banks, Citigroup and J.P. Morgan Chase (first and second), and Metlife, an insurance company-cum-bank. There are three banks located in other major money centres: Banc One Corp, based in Chicago; Wells Fargo, based in San Francisco;

Table 6.1 **Top ten US banks, 2001**

	Assets ($bn)
Citigroup	1,051
J.P. Morgan Chase	693
Bank of America Corp	621
Wachovia Corporation	330
Wells Fargo	307
Bank One Corp	268
Metlife	256
Washington Mutual	242
FleetBoston Financial Corp	203
US Bancorp	171

Source: *The Banker*, July 2002

and FleetBoston Financial Corp, based in Boston. And there are four super-regionals: Bank of America, based in Charlotte, NC; Wachovia Corporation, based in Winston-Salem, NC; Washington Mutual, based in Seattle, WA; and US Bancorp, based in Minneapolis, MN.

The complicated pattern of types of American commercial banks is more than mirrored in the industry's regulatory arrangements. There is a multiplicity of agencies with overlapping jurisdictions: the 3,000 national banks are regulated by the Office of the Comptroller of the Currency; the 1,000 state banks that are members of the Federal Reserve System are jointly regulated by the Fed and state banking authorities; bank holding companies are regulated by the Fed; the 6,000 state banks that are not members of the Federal Reserve System are jointly supervised by the Federal Deposit Insurance Corporation (FDIC) and state banking authorities; and the 500 or so state banks that do not have FDIC insurance fall under state banking authorities. From time to time attempts are made to rationalise and streamline the bank regulatory system through the creation of a single regulatory agency, but so far all have foundered in Congress.

Relationship with other financial-services sectors

The Glass-Steagall Act required the banking, securities and insurance sectors to operate separately. But in the 1970s and 1980s, a conjunction of new developments worked to the benefit of the securities industry firms and the disadvantage of the banking sector by simultaneously depleting banks' deposits and undermining their lending business. The depletion of deposits was the result of competition for funds from money-market mutual funds.

Money-market mutual funds
Launched in the early 1970s, money-market mutual funds (MMMF) provide investors with facilities that resemble an interest-bearing cheque account. Cheques can be written against balances and interest is paid from the proceeds earned by investments in short-term money-market securities.

As interest rates soared in the late 1970s and early 1980s, the rate of interest paid by MMMFs rose above the 5.25% ceiling permitted by the Federal Reserve's Regulation Q on savings accounts and time deposits. This made MMMFs very popular with the public. The value of MMMF assets rose from almost nothing in 1975 to $40 billion in 1979 and more than $500 billion in 1990. The growth of the MMMFs deprived the banks of a massive volume of deposits. Moreover, it disrupted their traditional business model, which was based on an abundant supply of cheap retail deposits to provide the funding for loans to businesses.

This business model was also under pressure from the demand side as corporations turned to cheaper non-bank forms of financing.

Commercial paper
The issuance of commercial paper – short-term debt securities issued by corporations and banks – is a money-market alternative to short-term bank borrowing, providing funds at cheaper rates than those available from banks. The issue of commercial paper by corporations, organised on their behalf by securities industry firms, rose rapidly in the 1970s and 1980s. The volume outstanding grew from $33 billion in 1970 to $124 billion in 1980 and $530 billion in 1990.

High-yield bonds
Traditionally, only corporations with an investment-grade credit rating could borrow in the long-term corporate-bond market, since there was no primary market for lower-rated bonds. Such lower-rated bonds as were traded had all been issued as investment-grade securities, but then the issuing corporation had hit hard times and the debt had been downgraded. The market slang for such bonds was "fallen angels".

Academic studies demonstrated that the default risk on a diversified portfolio of junk bonds was only slightly greater than on an investment-grade portfolio, but the yield was much higher. Michael Milken of Drexel Burnham Lambert, an investment bank, came to the conclusion that there was a market for new issues of junk bonds, both on the part of borrowers of below investment-grade status, often young and dynamic corporations, and investors who wanted higher-yield securities. The junk-bond market developed by Milken from 1977 quickly became a large and important dimension of the corporate-bond market, with $200 billion of bonds outstanding by the end of the 1980s. Like commercial paper, junk bonds provided a substitute for funding that would hitherto have been provided by bank borrowings.

Securitisation

The growth of securitisation – the bundling of financial assets such as mortgages, car loans or credit-card loans into securities that are sold to investors – developed rapidly from its introduction by Fannie Mae in 1970. This development had advantages for the banks in that it allowed them to free-up their balance sheets and focus on generating new business, thus increasing their fee income. But the standardisation of risk also allowed other parties to enter the loans business and eroded the banks' competitive advantage.

Financial services supermarkets

The outcome was a crisis in the banking industry in the second half of the 1980s and the early 1990s, when hundreds of banks failed and the survivors endured hard times. Under pressure from the banks to allow them to develop new lines of business, the Federal Reserve and the Office of the Comptroller of the Currency began to relax their interpretation of the Glass-Steagall legislation, allowing the banks bit-by-bit to undertake securities and insurance activities. The first big concession was in 1983, when they were permitted to buy discount securities brokers to enhance their services to customers. In 1987, securities underwriting was permitted, at first on a limited basis, but gradually the restrictions were relaxed.

Lastly, the proposed merger between Citicorp and Travelers Group led to the passage of the Financial Services Modernisation Act (Gramm-Leach-Bliley) by Congress and its ratification in November 1999. The legislation stated that its purpose was "to enhance competition in the financial services industry by providing a prudential framework for the affiliation of banks, securities firms and other financial service providers, and for other purposes". Permitting banks, securities industry firms and insurance companies to combine in whatever way they desired under a financial holding company, or to develop whichever financial-services activities they saw fit, opened the door to the consolidation and reconfiguration of the fragmented American financial-services industry. The era of the financial services supermarket had arrived in the US.

7 Insurance companies and pension funds

Institutional investors are professional financial custodians that invest funds arising from flows of money coming from insurance payments, pension-plan contributions or the sale of shares to investors. They are remunerated for their services by fees, often based on the size of the funds managed. The principal institutional investors are insurance companies, pension funds and mutual funds (see Table 7.1). They are the largest investors in the US securities markets, owning a growing proportion of stocks: 28% in 1970 and 47% in 2002.

Insurance companies

Insurance companies are the original institutional investors, having been active as investors since the 18th century. The business of insurance companies is to assume risks on behalf of their clients, both individuals and businesses. This is undertaken in exchange for a fee, known as a premium. Insurance companies invest the revenue from premiums in the financial markets so that they will be able to make payments when they receive claims. They make profits by charging more in premiums than they pay out in claims. Or so they hope – insurance differs from other products in that insurers must price and sell their policies before the full cost of what they have contracted to pay out is known.

Insurance is classified by the type of risk that is insured. The industry divides itself into two parts (both of which have many component products) life/health and property/casualty. In the US the life/health sector receives three-fifths of total premiums and the property/casualty sector two-fifths.

Life/health insurance

The product range of life insurance companies comprises life insurance, disability insurance, health insurance and annuities. Life insurance provides payments to a deceased person's heirs, who usually have a financial dependence on the deceased person. Disability and health insurance aim to give purchasers regular payments if they become unable to work or need medical attention. An annuity is an insurance product that pays the purchaser a future income in exchange for an initial fixed sum, such as a cashed-in defined-contribution pension plan upon retirement, or a

Table 7.1 **Assets of institutional investors, March 31st 2002** ($bn)

Insurance companies	
Life insurance companies	3,317
Other insurance companies	879
Total	**4,196**
Pension funds	
Private pension funds	4,183
State and local government employee retirement funds	2,205
Total	**6,388**
Mutual funds	
Mutual funds (equity, bond and hybrid funds)	4,245
Other investment companies	133
Money-market mutual funds	2,202
Total	**6,580**

Source: Federal Reserve Board, *Flow of Funds Accounts of the United States*

stream of payments. Many insurance policies provide both life cover and retirement benefits. Life products generate around two-thirds of life/health sector premiums. The business risk in life insurance is that the anticipated returns from investments are insufficient to meet life and annuity contracts, particularly for products that pay fixed rates.

The liabilities of life insurance companies are long-term and highly predictable through the use of actuarial tables that capture decades of experience of life expectancies. Accordingly their distribution of assets, with 61% in fixed-income classes, is designed to meet their long-term obligations (see Table 7.2).

As a result of industry consolidation, there are around 1,500 US life/health insurance companies, compared with 2,200 at the start of the 1990s. The leading US life/health insurance companies, ranked by premium income, are listed in Table 7.3.

Property/casualty insurance

This type of insurance protects property, such as buildings, automobiles and ships, against losses or damage from a wide range of possible causes, such as accident, fire, theft or hurricane. Property insurance protects property owners and businesses against risks deriving from the

Table 7.2 **Assets of life insurance companies, March 31st 2002**

	($bn)	*%*
Cash and money-market instruments	259	8
US government securities	310	9
Bonds and mortgages	1,733	52
Stocks and mutual-fund shares	982	30
Others	33	1
Total	3,317	100

Source: Federal Reserve Board, *Flow of Funds Accounts of the United States*

Table 7.3 **Top ten US life/health insurance companies, 2000**

	Premium income ($bn)
Metropolitan Life	30.6
ING	24.0
AIG	23.5
Aegon USA	23.0
Hartford Life	18.6
Nationwide	18.2
CIGNA	17.5
Prudential	17.0
Principal Life	15.6
New York Life	14.4

Source: Insurance Information Institute

ownership of property. This may include loss of earnings. Casualty insurance protects the policyholder against liability for harm caused to others resulting from accidents or product failure. For the policyholder, insurance substitutes a modest certain loss – the premium – for a large potential loss. For the property/casualty insurance company, the business risk is that claims may be more frequent and more costly than expected and that investment income may be insufficient to meet the shortfall in premium income.

Property and casualty insurance differs from life insurance in four ways:

Table 7.4 **Top ten US property/casualty insurance companies, 2000**

	Premium income ($bn)
State Farm Group	33.3
Allstate Insurance	21.6
Zurich/Farmers Group	16.8
American International Group	12.2
Berkshire Hathaway	10.4
Travelers PC Group	9.9
Nationwide Group	9.5
Liberty Mutual	8.7
C.N.A. Insurance	8.1
The Hartford Group	6.9

Source: Insurance Information Institute

- policies are usually short-term, often for a year or less;
- property and casualty insurance covers policyholders against many eventualities, whereas life insurance provides cover against a single risk;
- the likelihood of claims is often more difficult to calculate;
- the cost is more unpredictable.

Property/casualty insurance companies match these business features by maintaining a higher proportion of liquid assets than life companies.

Property/casualty insurance companies may choose to limit their risk exposure by transferring part of their liability to another insurance company, for a part share of the premium payment. This is called reinsurance; some 10% of property/casualty business is reinsured.

There are around 2,400 US property/casualty insurance companies, providing plenty of competition in the marketplace, to which foreign companies increasingly contribute. The leading US property/casualty insurance companies, ranked by premium income, are listed in Table 7.4.

The development of insurance companies

There are two types of insurance companies: stock companies and mutual companies. A stock insurance company operates for profit and is owned by stockholders, who have limited liability. A mutual insurance company is owned and controlled by the policyholders, the objective being to provide insurance at the lowest possible cost. America's first insurance company, the Friendly Society of Charleston, South Carolina, formed in 1735, was a mutual company. The first stock insurance company was the Insurance Company of North America, established in 1792.

Insurance companies are regulated principally at the state level. State statutes promote and enforce policies to ensure solvency and protect policyholders, placing restrictions on insurance companies' asset allocations and capital ratios. Companies are required to make annual financial filings with the insurance agencies of the states in which they operate. States also license agents, brokers and salesmen in order to promote competence and probity. Insurance companies must adhere not only to the regulations of the state in which they are registered, but also to those of any state in which they conduct business. New York, which passed the first general insurance law in America in 1849, requires any insurance company undertaking business in the state to comply with its investment standards. Virtually all do, since otherwise they would be unable to do business on Wall Street.

Insurance industry

The US insurance industry is much the largest in the world. In 2000, US life/health premiums were $442 billion, a 29% share of the world market, and property/casualty premiums were $423 billion, a 46% share. The combined total of $865 billion represented a 35% share of aggregate world premiums. However, per head of population, the US average of $3,152 places it fourth in the world, after Switzerland, Japan and the UK.

The US insurance industry has a nationwide workforce of 2.3m, 500,000 more than the banking industry, making it the largest financial-services employer in the country. The largest number, 960,000, work for life/health companies, 630,000 work for property/casualty companies and a further 760,000 work as agents, brokers and in other service personnel capacities.

In 1960, the insurance industry's total assets were $142 billion; by 2002, they had grown thirtyfold to $4,197 billion (see Figure 7.1). This substantial increase made insurance companies even more important as institutional investors. But in rate of growth and overall size of assets, pension funds and mutual funds have now overtaken the insurance industry.

The 1990s were fairly prosperous years for the insurance industry, with the life/health companies achieving an average return on equity of

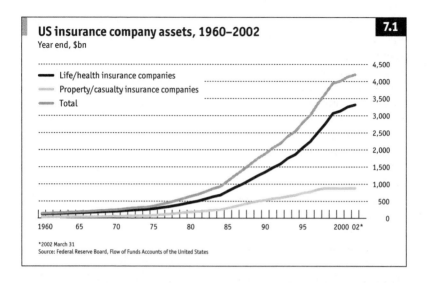

US insurance company assets, 1960–2002 `7.1`
Year end, $bn

- Life/health insurance companies
- Property/casualty insurance companies
- Total

*2002 March 31
Source: Federal Reserve Board, Flow of Funds Accounts of the United States

around 12% in the second half of the decade and the property/casualty companies almost 9%. However, these rates were considerably below the average of the *Fortune* 500 largest companies in those years. Then in 2001 the industry experienced "a perfect storm", as the chief economist of the Insurance Information Institute put it, reporting a negative return of -2.9% for the property/casualty sector. This was the outcome of a combination of "recession, underpricing, catastrophe losses, medical cost inflation, abuse of the legal system, Enron and, of course, the September 11 attack". Moreover, the crisis in corporate governance and the slump in stock prices from their spring 2000 peaks promised that, as large holders of equities, the insurance companies would continue to have problems.

Challenge from banks

The passage of the Financial Services Modernisation Act (Gramm-Leach-Bliley Act) in 1999 marked the end of the regulatory barriers enforcing the separation of not only the securities and banking industries, but also the insurance industry. Insurance had in fact been separated from banking since a federal act of 1916, which banned banks from selling insurance (except in small towns) and was reinforced by the Glass-Steagall Act 1933.

The problems encountered by the banks in the 1970s and 1980s through erosion of their retail deposits by competition from money-market mutual funds, which hit their retail business, and from growth in commercial paper, which hit their corporate lending business, led them to look around for other opportunities in financial services. The sale of insurance was an obvious source of expansion and from the late 1980s banks began to lobby for repeal of the regulatory impediments. Insurance companies opposed liberalisation, concerned about competition from an industry that they could not readily enter themselves. Federal legislation to amend Glass-Steagall stalled in Congress, becoming bogged down in the formidable complexities of a range of issues: How would the anticipated financial conglomerates be regulated? How would assets and deposits be protected against raids by other arms of a conglomerate? How would the financial privacy of consumers be protected? And how could they be safeguarded from the coercive bundling of insurance with lending?

The announcement in 1998 of the merger between Travelers Insurance (owner of Salomon Smith Barney, an investment bank and securities house) and Citicorp, a commercial bank, with the consent of the Federal Reserve, drove a coach and horses through Glass-Steagall. It turned reform from the abstract to the practical. Since banks were forbidden to underwrite insurance or securities, the combine would have to be unwound if the repeal of Glass-Steagall was not enacted within two years. Just in time, on November 12th 1999, President Clinton signed the legislation.

After the dramatic build-up to the Gramm-Leach-Bliley Act, the immediate impact on the insurance industry was less than expected. Initially at least, other companies did not rush down the trail blazed by the Travelers–Citigroup financial supermarket. Several reasons have been suggested, including the unanswered regulatory uncertainties; the low return on equity in the insurance industry that made insurance companies unattractive acquisition targets for banks; the timing, being soon followed by the downturn in the stockmarket and the collapse of mergers and acquisitions activity; the onset of recession and the sense of economic and financial uncertainty that was heightened by the September 11th terrorist attacks.

Instead of pursuing diversification through high-profile mergers and acquisitions, insurance companies focused on organic growth. First and foremost this meant the development of their own business. But there were also link-ups with banks, in the form of partnerships marketing each other's products. Moreover, many insurance companies took advantage of their new freedom to form their own bank subsidiaries, although it is too early to judge whether they will enjoy success.

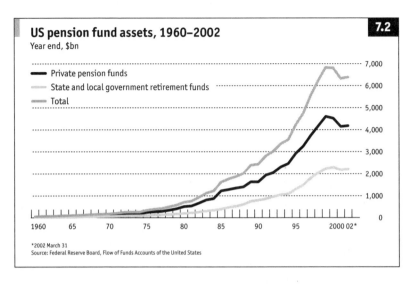

US pension fund assets, 1960–2002
Year end, $bn

7.2

- Private pension funds
- State and local government retirement funds
- Total

*2002 March 31
Source: Federal Reserve Board, Flow of Funds Accounts of the United States

Pension funds

In recent years, pension funds have been the most rapidly growing type of financial intermediary and are jointly the biggest owner of long-term securities. In 1960, the combined assets of US private pension funds and state and local government retirement funds totalled $61 billion; by 2002, it had increased more than one-hundredfold to $6.3 trillion (see Figure 7.2).

A pension fund is an accumulation of assets from which retirement benefits are paid. Pension funds are composed of many individual pension plans, which are pools of assets that are built up during working years and that entitle holders to pension payments in non-working years. A pension-plan sponsor is a body that sets up a pension plan; it may be a corporation, state or local government, union or other entity acting for its employees. Such pension plans are financed by contributions by an employer, mostly matched in some measure by employees. Contributions to qualifying pension plans are normally tax exempt until withdrawal. Usually, pension-plan investments cannot be used until retirement.

There are two types of pension plans:

- ◪ Defined-benefit pension plans, where the sponsor promises a specific benefit to employees when they retire, according to a formula based on final salary and years of service. This puts the onus on the sponsor to ensure that there are sufficient funds to make the promised payments. Plans with sufficient funds are known as fully funded. If there is a deficit a plan is underfunded, and if there is a surplus it is overfunded. The fund is managed by a fund manager appointed by the sponsor.

◪ Defined-contribution pension plans, where the sponsor is responsible only for making specified payments into the plan on behalf of employees, usually a set percentage of salary, which is matched by the employee. The plan does not guarantee any specific amount at retirement and the retirement benefits are entirely dependent upon the earnings of the fund. An insurance company or fund manager acts as trustee and invests the fund's income. Employees are generally permitted to direct how the funds in their individual plans should be invested. Upon retirement, the amount in the plan is transferred into an annuity, making the value of the pension dependent upon the performance of the fund at the point of retirement.

A distinction is made between private and public pension plans. A private pension plan has a private-sector sponsor. A public pension plan is one that is sponsored by a government entity. In the United States, state and local government pension plans cover 17m employees, the Federal Civilian Employees plan covers 6m federal workers and the Railroad Retirement Plan covers a further 1.1m persons.

The largest public pension plan is the Federal Old Age and Disability Insurance Program, colloquially known as Social Security. This was a New Deal measure, established in 1935, to provide a safety net for ageing workers. The programme operates on a pay-as-you-go basis, with payments to beneficiaries being paid out of current contributions. Workers contribute 7.5% of earnings, which is matched by employers, up to a ceiling wage. Although the programme currently has adequate resources, there are concerns that the forthcoming retirement of the populous baby-boom generation (born in 1946–60) will necessitate increased contributions or decreased benefits – probably both.

The distribution of assets in private pension funds and state and local government retirement funds in 2002 is shown in Tables 7.5 and 7.6. In both cases, stocks make up more than half the portfolio. Perhaps unsurprisingly, US government securities feature particularly prominently in the portfolios of the public servants' funds.

Table 7.5 **Assets of private pension funds, March 31st 2002**

	$bn	%
Cash and money-market instruments	288	7
US government securities	341	8
Bonds and mortgages	351	8
Stocks and mutual-fund shares	2,578	62
Others	625	15
Total	4,183	100

Source: Federal Reserve Board, *Flow of Funds Accounts of the United States*

Table 7.6 **Assets of state and local government employee retirement funds, December 31st 2001**

	$bn	%
Cash and money-market instruments	101	5
US government securities	393	18
Bonds and mortgages	374	17
Stocks	1,234	56
Others	103	4
Total	2,205	100

Source: Federal Reserve Board, *Flow of Funds Accounts of the United States*

The development of US pension plans

The first private pension plan in the US was established in 1875 by the American Express Company. Gradually, other major corporations followed its example, including Standard Oil of New Jersey in 1903, US Steel in 1911, General Electric in 1912, AT&T in 1913, Goodyear Tire and Rubber in 1915, American Can in 1924 and Eastman Kodak in 1929. By then, there were 397 functioning private-sector pension plans in the United States and Canada. A number of measures in the 1920s and 1930s enhanced the favourable tax status of pension plans. By 1940, 4m workers, 15% of the private-sector workforce, were covered.

A dynamic expansion of private pensions began in 1948, when the National Labour Relations Board, which was responsible for negotiations between corporations and unions, ruled that pensions were part of wages and had to be included in contract negotiations with employers if unions wished. Thereafter, union demands for pension benefits led to a proliferation of pension plans and a rapid growth in pension funds. By 1950, 9.8m private-sector workers, 25% of the workforce, were covered; by 1960, the number had risen to 18.7m workers, 41% of the workforce.

Under the terms of the Self-Employed Individual Retirement Act of 1962, called the Keogh Act, qualifying pension plans were made available to self-employed individuals, professionals in partnerships, farmers, and small businesses and their employees. This led to a further extension of coverage to 45% of the private-sector workforce by 1970.

A rash of failures of private pension funds, arising from corporate failures during the recessions of the early 1970s as well as a variety of unsatisfactory practices, led to the passage of the Employee Retirement Income Security Act (ERISA) in 1974. The purpose of ERISA, the most important and comprehensive legislation affecting pension funds, was to secure the benefits of participants in private pension plans through a set of standards regarding disclosure, reporting, eligibility and funding guidelines. It provided additional pension incentives for self-employed people and those not covered by pensions through the creation of individual retirement accounts (IRAS). It also established the legal status of employee stock ownership plans (ESOPS). Regulatory responsibility for pensions was assigned to the Department of Labour. Another provision was the establishment of the Pension Benefit Guarantee Corporation (PBGC), a government agency with a similar function to the Federal Deposit Insurance Corporation (FDIC): it insures defined-benefits plans (but not defined-contribution plans), up to a limit, should a company be unable to meet its obligations.

The ERISA legislation led to a substantial increase in the flow of money into pension funds, boosting their importance as institutional investors. But the increased regulation, combined with government measures to reduce pension funds' tax advantages, undermined the commitment of many corporations to costly defined-benefit plans. More and more employers went over to defined-contribution plans in the 1980s and 1990s, particularly 401(k) plans, a form of tax-sheltered retirement plan launched in 1981, shifting the risk and the plan-management responsibility to employees. By the beginning of the 21st century more than 50m private-sector or state and local-government employees were covered by a pension plan, the majority by a defined-contribution plan.

Asset management

The growth of pension funds boosted the expansion and development of institutional asset-management services. These services were supplied by insurance companies, banks, broker-dealers and, to its great advantage, the burgeoning mutual-fund industry. But the demand also gave rise to new institutions: specialist asset-management firms that were established expressly to service pension funds. These firms pioneered new investment strategies, sometimes specialising in particular asset classes, and generated a massive proliferation of investment approaches, setting the pace for insurance companies and mutual funds.

It is estimated that around 10,000 investment managers at money-management firms and mutual funds, supported by a similar number of securities analysts, determine the asset-allocation decisions of institutional investors. In the case of defined-contribution plans, some 35m beneficiaries have a say in their investment strategy through their decisions about how much to put into the various mutual-fund options offered by their employers. While stock prices were surging upwards in the 1990s, almost every strategy was a winner. But in a bear market, those who retire or lose their jobs during the downturn will have to cash in their pension entitlements at depreciated prices and face a less prosperous retirement than they had expected. Such disillusioned savers will almost certainly be looking for someone to blame – either on Wall Street or in Washington.

8 Mutual funds

Mutual funds are the largest of the institutional investors, with total assets of $6.9 trillion in 2001. They are a widely held form of saving, with 93.3m individual shareholders. Some 54.8m American households, more than half the total (105.5m households), are mutual fund shareholders. Individual investors own 76% of mutual fund assets, the other 24% being owned by institutional mutual fund investors. In 2001, there were 8,307 different mutual funds available to investors.

A mutual fund is an investment company that raises money by selling shares to investors, both individuals and institutional investors, and invests the proceeds in stocks, bonds and money-market instruments. By pooling resources through a mutual fund, investors gain the advantages of professional investment management, diversification of the portfolio to reduce risk, volume discounts on large brokerage commissions and liquidity.

Mutual funds are "open-end" investment companies, meaning that they are obliged to buy back shares whenever investors wish to sell, that the redemption price is based on the current value of the fund's net assets, and that new shares in the fund are continuously on offer to the public.

Three other types of investment companies are also regulated under the Investment Company Act of 1940:

- ▰ Closed-end fund. This issues a set number of shares (mutual funds, by contrast, can issue as many shares as demanded by investors) which are traded either on an exchange or over-the-counter. The assets are professionally managed and invested in securities in accordance with the fund's objectives.
- ▰ Unit investment trust (UIT). This buys and holds a fixed portfolio of securities. Units are bought by investors, who receive a proportionate share of the revenue generated by the investments in the portfolio. At a set termination date (other types of investment companies do not have set termination dates) investors receive a share of the UIT's net assets proportionate to their holding.
- ▰ Exchange-traded fund (ETF). This provides investment results that

Mutual fund structure

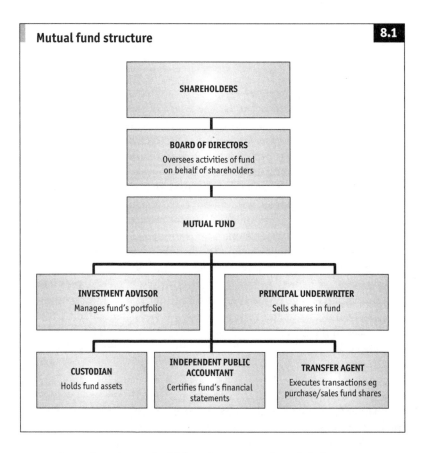

mirror the price and yield performance of stock indexes. ETF shares are bought and sold through a broker like regular stocks at the market-determined prices of their related indexes.

Mutual funds are established by large broker-dealers, investment banks, banks and independent asset-management companies. They are usually managed by the firm that set them up, but sometimes by independent contractors. The organisational structure of a mutual fund is depicted in Figure 8.1.

■ Shareholders have voting rights and receive regular reports on performance. The prospectus filed with the Securities and Exchange Commission (SEC) defines a fund's objectives, investment strategy, fees and expenses, and other important matters. Shareholder approval is required for any material change in the fund's policies or relationship with its investment adviser.

- Directors are appointed by the shareholders and oversee the management of their funds. The board of directors is required to ensure that the mutual fund is managed professionally and with reasonable prudence. Fulfilment of a director's fiduciary duty includes being properly informed about items that come before the board requiring the exercise of "business judgment". The SEC requires a mutual fund to have a majority of "independent" directors, individuals who do not have a significant relationship with the fund's investment adviser or principal underwriter and are able to scrutinise its operations independently.

- Investment adviser. Usually the firm that established the fund. It invests the fund's resources in accordance with the fund's objectives defined in the prospectus. Advisers receive fees based on a percentage of the fund's average net assets. The relationship between a fund and its investment adviser is regulated by many rules and legal restrictions. The contract between a fund and an investment adviser specifies the services performed by the adviser.

Some mutual funds are "actively managed", which means that adjustments are made to the contents of the portfolio to meet changing market circumstances based on the research and professional judgment of the investment adviser. Other funds are "passively managed", meaning that they are set up to track a market index, being composed of a set of securities that mirrors the index.

Typically, investment advisers also provide a variety of administrative services, such as office administration, accounting and the preparation of reports for shareholders.

- Principal underwriter. A broker-dealer that sells fund shares to the public, either directly or through other firms, on behalf of the mutual fund. Such underwriters are subject to National Association of Securities Dealers' rules governing mutual funds sales.

- Custodian. It is a legal requirement that mutual fund securities must be placed with a custodian for safekeeping. Custodians are usually major banks.

■ Transfer agent. Maintains records of shareholder accounts and provides a range of customer services, including sending out statements and notices to shareholders.

The development and regulation of mutual funds

The mutual-fund industry traces its origins to three pioneering funds established in Boston in 1924–25. It has been suggested that interest was aroused by an article about British investment trusts that appeared in the *Federal Reserve Bulletin* in 1921. The British-style investment trusts were closed-end funds, but the Boston funds were open-end funds providing the additional attraction for investors of redemption on demand. Incorporated Investors, which soon became the largest and best-known mutual fund, provided the prototype for the new industry: a free-standing fund whose trustees hired the services of a separate investment advisory firm that was owned by some of the trustees.

The launch of the Boston funds was well timed to catch the upswing of the Wall Street bull market of the second half of the 1920s. The mutual-fund concept spread quickly, with $1 billion shares being sold in 1924–28. In the first nine months of 1929 a further $2.1 billion shares were sold. It was estimated that in these months, the peak of the speculative frenzy, a new investment company of some sort was established every day.

Soaring stock prices and the virtual absence of regulation provided ample opportunities for unscrupulous practices or reckless optimism on the part of investment advisers. When the crash came in October 1929, even the best-run investment companies did poorly, and the fraudulent or just badly run ones fared disastrously. The post-crash Pecora hearings revealed that even leading Wall Street firms, such as Goldman Sachs, Dillon Read and National City Bank, had treated the investment trusts they managed as dumping grounds for unmarketable securities and otherwise abused investors. The revelations discredited closed-end investment trusts, but the Boston mutual funds emerged with relatively uncompromised reputations and henceforth were the dominant form of US investment company.

Investment Company Act 1940

Over the years 1935–1940, as required by the Public Utility Holding Company Act 1935, the SEC undertook an exhaustive investigation of US investment companies. Every company received a lengthy question-naire and a follow-up visit from SEC officials, and some managers were required to testify at public hearings. The outcome was the Investment Company Act 1940, the first federal regulation of investment companies. The act set the structure and regulatory framework for the development of the mutual-fund industry. Its provisions were both remedial, attacking abuses uncovered by the SEC inquiry, and positive, prescribing new standards and procedures. It conferred almost complete control of investment companies upon the SEC as the regulatory authority, and required the companies to keep proper accounts, file regular returns and comply with capital adequacy requirements. The act remains the basic framework for the regulation of the industry. It has kept abreast of developments because of the broad discretionary powers that it grants to the SEC to modify regulations in response to developments in the financial-services industry.

Mutual funds must also comply with the Securities Act of 1933, which requires registration with the SEC of all securities offerings, including mutual-fund shares. Mutual funds' principal underwriters, the broker-dealers that sell shares on their behalf, must register with the SEC under the terms of the Securities Exchange Act 1934, which also makes stipulations about their filings, accounts and other matters. Investment advisers, who manage the funds, are obliged to register under the Investment Advisers Act 1940, which sets reporting and other standards and contains a variety of anti-fraud provisions.

The Investment Company Act 1940 prompted the industry to establish its own trade association, the National Association of Investment Companies, which was set up in New York in the same year. It represents the interests of investment companies of all sorts as regards legislation, regulation and taxation. It promotes public understanding of investment companies and their products, collects and publishes statistics, and produces high-calibre economic and market research. In 1961 it was renamed the Investment Company Institute, and in 1971 it relocated to Washington DC.

Up, up and away

Mutual funds grew rapidly in the 1950s and 1960s as a means for small investors to participate in the rising stockmarket. Between 1950 and 1970, the number of funds grew from 98 to 361 and total net assets increased from $2.5 billion to $48 billion. Since the 1930s, mutual funds had been the foremost type of US investment company. In 1970, the combined net assets of closed-end funds, UITs and exchange-traded funds was $6 billion, one-eighth of the size of mutual-fund assets.

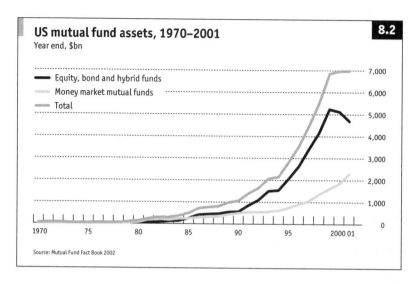

US mutual fund assets, 1970–2001

Year end, $bn

`8.2`

— Equity, bond and hybrid funds
— Money market mutual funds
— Total

Source: Mutual Fund Fact Book 2002

There were several developments in the 1970s that promoted the further expansion of mutual funds. The first, the launch of money-market mutual funds in 1972, developed an entirely new type of fund, which grew rapidly. The retirement savings market was opened up by a series of measures: the Self-Employed Individuals Tax Retirement Act of 1962, which created savings opportunities for the self-employed (Keogh plans); the Employee Retirement Income Security Act (ERISA) of 1974, which set up Individual Retirement Account (IRA) plans for workers not covered by employer-sponsored pension plans; and the Revenue Act of 1978, which permitted the creation of 401(k) tax-sheltered retirement plans.

The stock-price slump of the mid-1970s led to a temporary decline in mutual-fund assets, but by 1980 they had grown to $135 billion, almost three times as much as in 1970, and the number of funds had increased to 564. In the bull market of the 1980s, there was a strong advance in mutual-fund net assets that was almost unaffected by the October 1987 crash. In 1990, assets were $1,065 trillion, an eightfold increase over the decade, and the number of funds had grown sixfold to 3,079 (see Figure 8.2).

In the 1990s, there was further expansion of mutual-fund net assets, which grew to $6,974 billion in 2001, a 6.5 times increase over the decade, and the number of funds rose to 8,307, a 2.7 times increase. Underlying this growth was a strong rise in stock prices and other favourable factors, notably further legislative encouragement for

Table 8.1 **Mutual fund types, December 31st 2001**

	$bn	%
Equity funds	3,418	49
Bond funds	925	13
Hybrid funds	346	5
Money-market funds	2,285	33
Total	6,974	100

Source: Investment Company Institute, *Mutual Fund Fact Book 2002*

retirement saving that boosted retirement-plan purchases of mutual-fund shares. The enactment of the Economic Growth and Tax Relief Reconciliation Plan Act in 2001 significantly expanded retirement-savings opportunities for millions of working Americans. A new source of growth was exchange-traded fund shares, which were launched and developed by the American Stock Exchange from 1993. Encouragement of a different kind was provided by the SEC's initiation of investor-friendly disclosure reforms in 1998, requiring "plain English" mutual fund profiles and clearer risk disclosure.

Types of mutual fund and investment objectives

There are four types of mutual funds:

- Equity (stock) funds focus on investment in stocks.
- Bond funds concentrate on investment in bonds.
- Hybrid funds invest in a mixture of stocks, bonds and other securities.
- Money-market funds invest in short-term money-market instruments.

Equity funds and bond funds are long-term funds, favoured by investors with long-term investment objectives. Money-market funds have the characteristics of mutual funds, but for many investors they serve not as investment vehicles but as a substitute bank account that pays a better rate of interest. They also serve as repositories for investment cash flows at times of stock-price declines, as in 2002. The assets of the four mutual fund types in 2001 are shown in Table 8.1. Equity funds are the largest type of long-term fund.

Table 8.2 **Assets of equity, bond and hybrid mutual funds, December 31st 2001**

	$bn	%
Cash and money-market instruments	219	4
US government securities	376	8
Bonds and mortgages	689	15
Stocks	3,404	73
Others	1	0
Total	4,689	100

Source: Investment Company Institute, *Mutual Fund Fact Book 2002*

By definition, the total assets of money-market mutual funds consist of money-market instruments or cash. Among equity, bond and hybrid mutual funds, stocks make up much the largest proportion of assets (73%, see Table 8.2). This is a higher proportion than private pension funds (62%), state and local-government employee retirement funds (56%), or life insurance companies (30%). The $3.4 trillion-worth of stocks owned by mutual funds is slightly smaller than the $3.8 trillion owned by pension funds.

The Investment Company Institute classifies US mutual funds into 33 different types defined by investment objective.

Equity funds

Capital appreciation funds – the primary objective is capital appreciation, dividends are a secondary consideration.

- Aggressive growth funds
- Growth funds
- Sector funds

Total return funds – the objective is a combination of income and capital appreciation.

- Growth-and-income funds
- Income-equity funds

World equity funds – focus on investment in stocks of foreign corporations.

- Emerging market funds
- Global equity funds
- International equity funds
- Regional equity funds

Taxable bond funds
Corporate bond funds – the objective is current income through investment in high-quality debt issues by US corporations.

- Corporate bond funds – general
- Corporate bond funds – intermediate-term
- Corporate bond funds – short-term

High yield bond funds – seek a higher level of current income by investing two-thirds or more of the portfolio in below-investment-grade US corporate bonds.

World bonds funds – the objective is the highest possible income through investment in debt securities of foreign corporations and governments.

- Global bond funds – general
- Global bond funds – short-term
- Other world bonds funds

Government bond funds – the objective is to achieve high current income through investment in US government bonds of varying maturities.

- Government bond funds – general
- Government bond funds – intermediate-term
- Government bond funds – short-term
- Mortgage-backed funds

Tax-free bond funds
State municipal bond funds – the objective is high tax-free income for residents of particular US states through investment in bonds issued by the relevant state.

- State municipal bond funds – general
- State municipal bond funds – short-term

National municipal bond funds – the objective is high current income free of federal tax through investment in bonds of US municipal issuers.

- National municipal bond funds – general
- National municipal bond funds – short-term

Hybrid funds
Hybrid funds – seek high total return derived from a cocktail of stocks, bonds and derivatives.

- Asset allocation funds
- Balanced funds
- Flexible portfolio funds
- Income-mixed funds

Money-market funds
Taxable money-market funds – the objective is the highest income compatible with preservation of capital. They invest in short-term, high-grade money-market securities.

- Taxable money-market funds – government
- Taxable money-market funds – non-government

Tax-exempt money-market funds – the objective is the highest level of tax-free income (free of federal and sometimes state and local taxes). They invest in short-term municipal securities.

- National tax-exempt money-market funds
- State tax-exempt money-market funds

Mutual-fund shares and shareholders
Mutual-fund shares are a highly liquid form of investment since funds are required to redeem shares whenever investors wish. The price at which redemption is made is the net asset value (NAV): the current market value of the fund's assets, less liabilities, divided by the number of shares outstanding. New shares are available to investors at the price of NAV plus any sales charge.

The calculation of the current market value of a fund's assets is undertaken each day at the close of business using prices supplied by a pricing agency. Most mutual funds release their daily share price

Table 8.3 **Top ten mutual fund companies, 2000**

	Assets ($bn)
Fidelity	818.8
Vanguard Group	574.3
Capital Research	368.5
Putnam	242.6
Merrill Lynch	191.7
Federated Investments	177.0
Janus	176.6
AIM Group	172.2
Franklin Templeton	171.7
Citigroup	166.0

Source: Insurance Information Institute

through NASDAQ, which transmits them to subscribers including the wire services that forward them to the newspapers in which they are published the following day. Share prices are also available over the Internet and via toll-free telephone numbers.

Mutual-fund shares can be purchased through an investment intermediary, such as a financial adviser, broker or bank, who may provide advice on funds that meet an investor's objectives. Such investment intermediaries charge a sales commission or fee. Alternatively, investors can purchase shares directly from the principal underwriter, relying on their own research and the reputation of the mutual fund company. See Table 8.3 for the largest mutual-fund companies.

The typical mutual-fund investor is middle-aged, married and saving for retirement. Mutual-fund shares are offered as investment selections in many defined-contribution pension plans. More than 80% of mutual-fund-owning households participate in employer-sponsored defined-contribution pension plans.

Institution-managed US retirement assets in 2001 totalled $11.2 trillion, of which pension funds, insurance companies, banks and broker-dealer firms managed $8.6 trillion (78%) and mutual funds managed $2.4 trillion (22%). The latter consisted almost equally of $1.19 trillion in employer-sponsored defined-contribution plans, such as 401(k) tax-sheltered retirement plans, and $1.17 trillion in Individual Retirement Accounts (IRAs). Both types grew rapidly in the 1990s and early 2000s, especially IRAS, which cover individuals outside sponsored plans. The mutual-fund industry's share of the rapidly expanding IRA market grew from 14% in the mid-1980s to 49% early in 2002. Its share of the employer-sponsored retirement plan market is 14%. Overall, retirement assets comprise around one-third of total mutual fund assets.

It is anticipated that the increased amounts investors are able to contribute to IRAS and employer-sponsored retirement plans available under the Economic Growth and Tax Relief Reconciliation Act 2001 will boost retirement saving through mutual funds. The legislation is also expected to stimulate the emerging education savings-plan market, which was launched in the 1990s. With a 98% share of the $8.5 billion market, mutual funds would be the foremost beneficiaries of expansion. Thus it appears likely that the robust growth of mutual fund assets will resume with the recovery of stock prices.

9 Stock exchanges

Stock exchanges are organised markets for the purpose of conducting centralised trading in securities. They are institutions with a constitution, members and rules governing trading to ensure an efficient, attractive and legal marketplace. They also have rules about the listing of the securities that are traded on the exchange: corporations whose securities are listed are required to observe specified standards of accounting and reporting, which often go beyond statutory requirements.

Exchanges provide facilities for trading, they do not themselves undertake trading. The facilities include buildings, trading technology, market-information systems and professional staff. Stock exchanges assist the trading of securities by bringing together buyers and sellers, the large number of participants enhancing the liquidity of the market and promoting better prices. By collecting and publishing price and volume information, exchanges provide investors with important market information, and their rules and procedures ensure that the parties to transactions abide by their undertakings.

Stock exchanges are secondary markets where issued and outstanding securities are traded. They play a tangential yet significant part in the primary market process of raising new capital in two ways. First, by providing a listing for the securities of companies new to the market, such issues being known as initial public offerings (IPOs); and second, through the signals that a well-run market provides about the pricing and timing of new issues for borrowers seeking to raise funds.

Stock exchanges in the US are voluntary associations of members, rather like private clubs. They were brought under federal regulation by the Securities Exchange Act 1934 through the neat device of making it illegal for a broker, dealer or exchange to use the mail or any means of conducting interstate commerce to carry out a transaction in a security unless the exchange was registered as a national securities exchange with the Securities and Exchange Commission (SEC). The registration process involves the filing of a statement undertaking to comply with and enforce federal securities legislation through the rules of the exchange. In essence, the regulatory approach is to guide and oversee an exchange's own self-regulation. To promote open, fair and orderly securities markets, the act outlaws misrepresentation, manipulation and

Table 9.1 **US stock exchanges, market value of domestic securities, December 31st 2000**

	$m
	$m
New York Stock Exchange	11,632,885
American Stock Exchange	94,391
Pacific Stock Exchange	2,737
Boston Stock Exchange	1,644
Chicago Stock Exchange	233
Philadelphia Stock Exchange	195
Cincinnati Stock Exchange	0

Source: Securities and Exchange Commission, *Annual Report 2001*, Table 14

other abuses. Furthermore, under the terms of the Securities Act 1933, every corporation that has securities listed on an exchange must itself register with the SEC and file a range of reports disclosing financial and other information relevant to investors.

The SEC oversees seven US stock exchanges that are registered with it as national securities exchanges (see Table 9.1).

Many securities are traded in the over-the-counter (OTC) market. Most OTC stocks are issues that do not meet the listing requirements of the national securities exchanges. They are traded on the NASDAQ (National Association of Securities Dealers Automated Quotation System), a vast computer and telecommunications network operated by the National Association of Securities Dealers (NASD). The NASD is a nationwide association of securities broker-dealers representing virtually the entire US securities industry. In August 2001, the market value of securities quoted on NASDAQ was $2,558 billion.

Since 1978, the eight US securities markets have been linked together by the Intermarket Trading System (ITS), an electronic communications network. Since a stock may be listed – and traded – on more than one stock exchange, the ITS allows traders to check securities prices on the different markets on which they are quoted to get the best prices.

The New York Stock Exchange

The New York Stock Exchange (NYSE) is Wall Street's best known institution. It is also one of New York's leading tourism sites, attracting more than 700,000 visitors a year.

The NYSE is the world's foremost stock exchange. At the start of 2002, a total of 2,798 corporations (2,336 domestic and 462 foreign) were listed on the NYSE. The market capitalisation of domestic corporations alone is $11.1 trillion, more than America's gross national product, and that of foreign corporations is $4.9 trillion, making a total market capitalisation of $16 trillion. The NYSE is by far the largest of the world's stock exchanges – domestic capitalisation alone accounts for 41% of global stockmarket value, more than the three next largest exchanges, NASDAQ, Tokyo and London, added together.

Originally a private members' club, in 1971 the NYSE was incorporated as a not-for-profit corporation. The following year the board of governors was replaced by a board of directors, which consists of 12 directors from the securities industry, 12 other directors and two NYSE officers (the chairman and the chief executive officer, and the president and chief operating officer). The exchange has 1,400 employees working in its various business divisions – the Regulatory Group, Competitive Position Group, International and Research, Equities, Communications, Finance, Human Resources, Administration and Security, the Office of the General Counsel and the Corporate Secretariat. A small number work on the trading floor.

NYSE membership

The NYSE has 1,366 voting members (unchanged since 1953) who own a "seat", the traditional term for the right to trade on the trading floor. Additionally, 57 individuals are entitled to physical or electronic access to the trading floor through payment of an annual fee, making a total of 1,423 floor members. Seats can be bought and sold, the price being determined by supply and demand. The record is $2.6m, paid at the height of the bull market in summer 1999, although during the recession of the mid-1970s the price dipped as low as $35,000. Most members of the NYSE work for one of the large broker-dealer firms. In 2001 there were 365 member organisations of which 283 were corporations, the rest being partnerships or sole proprietors. Most member organisations conduct business with the public, although about one-quarter of them deal only with fellow members. Around 3,000 people (made up of members, their support staff and NYSE personnel) work on the trading floor.

There are three types of members – two types of floor brokers and dealers, known in New York as specialists – each with a distinct function.

- Commission brokers. These are employed by member brokerage firms to execute buy and sell orders on the trading floor on behalf of the firm's clients. They are paid salaries and commissions.
- Independent floor brokers. These operate on their own behalf. They handle orders for brokerage houses that do not have their own commission brokers or act for other firms whose personnel are too busy.
- Specialists. Each stock listed on the NYSE is allocated to a dealer, who makes a market in the assigned security, working at a designated trading post on the trading floor. There are ten specialist firms employing 482 specialist members, who make markets in 2,800 stocks. The specialist firms are independent entities; most of them are owned by corporations and others are partnerships.

Specialists play an important role in maintaining the market's integrity, efficiency and competitiveness. They have five functions:

- Auctioneer. At the start of each trading day, specialists set a buy and sell price based on supply and demand. As trading proceeds, they quote current bids and offers in their stocks to the floor brokers.
- Brokers' broker. Specialists execute "limit orders" entrusted to them by floor brokers on behalf of customers when the price of one of their assigned stocks reaches a specified price limit. They also act as agents for all electronically routed orders.
- Facilitator. Specialists use their extensive knowledge of the market in their assigned stocks to bring together potential buyers and sellers. This skill is especially important when large blocks of stock are brought to the market.
- Market stabiliser. Specialists are required to maintain "orderly markets" in their assigned stocks, ensuring that trading proceeds smoothly and without violent price fluctuations. Facilitator skills are important in the maintenance of an orderly market, making it possible for large orders to be moved through the market with minimum price disruption. Supporters of floor trading claim that this is one of its main advantages over electronic dealing.
- Principal. Three out of four transactions are executed by matching customers' buy and sell orders. But sometimes market conditions require specialists to provide liquidity to the market by

committing their firm's own money, acting as counterparty to a trade. For instance, if buy orders outweigh sell orders, or vice versa, the specialist is required to minimise the imbalance by acting against the market trend until a price is reached at which orders from the public are in equilibrium.

Trading on the NYSE

The buying and selling of stocks takes place on the main trading floor at 17 trading posts, at which the specialists operate. They are waist-high octagonal desks, surmounted by canopies of overhead screens displaying price and volume information about the stocks in which they deal. Each trading post is assigned at least 150 stocks.

The NYSE is an auction market. Floor brokers (commission brokers and independent brokers), representing buyers and sellers of a stock, gather at the trading post to which the stock is assigned to execute buy and sell orders. Bids to buy and sell are made by open outcry, providing every broker with an opportunity to participate. When the highest bid meets the lowest offer, a trade is executed.

Around the edge of the trading floor are hundreds of booths belonging to member firms. When a brokerage house receives an order from a client it transmits the instruction to its booth via computer or phone. The order is routed to a floor broker via a wireless device called the Broker Booth Support System (BBSS). The floor broker then presents the order to a specialist for execution.

Increasingly, orders arrive directly at trading posts from off-the-floor via an electronic order-routing system known as SuperDOT, but they are still handled by specialists on the trading floor, not by electronic matching. Upon execution, the specialist reports the trade directly to the broker firm via the SuperDOT circuit.

Most large US corporations list their securities on the NYSE. To obtain a listing, a corporation has to meet specified minimum levels of earnings, capitalisation and trading volume, and its stocks must be widely held by investors. To protect investors, candidates for listing must agree to satisfy the exchange's standards of disclosure, corporate governance and shareholder participation. Evidence is required that there is sufficient trading interest in the corporation's securities to warrant listing on the "Big Board".

Many corporations initially obtain a listing on NASDAQ or one of the other stock exchanges before transferring to the Big Board. The main reason for transfer is to enhance the marketability of a company's securities, as the NYSE provides greater market liquidity, trading activity and

Table 9.1 **NYSE stocks listed, December 31st 2001**

Industry sector	Number of corporations	Number of issues (bn)	Market value ($bn)
Industrial, services	1,444	1,500	7,865
Financial	1,052	1,094	2,650
Utilities	250	331	1,047
Transportation	52	59	151
Total	2,798	2,984	11,713

Source: NYSE, *Factbook 2002*

visibility and appeals more to investors. Corporate pride may be another motive.

Most stocks listed on the NYSE are common stocks (called ordinary shares in the UK). Despite the attention they receive in finance textbooks, preference and other stock types account for less than 1% of NYSE stocks by value. The distribution of NYSE listed stocks by sector at the end of 2001 is shown in Table 9.1.

Stock indexes

An indication of the movement of prices on the stockmarket as a whole is provided by stock indexes (see below), which are calculated by averaging the prices of a selection of stocks.

- Dow Jones Industrial Average. The original market yardstick, calculated since 1896. A price-weighted average of the stocks of 30 large industrial corporations.
- Standard & Poor's 500 Composite Index – a widely used market measure, based on the market value of 500 large corporations (400 industrials, 40 utilities, 40 financials and 20 transportation). It includes some OTC stocks. Standard & Poor's also publishes indexes for specialised stock sectors.
- New York Exchange Composite Index. An average of the price changes of all the common stocks listed on the NYSE weighted by market value. It is the only measure of the market as a whole. It is computed continuously after every transaction and is transmitted electronically to the trading floor and brokerage houses every 15 seconds. The NYSE also calculates specialised sector indexes.

▪ Others. The "US Market Statistics" report in the *Wall Street Journal* lists 29 "Major Stock Indexes". Each index covers a different set of stocks and there are also differences in the ways they are computed. Together they provide a spectrum of stockmarket yardsticks for a range of reference purposes.

Foreign stocks

The scale of holdings of non-US equities by US investors increased rapidly during the 1990s, from $100 billion in 1990 to $1.5 trillion in 2001, as they diversified their portfolios internationally. As a proportion of total equity holdings, non-US equities increased from 4% in 1987 to 11% in 2001. In response to the growing interest of US investors in foreign securities, the number of non-US companies listed on the NYSE rose from 290 in 1996 to 462 in 2001.

At the beginning of 2002, the market capitalisation of the NYSE's non-US companies was $4.9 trillion. Europe was the main region of origin – 174 companies with a combined capitalisation of $3.4 trillion, 69% of the total. Other significant regions were Latin America, 210 companies, and Asia-Pacific and Canada, 74 companies each. The value of trading of non-US equities on the NYSE grew from $335 billion in 1996 to $1.1 trillion in 2000, falling back to $788 billion in 2001 because of lower stock prices. Non-US equities accounted for 7.5% of the total value of trading in 2001. Only the London Stock Exchange has a higher dollar turnover of trade in foreign equities.

Bonds

The NYSE operates the largest centralised bond market of any exchange, with a total par value of $1,654 trillion in 2001. It lists a broad spectrum of maturities and comprises 1,447 outstanding issues by 392 borrowers. Much the biggest borrowers are the US government and US corporations, with borrowings accounting for, respectively, 82% and 14% of the market's par value (see Table 9.2).

Bond trading volume on the NYSE totalled $2.7 billion in 2001. Straight or non-convertible bonds accounted for 86% of volume in 2001, the remaining 14% of trades being in convertibles. Bond trading is conducted through the exchange's Automated Bond System (ABS), a fully automated trading and information system that allows subscribing firms to enter and execute bond orders directly through terminals in their offices. ABS displays current market data, and provides subscribers with immediate execution reports and trade comparisons. At the begin-

Table 9.2 **NYSE listed bonds, December 31st 2001**

	Number of issuers	Number of issues	Par value ($ trillion)	% of par value
US government	1	406	1,355	82
US companies	304	683	225	14
International banks	5	117	38	2
Foreign companies	48	73	26	1
Municipals	6	162	9	0
Foreign governments	5	6	1	0
Total	369	1,447	1,654	100

Source: NYSE, *Factbook 2002*

Table 9.3 **Stockowners in US, 1989–98** (m)

	1989	1992	1995	1998
Individuals owning stock directly, through mutual funds, retirement saving accounts or defined-contribution pension plans	52	61	69	84
Individuals owning stock directly, through mutual funds or retirement saving accounts	42	52	60	76
Individuals owning stock directly or through mutual funds	32	35	39	49
Individuals owning stock directly only	27	29	27	34

Source: NYSE, *Factbook 2002*

ning of 2002, ABS had 45 subscribers operating a total of 164 installed terminals.

Investors

The NYSE's latest survey of US investors, *Shareownership 2000*, revealed that in 1998, some 84m Americans (44% of the adult population) owned stocks, either directly or indirectly via a mutual fund or pension plan (see Table 9.3). This was a further increase on previous surveys that had identified 52m individual stockholders in 1989, 61m in 1992 and 69m in 1995. Around 60% of stockholders own stock indirectly through mutual funds or pension plans (some of them also own stock directly), and 40% are direct owners only.

There are several reasons for the growth of stock ownership in recent

Table 9.4 **Ownership of corporate equities in the US, 1950, 1990, 2001 ($bn)**

	1950	1990	2001
Institutional investors			
Mutual funds	3	233	2,442
Private pension funds	1	606	1,591
State and local pension funds	0	271	1,100
Life-insurance companies	2	82	821
Bank personal trusts	0	190	206
Other insurance companies	3	80	170
Closed-end funds	2	16	28
Subtotal	11	1,478	6,358
Household and foreign			
Households	28	1,795	5,472
Foreign ownership	3	245	1,524
Others	1	25	271
Subtotal	32	2,065	7,267
Total equities outstanding	43	3,543	13,625

Source: Federal Reserve Board, *Flow of Funds Accounts of the United States*

years. One has been the growth of self-directed retirement accounts, particularly 401(k) plans. Others include the spread of stock options in remuneration packages and staff stock-ownership plans and the popularity of saving though equity mutual funds. The well-publicised upward movement of stock prices during most of the 1980s and 1990s was also a powerful inducement.

Institutional investors – principally mutual funds, pension funds and insurance companies – own a growing proportion of US stocks. In 1950, institutional investors owned just 7% of stocks; by 2001, the proportion was 47%, with a value of $6.4 trillion (see Table 9.4).

Regulation
The integrity of the market is crucial for securities markets. The NYSE safeguards the interests of investors, listed companies and members through a combination of the self-regulation of member firms, exchange rules and external oversight.

◪ Each of the 500 or so member firms has responsibility in law, and as a member of the exchange, for the conduct of their staff and for their training to meet industry standards. Like bank depositors, retail clients of securities brokerage firms have some federal government protection. Cash and securities in customer accounts at brokerage firms is insured by the Securities Industry Protection Corporation (SIPC), created by Congress in 1970, against the failure of brokerage firms for losses up to $500,000 per customer.

◪ The NYSE has an extensive set of rules, running to more than 1,000 pages, on policies and standards of conduct for member firms and individuals. Disclosure rules for listed companies provide investors with important financial information about all NYSE-listed corporations. Member firms are required to submit regular reports every few months providing detailed information about their financial condition, managers and sales practices. Around 95% of all client cash and securities in US brokers' accounts is held by members of the NYSE over which it has regulatory responsibility. In-house regulators police the NYSE's rules, checking market transactions through computer surveillance and conduct investigations. The fully automated Stock Watch system continuously monitors trading activity in all stocks, looking out for suspicious price movements. Regulatory staff are alerted if the trading pattern in a stock deviates from set price or volume guidelines, and an inquiry is carried out to determine whether a violation has taken place.

◪ The SEC supervises every national exchange, including the NYSE, and every company or organisation that participates in the securities market. Part of its job is to ensure that the NYSE's rules conform to statutory standards and that they are strictly enforced. Individuals or organisations that violate SEC rules and standards are liable to penalties, including fines, suspension of licence and permanent expulsion from the securities market. The SEC also recommends the enactment of new legislation it believes necessary to protect investors and the integrity of the markets.

◪ Arbitration is increasingly viewed as an attractive alternative to lengthy and costly litigation for the settlement of disputes. It enables a dispute to be resolved quickly and fairly by impartial expert arbitrators. In disputes involving NYSE members, an investor has the right to require a broker to submit to the arbitration process, so long as the claim is filed within six years of the event in dispute. In choosing arbitration as the means of dispute resolution, the parties waive the right to pursue the matter through the courts.

The development of the NYSE

The NYSE traces its origins to May 1792, when 24 of the most active traders in the fledgling American securities market agreed to do business only with one another and to trade on a common minimum commission basis. Their written compact was known as the Buttonwood Agreement, after the tree at 68 Wall Street beneath which their trading took place (except in bad weather, when they repaired to the nearby Tontine Coffee House).

By 1817, the securities market had developed sufficiently – 30 securities were being traded – for the Buttonwood brokers to move indoors to a rented room at 40 Wall Street and to create a formal organisation, the New York Stock & Exchange Board. They drew up a constitution and a set of rules governing the conduct of trades, commission rates and contracts for delivery, and outlawing fictitious sales and other sharp practices. Membership was by election with defined criteria for eligibility. The new exchange operated as a call market. Twice a day, the president of the Board read the list of securities and an auction took place with members, sitting on chairs assigned to them, shouting out bids and offers. This was the origin of the term "seat", meaning membership of the exchange.

The civil war of 1861–65 led to a large increase in government borrowing through bond issues and hence an upsurge in stockmarket activity. Its rented accommodation became crowded and inadequate, so the Board decided to construct its own building on Broad Street, just south of Wall Street. This opened in 1865, and at around the same time the name New York Stock Exchange was adopted.

Telegraph and railroads

The conduct of trading in the mid-19th century was transformed by radical developments in communications technology, notably the telegraph, which reduced the time it took for information to reach New York from days, weeks or even months, to minutes – the most radical communications revolution ever. Telegraph communication between New York and Philadelphia began in 1846, with the cotton market in New Orleans in 1848 and with the international capital market in London, by undersea cable, in 1866. The following year saw the introduction of the telegraphic stock ticker, which for a weekly rental fee of $6 sent price information from the trading floor to brokers' offices throughout the country. The exchange was also an early adopter of the telephone. Lines were installed in 1878, allowing staff in brokerage firms' offices to speak to their colleagues on the trading floor.

The completion of the transcontinental railroad in 1869 was a vivid manifestation of the frenzy of railroad construction that created a national economy and drove rapid economic growth and increased prosperity in the post-civil war decades. The railroad also transformed the pattern of trading on the NYSE, with railroad stocks and bonds becoming the biggest category of securities.

The call-market system was dropped in 1876 in favour of continuous trading. Under the new system, stocks were assigned to dealers, called specialists, who operated from fixed trading posts, whereas brokers circulated around the trading floor placing bids and offers. Every day the start and finish of trading was heralded by the chimes of a Chinese gong. This was replaced in 1903, after the rebuilding of the exchange, by the 18-inch diameter brass bells that are used to this day. An invitation to ring the opening or closing bell became an honour conferred on visiting dignitaries, companies listing for the first time and retiring members.

The "Gilded Age"
During the "Gilded Age", as the years from the end of the civil war to the early 20th century became known, stockmarket manipulation was rampant. It was orchestrated by a notorious band of financial buccaneers, such as "Commodore" Cornelius Vanderbilt, Daniel Drew, Jay Gould and Edward Harriman, whose outrageous scams and speculations, mostly in railroad stocks, made them celebrities. Then in the 1880s and 1890s came the "trusts", giant industrial corporations created to control entire industries and thus able to manipulate output and prices. Their size and the volume of securities they issued transformed the scale of stock-trading activity – the first 1m-stock trading day was in 1886. To cope with the vastly expanded volume of transactions, a stock clearing house was established in 1892 to streamline transfers from broker to broker. It was against this background of surging trading volume that the *Wall Street Journal* began publication of the Dow Jones Industrial Average in 1896. In 1865, 500 securities issues had been listed on the exchange; by 1900 there were 1,000.

Again the exchange needed more room, and a much larger new building, the present one on the corner of Broad Street and Wall Street,

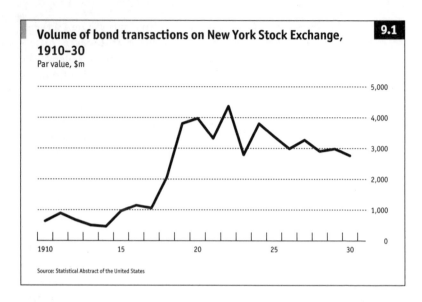

Volume of bond transactions on New York Stock Exchange, 1910–30 `9.1`

Par value, $m

Source: Statistical Abstract of the United States

opened in 1903. It was designed in the classical-revival style favoured at the time for public buildings. Faced with gleaming white marble, the facade features six colossal fluted Corinthian columns topped by a monumental triangular pediment. The sculptural ensemble in the pediment, entitled "Integrity Protecting the Works of Man", features a buxom goddess in a flowing robe presiding over ten toiling figures representing agriculture, industry, mining, science, invention and other productive activities. Inside, the vast new trading floor, with its marble walls and ornate gilt ceiling, looked more like a basilica than a place of business. The NYSE's new home was a forthright expression of Wall Street's confidence and prosperity at the dawn of the new century.

First world war, boom, crash

The outbreak of the first world war in Europe in summer 1914, a conflict on an unprecedented scale with perhaps apocalyptic consequences, led to fears of a stock-price melt-down that prompted the closure of the NYSE from the end of July until mid-December, the longest in its history. By the time the exchange reopened the panic was over, but securities were still regarded warily. That circumspection disappeared with the US government's massive Liberty Bond issues after America's entry into the war in 1917. The issues boosted bond-trading volumes and introduced a broad public to buying securities for the first time (see Figure 9.1).

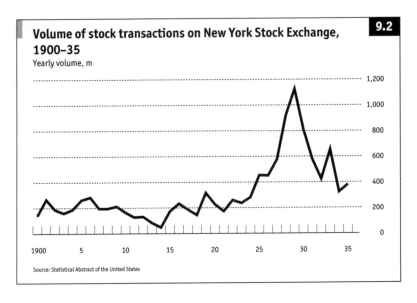

9.2

Volume of stock transactions on New York Stock Exchange, 1900–35

Yearly volume, m

Source: Statistical Abstract of the United States

After the war, Liberty Bond veterans became enthusiastic partici-pants in the bull market of the 1920s. Besides soaring stock prices, which sent the value of listed stocks up from $27 billion in 1925 to $90 billion in 1929, there were large increases in new issues, which rose from 1,800 in 1921 to 6,500 in 1929, and in stock transaction volume, which rose from 173m a year in 1921 to 1.1 billion in 1929 (see Figure 9.2).

The 1929 crash led to a collapse in the market value of NYSE-listed stocks, which by 1932 had fallen to $16 billion, one-sixth of the 1929 peak. Trading volume also fell massively, and there was no market whatsoever for new issues. Criticism of the conduct of the securities industry led to the passage of the Securities Act 1933, which regulated new issues, and the Securities Exchange Act 1934, which established the SEC as the industry's regulator. The NYSE registered with the SEC as a national securities exchange in 1934. In 1938, prompted by the SEC, the NYSE professionalised the running of the exchange with the appoint-ment of a full-time paid president and a salaried administrative staff. The opening the following year of a viewing gallery, affording a bird's-eye view of activity on the main trading floor, marked the start of the exchange's efforts to educate the public about its function and activities and cultivate a better image.

During the second world war, the NYSE and its members actively assisted the US Treasury in the sale of seven large war loans to finance

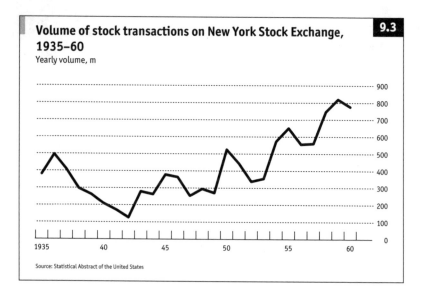

Volume of stock transactions on New York Stock Exchange, 1935–60 `9.3`

Yearly volume, m

Source: Statistical Abstract of the United States

the war effort. Conscription depleted the male staff of brokerage firms, leading to the appearance of women on the trading floor for the first time. Trading volumes fell further in the early years of the war to 171m stocks in 1941, but thereafter both transactions and stock prices picked up; in 1945 market volume was 378m stocks (see Figure 9.3).

Post-war prosperity

Stock prices and the volume of trading rose in the 1950s, particularly in the second half of the decade. This owed something to the exchange's efforts to woo private investors, then the principal purchasers of securities. In 1952, it sponsored the first census of stock ownership, which revealed that 6.5m Americans were stockholders. Aiming to increase this number, in 1954 it launched a public education programme with the slogan "Own Your Share of American Business". To boost investor confidence, listing requirements were made more demanding and trading was regulated more stringently. The exchange also lobbied successfully for legislative reforms that would allow institutional investors to increase their weightings of stocks.

In the 1960s, stock trading volume on the NYSE grew rapidly. In 1963, for the first time, market volume exceeded the record 1.1 billion stock transactions of 1929. Over the decade as a whole, market volume rose from 776m to 2.9 billion (see Figure 9.4). With fixed-rate commissions,

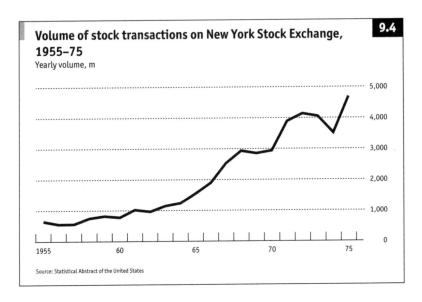

Volume of stock transactions on New York Stock Exchange, 1955–75
Yearly volume, m

9.4

Source: Statistical Abstract of the United States

the quadrupling of volume combined with rising stock prices meant a big hike in NYSE members' commission earnings, bestowing on them a prosperity not seen since the 1920s.

Social and technological progress

As ever, most of those who contributed to and shared in that prosperity were white and male, but not quite all. The social changes that swept through America in the 1960s were in evidence at the NYSE too. The first woman member of the exchange was elected in 1967, and the first black member in 1970. The first black-owned member firm, Daniels & Bell, joined in 1971.

The 1960s saw the beginnings of the electronic transmission and storage of information. In 1966, almost exactly a century after the introduction of the stock ticker, the transmission of trade and quote data from the trading floor was "fully automated", as the exchange put it, being entered on punch cards which were fed into optical scanners at the trading posts. A new Central Certificate Service was initiated to computerise stock transfers. Despite these efforts, the relentless growth in trading volume culminated in the "paper crunch" of the late 1960s, which caused the closure or sale of 100 member firms owing to settlement problems, because their back offices were unable to cope with the flood of paperwork. The crisis was relieved temporarily by the market dip of

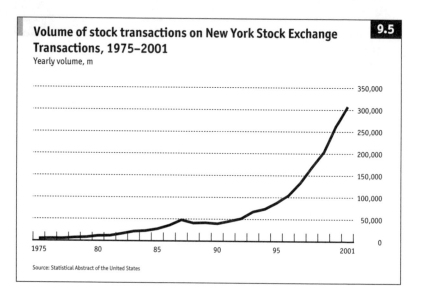

Volume of stock transactions on New York Stock Exchange Transactions, 1975–2001 `9.5`

Yearly volume, m

Source: Statistical Abstract of the United States

1969–70, and was then resolved by the implementation of upgraded electronic clearing and depository arrangements for securities in the mid-1970s. Computerisation also allowed the introduction of the Stock Watch system, which enables exchange officials to monitor and investigate unusual movements in stock volumes or prices, greatly enhancing market supervision.

Capital and commissions

Member firms had been allowed to incorporate as private companies since the early 1950s and many did so to increase capital. Developments during the 1960s – the increased volume of business, the burgeoning size of trades and the need to invest in the computerisation of the back office – led securities firms to require yet more capital. In March 1970, the exchange approved public ownership of member firms; a month later Donaldson, Lufkin & Jenrette became the first member firm to go public, and Merrill Lynch had the honour of becoming the first member firm to be listed on the NYSE. In 1971 the NYSE itself incorporated.

From the late 1960s, there was mounting Congressional pressure for the abolition of the minimum fixed commissions that the NYSE had operated since 1792. In 1971, the launch of NASDAQ, an electronic over-the-counter market with negotiated commission rates, increased the pressure for change. Following the publication of a Congressional report advocating abolition in 1972 the NYSE capitulated, and May 1st 1975 was set as the date for the abolition of fixed commissions. This coincided with the mid-1970s bear market and initially had little impact on trading volume. But the late 1970s saw the beginning of a surge in volume that continued almost without interruption through the 1980s and 1990s and beyond (see Figure 9.5).

Trading system developments

A further reform of 1975 was the passing by Congress of legislation to authorise the SEC to work with the industry to create an effective and competitive National Market System for securities trading. The first step was the introduction of the Consolidated Tape System, which electronically collects and reports trades in NYSE stocks from all markets the moment they occur. Then in 1978 the Intermarket Trading System became operational, linking all the US stock exchanges by computer and allowing brokers to execute a trade wherever the best price was available.

Instead of abandoning floor trading in favour of NASDAQ-style screen-based dealing from trading rooms in banks and brokers' offices, as the European exchanges have done, the NYSE chose to apply technology to bolster the floor-based auction-market system and the traditional role of the specialists. In 1979, it undertook a major upgrade of its trading floor, scrapping the 50-year-old trading posts and introducing overhead display monitors. The electronic order-routing system for off-floor orders, SuperDOT, launched in 1984, retained and strengthened the role of on-floor specialists, who continued to handle trades. In 1993, an Integrated Technology Plan was unveiled to harness the power of technology to the auction-market system. A further major upgrade of the trading posts in 1995 was one outcome. The launch of the NYSE's Wireless Data System in 1997 placed a new communication tool in the hands (literally) of brokers, allowing them to receive orders and send reports electronically from the trading floor.

The bull markets of the 1980s and 1990s put the new technology to the test. In 1982, the exchange had its first 100m stock-transactions day; in 1984, daily volume exceeded 200m; and in 1987, it exceeded 300m. The market crash in October 1987 brought the run to an abrupt, though temporary, end. The speed and savagery of the rout – the Dow fell 23% on "Black Monday", October 19th 1987, its biggest one-day fall – led to a search for culprits. The prime suspect was program trading (computer-driven trading that had been developed since the early 1980s to arbitrage between stocks, stock-index futures and options). The White House set up a task-force, chaired by Nicholas Brady, a future Treasury Secretary, to investigate the causes of the crash. The report was inconclusive about the culpability of program trading, but observed that all concerned had paid insufficient attention to the convergence and integration of Wall Street's many markets. This was attributed primarily to the growth of derivatives, and the authorities, regulators and practitioners were advised to embrace a "one-market concept". Perhaps they did, but it put no brake on the use of program trading, which continued to grow, rising from 11% of NYSE volume in the early 1990s to 13% in 1996 and 28% in 2001.

The NYSE's introduction of "circuit breakers" was an outcome of the Brady task-force's report. Circuit breakers are limits relating to changes in price that, if they are breached, trigger an automatic suspension of trading on selling if the market is falling sharply and on buying when it is rising sharply. The idea came from Japan, a fashionable fount of wisdom at the time, where circuit limits were a feature of financial markets. Some have credited them with curbing market volatility, although many are sceptical.

Into the new millennium

The expansion of market volume resumed in 1991 and powered ahead for the rest of the decade and into the new century. The NYSE had its first 1 billion-stocks day in 1997 and its first 2 billion-stocks day in 2001. Another milestone of 2001, instigated by the SEC, was the conversion of the NYSE and the other US stock exchanges from trading in fractions to decimal pricing. This brought them into line with international practice and cleared an obstacle to participation in an increasingly globalised securities market.

NASDAQ

The National Association of Securities Dealers Automated Quotation System (NASDAQ) is a large and sophisticated computer and telecommunications network for trading securities. The market value of stocks quoted on NASDAQ in August 2001 was $2.5 trillion, making it the second largest domestic equity market in the world, although it is only about one-fifth of the size of the $11.6 trillion market value of stocks quoted on the NYSE. However, in 1999, powered by the dotcom stocks boom, NASDAQ overtook the NYSE in trading value. In 2001, NASDAQ's market turnover was $10.9 trillion, whereas turnover at the NYSE was $10.5 trillion. As a screen-based trading system, NASDAQ has no physical trading floor. But it does have a large office building in New York's Times Square, where it ostentatiously draws attention to the market on the world's largest video screen.

NASDAQ was created by the National Association of Securities Dealers (NASD), a country-wide organisation of securities brokers and dealers that was established by statute in 1938. The NASD, which itself is regulated by the SEC, regulates the over-the-counter (OTC) securities market. In 1961, at the behest of Congress, the SEC conducted a study of the OTC market which proposed automation as the solution to the problem of the market's fragmentation. The NASD was charged with implementation, and in February 1971 NASDAQ commenced trading.

Safeguarding the integrity of the OTC market

The NASD fulfils its regulatory responsibilities for securities industry firms by annual site inspections of member firms and the qualifications testing of staff. The NASD's Rules of Fair Practice set strict standards of honesty, integrity and fair dealings with customers, including faithful adherence to customers' instructions and prompt delivery of funds and securities. The rules list a variety of unacceptable practices that violate the responsibility for fair dealings. The NASD also enforces federal securities law and SEC rules.

Trading on the OTC market is policed by the NASDAQ MarketWatch Department, which is responsible for protecting the integrity of the market. It fulfils its function through two separate operations: StockWatch and TradeWatch. The StockWatch section monitors issuer activity, news and market information disseminated to the public, as well as price and volume activity in NASDAQ securities. The TradeWatch section undertakes centralised, computerised surveillance of trading using automated detection systems. Any suspicious activity is immediately referred to NASD for review and investigation.

To be traded on NASDAQ, a company must meet NASDAQ National Market Quantitative Standards. To qualify, a company must adhere to an array of corporate governance standards designed to safeguard investors but that are less demanding for companies than those of the NYSE. As a result, it attracts a continuous flow of small or medium-sized companies making the transition from private company to public corporation. Hence many stocks traded on NASDAQ are little known to the general public; exceptions include Microsoft, Starbucks, Intel and Amgen. The NASD monitors underwriting arrangements for the public distribution of securities.

Trading on NASDAQ

The securities of 4,100 corporations are listed on NASDAQ. There are 1.3m users in 83 countries (although most are in the United States) who access its real-time quote and trade data. In theory, NASDAQ's "open market" structure allows a virtually unlimited number of participants to trade a company's stock. Both brokerage firms acting on behalf of clients and individual investors buy and sell securities on NASDAQ.

The key element of NASDAQ's trading structure is the 500 or so firms that are registered to act as market makers (dealers). These firms are required at all times to post their bid and sell prices on the NASDAQ network, where they can be seen and acted on by all participants. They commit their own capital to the purchase and sale of securities, buying for inventory when holders want to sell and selling from inventory when investors wish to buy. By being always willing to buy or sell – to make a market – these dealers add liquidity to the NASDAQ market, enabling trades to be executed promptly and efficiently. This is particularly important in the case of NASDAQ's many small and infrequently traded stocks as it provides them with essential liquidity.

There are four types of market-maker firms: retail, wholesale, institutional and regional. Retail market makers are broker-dealers with brokerage networks that serve both retail and institutional investors. Wholesale market makers primarily trade on behalf of institutional clients and other broker-dealers that are not registered as market makers in a corporation's stock but need to fulfil customers' orders. They are an important source of market liquidity. Institutional market makers specialise in executing large block orders for insurance companies, mutual funds, pension funds and asset-management companies. Regional market makers focus on servicing the companies and investors of particular regions, giving specialised attention to their requirements.

The reputation of NASDAQ's market makers was tarnished by the October 1987 crash. Allegations were made that when prices were plummeting, many of them refused to take phone calls from customers or fulfil their responsibility to make a market. The criticism led to rule changes with the intention of preventing dealers from failing to deal in future falling markets.

Tech stocks boom and bust

Many small or medium-sized companies make the transition from private ownership to public ownership via a listing on NASDAQ. During the technology stocks boom of the second half of the 1990s, many telecoms and Internet companies listed on NASDAQ and it was there, rather than the NYSE, that the trading frenzy reached its zenith in 1998–2000.

In June 1999, the NASDAQ Composite Index, the most widely cited market yardstick, stood at 2,550, at the time an all-time high but prices were still advancing. The following month the market value of Microsoft, the largest NASDAQ quoted stock, reached $500 billion. It was the first corporation to breach that benchmark, which made it worth more than the entire national product of the Netherlands. By mid-October the NASDAQ Composite was standing at 2,730, but then it really took off, staging an 11-week streak of straight increases and finishing the year at 4,069, an 85.6% increase for the year and the best ever performance for a major index. With such a backdrop, late 1999 was a favourable time for IPOs, including a $5 billion issue for United Parcel Service (UPS), the largest to date. Another record was set by the IPO for VA Linux, which was priced at $30 per share but soared to $320 and closed at $239, making it the biggest first-day increase.

The year 2000 began bumpily, with the NASDAQ Composite yo-yoing around the 4,000 level. An analysis at this time of the top 50 NASDAQ stocks with the highest price increases in 1999 revealed that only 15 of the companies were profitable. Moreover, the average annual turnover of this group of stocks was 600%, seven times the average for NYSE stocks, indicating that they had become gambling counters rather than investments. In February 2000, the NASDAQ Composite set off on its final run, leaving behind the Dow, which peaked in January. In mid-February it reached 4,411, towards the end of the month 4,590, and finally in mid-March it breached the 5,000 barrier, peaking at 5,048. Again, there were plenty of IPOs, including Palm, a manufacturer of handheld electronic organisers, which was priced at $38 but soared to $165 when trading opened. Strikingly, the rises occurred against a background of tightening by the Federal Reserve, which had begun raising rates on June 30th 1999. But this had no effect on the "irrational exuberance" that had taken hold among the NASDAQ punters.

The return to earth of the NASDAQ Composite began at the beginning of April 2000. By the middle of the month it was down to 3,320, 35% lower than the peak a few weeks earlier, a record slump for a major index. Many individual stocks were down even further, as the "tech wreck" took its toll. The rest of the year saw roller-coaster gyrations, but there was no sustained recovery. By summer 2002, the NASDAQ Composite stood at 1,205, 76% lower than the peak, and many of the shooting-star tech stocks of 1998–2000 were worthless.

New trading platform

In summer 2002 NASDAQ's new high-powered trading system, Super-Montage, was launched. The outcome of years of investment and development, this fully integrated electronic order-display and execution system promised, according to NASDAQ, much greater "efficiency, speed and depth of information to trading", resulting in "a dramatic enhancement of transparency, liquidity and trading environment stability". If the new screen-based system turns out to be as good as claimed, it may be time for floor trading to go the way of the dinosaurs.

The American Stock Exchange

The American Stock Exchange (Amex) is the third largest US securities market. By the yardstick of market value of listed domestic corporations, it is distinctly junior league compared with the NYSE and NASDAQ, its $94 billion market value being just 1% of the former and 4% of the latter. But this measure does not capture its significant role in listing new companies, or its successful development of financial options and exchange-traded funds.

Like the NYSE, Amex is a floor-based auction market. It has a similar set-up of specialists working at trading posts and brokers buying and selling on behalf of clients. The market is policed by a Stock Watch surveillance system, and suspected violations are investigated and reported to the NASD. Amex became an independent subsidiary of the NASD in 1998.

Amex traces its origins to the lively outdoor "curb market" in unlisted OTC securities that was conducted on Wall Street's sidewalks in the 19th and early 20th centuries. The formation of the New York Curb Agency in 1908 was the first attempt to organise this market and to list the securities of the smaller companies that were traded in it. Then in 1921, the curb brokers moved indoors into their own building in Trinity Place, which is still their home. The present name was adopted in 1953.

The turbulent 1970s were difficult years at Amex as at other exchanges. Over the decade, stock trading registered only a modest increase in volume, from 840m in 1970 stocks to 1.1 billion in 1979. The introduction of exchange-traded options in 1975 was an important initiative, and Amex soon became the second largest US options exchange, after the Chicago Board Options Exchange (CBOE), which pioneered exchange-traded options in 1973. During the bull market of the 1980s, there was a substantial increase in Amex market volume, which peaked in 1987 at 3.5 billion. There was also an energetic development of the options business, with the introduction of new contracts, such as US Treasury notes and bills in 1982 and index options in 1983. By 2001, Amex options volume was 205m contracts, a 29.5% share of the US market and not so far short of the CBOE's 35% market share. Stock trading volume in 2001 was 16 billion contracts, with a value of $817 billion.

In 1993, Amex pioneered trading in exchange-traded funds (ETFs), stock-index-based financial products that allow investors to buy or sell shares in entire portfolios of stock in a single security. Offering, as Amex puts it, "the diversification of traditional mutual funds but with trading flexibility, tax efficiencies and generally lower expense ratios, ETFs have become the fastest-growing securities product available". By 2001, the exchange listed 116 ETFs, with an underlying asset value of $87 billion. Moreover, it was a market in which Amex enjoyed a massive first-mover advantage with a 98% market share. But the NYSE is entering the market place with its own ETF products.

Regional stock exchanges

There are five regional stock exchanges in America. Originally, they were established to trade in the stocks of local corporations, but today they mostly trade in national stocks and options contracts.

The Pacific Exchange, the largest of the regional exchanges by market value of listed stocks, was founded in 1882. Besides trading equities, since 1976 options have been a large part of its business; the exchange lists options contracts on 1,200 stocks. The Boston Stock Exchange, established in 1834, trades 2,000 nationally traded US stocks as well as 125 exclusive listings. It is an integral part of the Boston money centre, the third largest asset management centre in the world. The Chicago Stock Exchange, created in 1882, trades 3,800 stocks, more than any other floor trading US stock exchange. The Philadelphia Stock Exchange, founded in 1790, is the oldest in America. It lists 2,200 stocks and a substantial number of options contracts. All these regional exchanges feature floor-based auction trading, although they have also adopted electronic trading technologies.

The distinguishing feature of the Cincinnati Stock Exchange, with headquarters in Chicago, is that it is an electronic stock exchange. In 1976, the centralised physical trading floor was replaced by a geographically dispersed electronic trading floor. Uniquely, it retains an auction form of trading, featuring, it elucidates, "a competing specialist system with preferencing capability". Overall volume averages almost 170m stocks a day. The Cincinnati Stock Exchange sees itself as a challenger to

NASDAQ, claiming to have captured 20% of trades in NASDAQ-listed securities in 2001.

Also chasing after NASDAQ's business are a number of large automated trading platforms known as electronic communications networks (ECNs). These independent for-profit corporations, of which the best known are perhaps Island and Instinet, have now attracted enough liquidity to be considered a real challenge to the established US securities markets.

Challenges

In common with other exchanges around the world, some US stock exchanges are converting from member-owned mutual organisations to for-profit shareholder-owned corporations. The Pacific Exchange has proceeded furthest along the track to demutualisation, becoming in 1999 the first American stock exchange to establish a for-profit subsidiary. Both NASDAQ and Amex are in the process of becoming independent from the NASD, which will provide the option of a public offering. These divestitures are the outcome of a strategic decision by the NASD to focus on its regulatory function.

The attention of the NYSE's management has focused on physical expansion and upgrading the facilities for trading. In 1998, it reached an agreement with New York City to move to 23 Wall Street, the old J.P. Morgan building, which was to be redeveloped as a 60-storey, 900-foot tower. But these plans were thrown into disarray by the terrorist attacks on September 11th 2001. As Richard Grasso, the NYSE chairman, put it: "The 900-foot tower is not a saleable transaction." Whatever the solution, the displacement of the NYSE from the Wall Street area has been ruled out as an option.

Around the world, the big stock exchanges are seeking ties with foreign exchanges to expand the services they offer clients and to position themselves strategically in the global marketplace. In 1999, NASDAQ formed NASDAQ Japan in conjunction with a Japanese partner, and in 2001 it established NASDAQ Europe. In the same year, Amex began trading ETFs on the Stock Exchange of Singapore, its first international joint venture, and agreements were reached with Euronext and the Tokyo Stock Exchange to list and trade each other's ETFs. The NYSE, however, has gone global by a different route, attracting listings from a growing number of the world's leading corporations that want to have their stock quoted on the Big Board, the world's leading stock exchange.

The respective merits of auction-market floor trading and dealer-based screen trading on electronic platforms have been debated since the advent of NASDAQ in 1971. For the moment, the NYSE, Amex and the Chicago exchanges remain fully committed to the retention of floor-based auction trading, investing millions of dollars in communications technology to strengthen the auction market, not replace it. Salvatore F. Sodano, Amex's chairman and CEO, says:

> Auction markets are better and stronger than dealer markets. Trading is more efficient when buyers and sellers trade directly with each other. Spreads are narrower, pricing is more precise and execution costs are lower. Bringing buyers and sellers together in one-to-one relationships increases liquidity and true price discovery. Trading is more orderly, so there is less price volatility.

But trading from a centralised location also has perils, as Amex was reminded on September 11th 2001. Located just 100 yards from the World Trade Centre, its building, though fortunately not the personnel, was devastated by the terrorist attacks. Helping hands were extended by the Philadelphia Stock Exchange and the NYSE, which provided temporary accommodation that allowed trading to resume on September 17th along with other US exchanges. Amex was able to move back into its own building in October.

The terrorist attacks revitalised the long-running debate about the concentration and decentralisation of financial markets in the United States. Although at present there is no doubt about the commitment of the floor-based exchanges to auction trading, were they to find themselves the target of further terrorist outrages it might just be the factor that tips the balance in favour of dispersed electronic screen-based trading.

10 Futures and options exchanges

Some 1,600 commodity exchanges were established in America in the decades just before and after the civil war, trading every conceivable type of produce. They were formed by farmers, merchants, prospectors and businessmen to provide an honest and structured forum for the purchase and sale of goods, setting quality and quantity standards, and with fair rules for the conduct of trading. Commodity markets began as spot (cash) markets, but most soon developed futures contracts as well; and it was as futures markets that the successful ones grew and prospered.

Trading in the commodity markets was invariably conducted by "open outcry" on the floor of the exchange. In open-outcry trading, traders stand in a trading pit (ring) and call out prices and quantities that indicate their willingness to buy or sell. A trade takes place when a seller accepts a bid price or a buyer takes an offer price. This procedure, which simultaneously conveys the latest price information to all traders, constitutes a transparent public price discovery mechanism, which is a prized benefit of open-outcry trading. Naturally, the price of subsequent bids and offers reflects the prices at which previous transactions have taken place.

Federal regulation of futures trading began in 1922 with the establishment of the Commodity Exchange Commission under the Department of Agriculture. This body was superseded in 1974 by the Commodity Futures Trading Commission (CFTC), which was given enhanced authority and responsibilities by Congress. The CFTC regulates US commodity exchanges, commodity exchange members and commodity futures contracts. All firms and individuals engaged in futures trading are required to register with the CFTC. It also regulates options transactions in commodities, gold and silver, foreign currencies and mortgage securities.

The CFTC's statutory responsibilities are to prevent price and trading manipulation, and the dissemination of false and misleading market information. It protects market users against fraud and abusive market practices and safeguards the handling of margin money. Based in Washington DC, the CFTC has regional offices in the four cities that host futures exchanges – Chicago, New York, Kansas City and Minneapolis – and in Los Angeles for enforcement purposes.

Options in exchange-traded form did not exist before the mid-1970s. Although some speculators were able to make private over-the-counter options deals, the regulatory authorities took a dim view of options, regarding them as devices for defrauding naive investors. But members of the Chicago Board of Trade, the leading futures exchange of the day, believed that there was a potential demand for standardised and listed options on stocks (equities) and began planning a specialist exchange to trade such products. Eventually, regulatory approval was received from the Securities and Exchange Commission (SEC), the regulatory authority of the securities markets, and a new market, the Chicago Board Options Exchange, began trading in April 1973.

Exchange-traded equities options give the holder the right to buy (or sell) from the Options Clearing Corporation (OCC – a central clearing organisation created for this purpose at the outset of the market) a number of stocks (typically 100) of the underlying security covered by the option at the stated exercise price. The settlement procedures of the OCC ensure that for every option there is a writer who is responsible for its fulfilment and is required to post deposit margin with the broker.

Options contracts proved immediately popular with investors, prompting the other securities markets to scramble to launch their own options products. Alarmed at the galloping proliferation of financial derivatives, in 1977 the SEC imposed a moratorium on new options contracts pending a thorough review. The SEC moratorium was lifted in March 1980, and the options market immediately began to expand rapidly. The first stock-index options contract was launched in 1983. Options contracts have also been introduced on the securities exchanges on US Treasury rates and foreign currencies.

In the early 1980s there was another twist in the story: the launch by the futures exchanges of options on their futures contracts. Henceforth, most new futures contracts offered by the futures exchanges had a companion options-on-futures contract. But the volume of trading on the options-on-futures contracts has never been as high as on the underlying futures contracts.

Futures exchanges

In America there are ten futures exchanges registered with the CFTC on which trading takes place. The big five, those with a place in the world's top 40 futures exchanges by volume of contracts traded, are listed in Table 10.1.

Table 10.1 **Top five US futures exchanges, 2001**

	Volume of contracts traded (m)	Global rank
Chicago Mercantile Exchange	315.9	2
Chicago Board of Trade	209.9	3
New York Mercantile Exchange	85.0	6
New York Board of Trade	14.0	17
Kansas City Board of Trade	2.3	36

Source: *Futures Industry Magazine*, Jan/Feb 2002

Chicago Mercantile Exchange

The Chicago Mercantile Exchange (CME) was established in 1898 as the Chicago Butter and Egg Board, adopting its present name in 1919. By then, in addition to spot trades, futures contracts were offered on a variety of agricultural products. As the years went by the list lengthened, including frozen pork bellies in 1961, random-length lumber in 1969 and lean hogs in 1995.

But the CME's real claim to fame is for having pioneered financial derivatives. In 1972, through the perspicacity and persistence of Leo Melamed, the CME's chairman, it launched, via its International Monetary Market division, the world's first financial futures contracts on seven currencies: sterling, yen, D-mark, lira, Mexican peso, Swiss franc and Canadian dollar. The timing was perfect, coming in the wake of the collapse of the Bretton Woods system of fixed exchange rates when currencies were behaving like yo-yos, and the new currency futures contracts immediately took off. So began the era of the derivatives markets.

The 3-month eurodollar contract introduced by the CME in 1981 was another milestone in the development of financial futures, being the first futures contract to be contractually settled in cash. The CME eurodollar contract quickly became the benchmark short-term interest-rate contract and the most actively traded futures contract in the world. Trading volume in 2000–01 was 162m contracts, around 30% of the US total.

The first successful equity-index futures contract, based on the Standard and Poor's 500 Index, was launched by the CME in 1982. An options contract based on the Standard and Poor's 500 Index futures contract was introduced in 1983. Subsequently, other futures contracts were matched with options-on-futures contracts, and most new products were launched in both futures and options-on-futures forms. In

2001, the volume of options-on-futures contracts traded on the CME was 96m, about one-quarter of the total.

In 2001, the aggregate volume of futures and options contracts traded on the CME was 412m with an underlying value of $294 trillion. There are four principal product areas: interest rates, 274m contracts; stock indices, 107m contracts; foreign exchange, 22m contracts; and commodities, 9m contracts. Besides the 3-month eurodollar contract, the other large futures contracts traded on the CME are the Standard and Poor's stock index, 65m contracts in 2000–01; the NASDAQ 100 index, 33m contracts; and a variety of currency futures, the biggest being euro, 5m contracts, and yen, 4m contracts.

The CME, which in 2001 overtook the Chicago Board of Trade to become the largest US futures exchange by trading volume, was the first US futures exchange to convert from a traditional not-for-profit membership organisation to a for-profit shareholder-owned corporation. In November 2000, membership interests were converted into common stock that can trade separately from exchange-trading privileges. For the moment, the stock of the new holding company, CME Holdings, is owned by trading firms and members, but an initial public offering (IPO) is envisaged.

Most trading on the CME is by open outcry, but a growing proportion – 20% in 2001 compared with 15% in 2000 – was being conducted on CME's electronic trading platform, Globex. Launched in 1992, Globex was significantly upgraded in 1998 when it adopted a modified version of the NSC trading system developed for Euronext, the amalgamated Paris, Amsterdam, Brussels and Lisbon securities exchanges. This electronic technological compatibility allows the members of the "Globex Alliance", as the CME calls its network of link-ups with other exchanges, to offer a greater variety of contracts to each other's members and customers.

Besides the CME and Euronext, the Globex Alliance embraces SIMEX, the Singapore derivatives exchange with which the CME has had a mutual offset agreement since 1984, and exchanges in Spain, Canada and São Paulo. The CME also has a partnership agreement with the London International Financial Futures and Options Exchange (LIFFE), allowing cross-margining of products. A corporate publication proclaims:

> With customers all over the world, a global product line,
> nearly around-the-clock electronic trading and strategic

alliances with other exchanges, CME is truly a global marketplace.

Chicago Board of Trade

The Chicago Board of Trade (CBOT) was established in 1848 as a central marketplace for trading the prodigious agricultural output of the Great Plains, especially wheat, corn and oats. In 1865, the CBOT invented the modern exchange-traded futures contract when it formalised grain trading by introducing standardised agreements, which it called "futures contracts". It also began to require performance bonds, called "margin", to be posted by buyers and sellers in its grain markets. It is now the most important US grain exchange, and around 90% of the world's grain futures trading takes place on its floor. It is also the largest spot market for corn and soybeans and trades many other agricultural products. In 2001, the CBOT's total trading volume was 260m contracts, 209m futures contracts and 51m options-on-futures contracts.

It was not until 1968, the year of CBOT's 120th anniversary, that trading began in a non-grain related product: iced broilers. The following year saw the introduction of silver futures, the exchange's first precious-metals contract. The turmoil in the financial markets in the early 1970s led to the creation by CBOT members of a separate exchange to specialise in trading options on securities – the Chicago Board Options Exchange (CBOE), which opened in 1973.

For its own trading floor, the CBOT focused on developing interest-rate futures, beginning with a contract on Ginnie Mae mortgaged-backed certificates in 1975. In August 1977, it introduced a US Treasury-bond futures contract that proved highly successful and established the CBOT's pre-eminence at the long end of the yield curve, whereas CME products dominate the short end and currencies. Options on the US Treasury-bond futures contract were launched in 1982, and the success of this contract opened the way for options on other financial-futures contracts as well as the CBOT's agricultural-futures contracts. Another notable move in the development of the CBOT's financial-derivatives business was the launch of futures and options-on-futures contacts on the Dow Jones Industrial Average in 1997. The principal financial-futures contracts traded on the CBOT in 2000–01 were US Treasury bonds, 57m contracts; 10-year US Treasury notes, 53m contracts; 5-year US Treasury notes, 28m contracts; and the Dow Jones Industrial Average index, 5m contracts. Among commodities, the major contracts were corn, 17m contracts, and soybean, 12m contracts.

CBOT members have traditionally been strong supporters of open-outcry trading, and the exchange proceeded cautiously with the introduction of electronic trading. An electronic trading system, Project A, was introduced in 1994, permitting what the exchange called "side-by-side open outcry and electronic trading". CBOT members were also cautious about demutualisation; a restructuring strategy was approved in 2000, but implementation proceeded gradually.

As the largest US and global futures exchange, the CBOT set a series of world trading-volume records in the 1980s and 1990s, with total contracts rising from 154m in 1990 to 220m in 1994 and 281m in 1998. But the creation during 1998 of Frankfurt-based Eurex, through the amalgamation of the Swiss and German futures exchanges, relegated the CBOT to second place in the global league table, and the rapid expansion of the CME since the late 1990s has pushed it into third place.

Negotiations between the CBOT and Eurex for the formation of what they refer to as a "strategic global alliance" began in 1998. CBOT members rejected the proposal initially, but after a second vote it won consent. August 2000 saw the launch of a new trading platform a/c/e – alliance/cbot/eurex – based on Eurex technology. The new electronic platform provides a common gateway to each exchange's products through a single trading screen, although the allies retain independent rights to launch new products.

New York Mercantile Exchange

The New York Mercantile Exchange (NYMEX) was established in 1872 by a group of Manhattan dairy merchants as a marketplace for trading in cash and futures contracts of agricultural produce. It later developed into the foremost US energy futures market. In 1994, NYMEX merged with the Commodity Exchange (COMEX), another New York futures exchange, which specialised in trading metals futures. The total number of contracts traded in 2001 was 103m: 85m futures contracts and 18m options-on-futures contracts.

The largest trading volumes are in energy futures, notably crude oil, 38m contracts in 2000–01, and natural gas, 16m contracts. The COMEX division's biggest business is gold futures, 7m contracts, and copper, 3m contracts. The NYMEX began trading currency futures in 1978, but discontinued the contracts in 1980. Although it lists a couple of index contracts, trading financial derivatives is not a significant part of NYMEX's business.

New York Board of Trade

The New York Board of Trade (NYBOT) came into existence in 1998 through the merger of the New York Cotton Exchange (NYCE), founded 1870, and the Coffee, Sugar & Cocoa Exchange (CSCE), founded 1882. In 2001, the total number of contracts traded was 18m, of which 14m were futures contracts and 4m options-on-futures contracts. Around four-fifths of NYBOT's trading volume consists of agricultural commodity contracts, notably sugar, 5m contracts, and coffee, cocoa and cotton, 2m contracts each.

Financial futures, mostly currency futures and index futures, make up the rest of its business. The currency side was developed by FINEX, which was formed by the NYCE in 1985 and now constitutes NYBOT's currency division. In 1988, the NYCE acquired the New York Futures Exchange (NYFE), which became NYBOT's index products division. The NYFE was formed in 1980 by the NYSE to trade futures contracts based on foreign currencies, US government securities, bank certificates of deposit and its own NYSE Composite Index. The last contract was eclipsed by the CME's Standard and Poor's 500 Index futures contract, and the NYFE proved unable to catch up with the Chicago exchanges. As regards financial futures, it is Chicago, not New York, that is the leading US financial centre.

Although continuing to have confidence in "the essential and proven benefits of open outcry", NYBOT has actively sought to apply technology to promote "modernised" open outcry and apply technology to achieve efficiencies and cost savings.

NYBOT and NYMEX were both physically damaged by the terrorist onslaught on September 11th 2001. NYBOT's offices in a World Trade Centre building, adjacent to the twin towers, were completely destroyed. The exchange activated a crisis back-up facility that it had established eight years earlier in the suburb of Queens. Although cramped and hot, with only two trading rings instead of 13, trading resumed on Monday September 17th. NYMEX's building two blocks away from the twin towers had to close temporarily because of blast damage and destruction to the surrounding area, but it was able to start trading again four days after the attack via its Internet site.

Remarkably, the attacks had a negligible effect on the business of either exchange or the futures industry overall. Both reported strong volume in the last two weeks of September, and for global business as a whole it was a strong month. Indeed, volume on some products surged on fears of war and economic repercussions.

Two leading futures industry firms with offices in the twin towers, Cantor Fitzgerald and Carr Futures, suffered catastrophic casualties in the attacks. Cantor responded by focusing its resources on trading on the electronic platform for Treasury-bond futures it had developed with NYBOT. Carr's business was handled by its Chicago and London offices. "In times of great turmoil, traders turn to the futures markets for all the right reasons," a Carr manager defiantly told *Futures Industry Magazine*. "Our markets remain liquid. Our credit is the best there is."

Kansas City Board of Trade

The Kansas City Board of Trade (KCTB) was formed in 1876. Located in the heart of America's wheat lands, grain trading was from the outset and remains the core business of its members. Initially, business was for cash, but wheat futures were traded from early on. In 1984, the KCTB began trading options on wheat futures. Its original contribution to the development of derivatives was the launch in 1982 of Value Line stock-index futures, the world's first stock-index futures contract. Another pioneering venture was the introduction of futures and options contracts on the ISDEX Internet stock index in 1999. Total trading volume in 2001 was 2.6m contracts, 2.3m futures contracts and around 300,000 options-on-futures contracts.

Smaller futures exchanges

There are five smaller US futures exchanges that are registered with the CFTC and on which trading takes place.

- BrokerTec Futures Exchange (BTEX) started trading in November 2001. It is affiliated with BrokerTec Global and provides an electronic trading platform for trading government securities.
- Cantor Financial Futures Exchange (CX) is a joint venture between NYBOT and Cantor Fitzgerald, established in 1998. It provides a proprietary electronic trading platform for US Treasury and agency notes.
- Merchants' Exchange (ME) gained approval as a contract market in 2000. It was originally established in 1836 as a cash commodity market. It operates as an electronic exchange offering contacts in barge freight service futures.
- MidAmerica Exchange (MIDAM) is a subsidiary of the CBOT, trading many of the same contracts as its parent but in smaller contract sizes. The principal contracts are soybeans, wheat, corn

Table 10.2 **US options exchanges, 2001**

	Volume of contracts traded (m)
Chicago Board Options Exchange	307
American Stock Exchange	208
Pacific Stock Exchange	103
Philadelphia Stock Exchange	96
International Stock Exchange	25

Source: Annual reports

and US Treasury bonds. The annual volume of contracts traded in 2001 was about 300,000.

◼ Minneapolis Grain Exchange (MGE) was originally established in 1881 as the Minneapolis Chamber of Commerce, a regional cash marketplace to promote trade in wheat, corn and oats and to prevent market abuses. The first futures contract, in hard red spring wheat, was introduced in 1883. The name was changed to the MGE in 1947. Futures and options contracts are traded in wheat, corn and soybeans.

Options exchanges

Options are traded on five US securities exchanges: the Chicago Board Options Exchange, which pioneered options trading; the American Stock Exchange; the Pacific Stock Exchange; the Philadelphia Stock Exchange; and the International Stock Exchange. Three other securities exchanges that entered the market have withdrawn, NASDAQ, the Midwest Stock Exchange (Chicago Stock Exchange) and the NYSE, which in 1997 sold its options business to the CBOE.

The volume of options contracts traded on the US options exchanges is shown in Table 10.2.

Chicago Board Options Exchange

The Chicago Board Options Exchange (CBOE) was formed by the CBOT following a four-year feasibility study, but it is managed and regulated as an independent entity. It opened for business in April 1973, specialising in providing facilities for trading in options on stocks that were actively traded on the NYSE. It had 284 members, representing 121 firms.

At the outset, the CBOE traded call options on 16 stocks (puts were added in 1977). Options trading boomed, and in just three years the CBOE grew from being the smallest US securities exchange to the second largest by trading volume. The other US securities exchanges soon entered the market. The American Stock Exchange began options trading in January 1975, followed by the Philadelphia Stock Exchange in June 1975 and the Pacific Stock Exchange in 1976. The sudden deluge of options trading and applications for additional listings led the SEC to impose a moratorium on further expansion, pending completion and implementation of its *Special Study of the Options Market*. This review of the structure and regulatory procedures of options exchanges resulted in significant improvements in customer protection.

The SEC moratorium was lifted in March 1980 and the expansion of the options market resumed. The CBOE immediately raised the number of options on listed stocks to 120 and commenced trading in options on US Treasury bonds and notes in 1982. It also did a deal with the Midwest Stock Exchange (now the Chicago Stock Exchange), adding its 411 members to the CBOE floor.

In 1983, the CBOE pioneered another innovation in financial derivatives – stock-index options. The first were based on the Standard and Poor's 100 and 500 indexes, the former becoming much the most actively traded options-index product. Business expanded rapidly, and in 1984 the CBOE left the CBOT building and moved into its own premises.

Subsequent years saw further innovations. Currency options were introduced in 1985, interest-rate options in 1989, LEAPS (long-term options) in 1990, FLEX (flexible exchange options) in 1993, and so on. The CBOE now lists options on around 1,500 widely traded stocks and a host of index and other products. It accounts for two-fifths of all US options trading and 90% of index-options trading.

American, Pacific and Philadelphia stock exchanges
The American Stock Exchange was the second options exchange to get going and built up the second largest US options business. It has been close behind the CBOE in launching new products, and in recent years has been narrowing the CBOE's lead, especially in equity options. Substantial options trading also takes place at the Pacific and Philadelphia exchanges, much of it in the same stocks as the CBOE. The Philadelphia Stock Exchange has a leading position in sector index options.

International Stock Exchange

At the CBOE, American, Pacific and Philadelphia exchanges, the bulk of trading is conducted on the trading floor. The International Stock Exchange (ISE), based in the Wall Street area, was launched in May 2000 and is an electronic options exchange, trading being conducted exclusively on screen. By the end of its first year of business, it listed 436 issues, had signed up 85 broker-dealers and claimed to have taken a 15% overall market share of US options trading. That is the record of an operation to be reckoned with.

Floor trading versus electronic trading platforms

In Europe, floor trading has been largely discontinued in both securities and futures exchanges because screen trading has been found to be cheaper. In the United States, NASDAQ has operated as a screen-based securities trading system since 1971, and the ISE has demonstrated that there are customers for electronic options trading. But floor trading continues at all the other US futures and securities exchanges. Supporters of open outcry contend that it provides superior execution, particularly of large trades. The exchanges have sought to harness technology to bolster floor trading, for instance in the delivery of orders and the clearing of trades. Nonetheless, many observers believe that ultimately the open outcry versus electronic platform issue will be resolved by cost, and that, as in Europe, machines will prevail.

Demutualisation

The demutualisation of exchanges is an international phenomenon. Conversion from mutual, not-for-profit, trader-owned clubs to shareholder-owned for-profit corporations allows exchanges to raise external funding to spend on all that expensive technology. It is also argued that it improves the quality of management and the delivery of services to users. Moreover, it transforms strategic thinking: "If exchanges are publicly listed," says a former CBOT manager, "you're going to see them start to act like regular companies." While not disputing the power of these propositions, most US exchanges have proceeded gingerly along the road to demutualisation.

Alliances and consolidation

Recent years have seen the forging of international alliances amongst both stock and futures exchanges. One motive has been to satisfy the increasing global outlook of investors and market participants. Another has been a desire to share the increasing cost of technology. In Europe, there has been the merger of the German and Swiss derivatives exchanges to form Eurex; the amalgamation of the Paris, Brussels and Amsterdam exchanges into Euronext; and a bidding war between them for LIFFE, which was won by Euronext. Further consolidation is expected as the remaining national exchanges join up with one of the large groups, or the groups themselves combine.

Consolidation among US futures exchanges is also on the cards. In May 2001, the famously independent and competitive Chicago exchanges, the CBOE, the CME and the CBOT, signed a letter of intent to create a joint venture to introduce single-stock futures, the industry's newest product. Some see it as a first step in a logical combination that would put the combined Chicago derivatives exchanges back in the world's top spot. Others are sceptical. "That's been talked about forever," says a senior manager at a big Chicago trading firm. "I can't just see it happening."

11 Payments system, clearing houses and depositories

The clearing and settlement of payments and the custody of financial securities are crucial, though often little appreciated, dimensions of the operations of Wall Street or any other financial centre. Every business transaction generates a transfer of financial value, or a payment. The flow of payments is aided by the mechanisms – the institutions, technology, people and rules – that constitute the national payments system.

US payments system

The US payments system, like the US economy, is large and complex. The average daily volume of transfers through the payments system is $3 trillion. To put this in perspective, US GDP – the annual output of the US economy – is $8.2 trillion. So in less than three days, payments equivalent to the yearly output of the US economy are made through the US payments system.

There are two levels of payments, retail and wholesale. Retail payments are small-value payments for goods or services. Wholesale payments are large-value payments made among corporations, financial intermediaries, the government and government agencies. The latter include large corporate and financial-market payments for securities, such as stocks and bonds, money-market instruments or foreign exchange.

Retail payments by cheque or card account for more than nine-tenths of the number of payments made in the United States each year (see Table 11.1).

In terms of value, large-value payments account for almost nine-tenths of total US payments (see Table 11.2).

The Federal Reserve, the US central bank, is the central component of the US payments system, although certain private-sector institutions also have important roles. One reason for the creation of the Federal Reserve in 1913 was to provide a safe and efficient mechanism for the transfer of funds within the banking system. The Fed's role includes the provision of coin and currency, processing and clearing cheques, wire

Table 11.1 **Number of payments in the United States, 2001**

	Number (m)	%
Cheques	67,000	70.0
Cards	23,255	24.0
Automated clearing house	5,344	5.8
Large-value payments	157	0.2

Source: Federal Reserve Bank of New York

Table 11.2 **Value of payments in the United States, 2001**

	Value ($bn)	%
Large-value payments	679,121	87.5
Cheques	79,000	10.2
Automated clearing house	16,400	2.1
Cards	1,395	0.2

Source: Federal Reserve Bank of New York

transfers of funds and securities, and provisions for the settlement of cheques and other types of payments. Charges are made for the provision of many of these services to recover the costs of providing them.

Any payment is made in two stages: clearance and settlement. Clearance is the process of transmitting, reconciling and confirming payment instructions. Settlement is the last step in the transfer of value that constitutes payment. There are a number of ways in which payments are made at both the retail and wholesale levels.

Retail payments system

- Cash. The transfer of value is inherent in payment by cash; this constitutes settlement.
- Cheques. There are three routes for clearing and settling cheques: the Federal Reserve's cheque services; via correspondent banks (usually large money-centre banks); and through a bank clearing house – a private body set up by a group of banks whose members net their payments against each other. The last reduces

the number and scale of transactions since only outstanding balances are settled at the end of the business day. The New York Clearing House has traditionally served Wall Street in this capacity.

◪ Bank cards. Credit cards, debit cards, automated teller machine (ATM) and point-of-sale (POS) cards.

◪ Automated clearing house (ACH). An automatic electronic funds transfer method of payment primarily used for high-volume, low-value recurring payments, such as salaries, regular bill payments and social-security benefits. There are four ACH processors in the United States: the Federal Reserve System; VISANet ACH; the American Clearing House Association; and the Electronic Payments Network (EPN), operated by the New York Clearing House. In the Federal Reserve ACH service, transactions are cleared and settled through the accounts that financial institutions maintain at their regional Federal Reserve Bank. The three private-sector processors clear transactions among their members and use the Federal Reserve's ACH service for transactions with non-members. These processors use settlement services provided by the Federal Reserve.

Wholesale payments system

There are two large-value payments mechanisms in the United States.

◪ Fedwire. An electronic funds and securities transfer service operated by the Federal Reserve. Banks use Fedwire to make payments related to interbank overnight loans and interbank settlement transactions, and to send funds to other institutions on behalf of customers. Transfers on behalf of bank customers include funds used in the purchase or sale of government securities, deposits and large, time-sensitive payments. The Treasury and other federal agencies use Fedwire extensively to disburse and collect funds. Fedwire is used by the Federal Reserve Banks and their branches, the Treasury and other government agencies and around 9,500 depository institutions.

Fedwire is a fully automated real-time gross settlement system. When a sender of funds initiates a transfer, Fedwire clears the transfer and, simultaneously and almost instantaneously, debits the sending institution's account at its Federal Reserve Bank and credits the receiving institution's reserve account. The transfer becomes final as soon as the Federal Reserve Bank posts the credit. Any deposit-taking institution that maintains an account on the books of the Federal Reserve Bank may use Fedwire. Around 410,000 such payments are made daily, totalling on average $1.35 trillion.

◪ CHIPS (Clearing House Inter-Bank Payments System). A private-sector electronic funds payments service that transfers funds and settles transactions in US dollars. It was created in 1970 by the New York Clearing House to replace paper-based payments clearing arrangements, principally cheques. Like Fedwire, a sender must initiate a payment. CHIPS operates both real-time payments and a multilateral net system – payment transactions are netted multilaterally throughout the day and net balances are settled at the end of the day. In 2002, CHIPS had 59 participant members, including the main money-centre US banks, the US branches of large foreign banks and the Federal Reserve System. CHIPS transactions are typically related to international interbank transactions, such as dollar payments from foreign-currency transactions. Around 240,000 such payments are made daily, totalling about $1.2 trillion. CHIPS is estimated to handle 95% of all US dollar payments moving between countries.

Depositories and clearing houses

The clearance and settlement of trades in financial instruments – corporate stocks and bonds, US government securities, money-market instruments, municipal securities and derivatives – is undertaken by a variety of specialist clearing agencies. There are two types of clearing agencies registered with the SEC: depositories and clearing corporations. Depositories act as custodial agents for securities, allowing securities transfers via book-entry. They may also offer funds accounts and permit funds transfers as a means of payment. Depository institutions that maintain funds accounts at a Reserve Bank are also eligible to maintain book-entry securities accounts at a Reserve Bank. The National Book-Entries Securities system (NBES) is operated by the Federal Reserve as part of the Fedwire service. It services all marketable US Treasury securities, many federal agency securities and some international agency securities. Each day the NBES handles transfers of, on average, 48,000 securities, with a value of $643 billion.

The Depository Trust Company (DTC), a private company owned by the main money-centre banks, is the largest US securities depository, holding the bulk of the stocks, corporate bonds and money-market instruments issued in the United States.

Clearing corporations (clearing houses) provide a central processing mechanism through which dealers record trades with each other, account for them (usually through a netting system that reduces the number of securities deliveries) and settle interdealer security and money obligations. The majority of transactions are netted, with the movement of securities taking place at the depository or electronically. The clearing corporation also guarantees that transactions will be completed, itself assuming the risk that payments will not be made.

The principal clearing corporations are the following.

- Board of Trade Clearing Corporation (BOTCC), which clears and settles exchange-traded derivatives.
- Chicago Mercantile Exchange (CME), which clears and settles exchange-traded derivatives.
- Government Securities Clearing Corporation (GSCC), which clears and settles US government securities.
- Mortgage Backed Securities Clearing Corporation (MBSCC), which clears and settles mortgaged-backed securities.
- National Securities Clearing Corporation (NSCC), which clears and settles corporate stocks and municipal securities.
- New York Mercantile Exchange (NYMEX), which clears and settles exchange-traded derivatives.
- Options Clearing Corporation (OCC), which clears and settles exchange-traded derivatives.

Cross-border payments and international payments systems

These are payments and payments systems between the US and the rest of the world. Cross-border retail payments are largely made with cash, credit and debit cards. Wholesale, large-value cross-border payments are transmitted through networks operated by consortiums of international banks. The Society for Worldwide Interbank Financial Telecommunications (SWIFT) is the leading example. Settlement of dollar obligations arising from international transactions is usually made through correspondent banking relationships or a large-value payment system, notably CHIPS and Fedwire.

Federal Reserve Bank of New York

As the operating arms of the US central bank, the Federal Reserve Bank of New York (FRBNY) and the other regional Federal Reserve banks pro-vide important payments services for the federal government and the banking system. In its role as banker for the federal government, the Federal Reserve clears cheques drawn on the Treasury's account. Acting as fiscal agents for the government, the Reserve banks sell, redeem and act as paying agent for Treasury securities. They are also responsible for adjusting the volume of notes and coins in circulation in response to seasonal and cyclical movements in the public's requirement for cash.

The FRBNY has responsibility for the Federal Reserve's Second Dis-trict, which includes lower Manhattan. This means a special role in the provision of services to money-centre banks and financial firms. It oper-ates the Second District's cheque-clearing centre, which in conjunction with the New York Clearing House (see below) and correspondent banks processes Wall Street's cheques. Some banks use its facilities for the safekeeping and transfer of funds and securities.

The FRBNY plays a leading role in the Fedwire system, hosting the Wholesale Payments Product Office, which is responsible for running the Fed's large-value funds and securities transfer and net settlement services. Most US Fedwire transactions originate from Second District financial institutions. In 2001, total Fedwire transfers were $1.7 trillion per day of funds, of which $1 trillion originated in the Second District, and $873 billion per day in securities, of which $758 billion came from the Second District. Total Fedwire transfers in 2001 by the 12 regional Federal Reserve banks were $643 trillion-worth of funds and securities; the Second District's share was $445 trillion or 69%. The New York Fed also services CHIPS, the privately owned large-value payments system, through which transfers of $1.2 trillion per day were settled in 2001.

The Federal Reserve banks operate automated clearing house (ACH) facilities for transactions they process themselves and for all ACH pay-ments by the US government. They process around 75% of all items han-dled by ACH clearing houses in the US. In 2001, the 12 Federal Reserve banks processed 5.5 billion ACH transactions worth $15 billion. The New York Fed's share was 633m transactions (12%) valued at $3.5 trillion.

New York Clearing House

Established in 1853 to bring order to the chaotic state of New York bank settlements, the New York Clearing House (NYCH) is the oldest and largest US bank payments clearing corporation. It is privately owned by New York banks and processes $1.4 trillion payments per day for more than 1,000 institutions in the United States and around the world. Before its formation, interbank settlement was in cash, with porters travelling from bank to bank each day with bags of gold coins and bank notes, making or receiving payments to settle balances. Not only was this expensive and dangerous, it was also a highly inefficient banking practice. The appearance of lots of new Wall Street banks following the California gold-rush boom of 1849 (the number grew from 24 to 57 in four years) exacerbated the problem.

A bank cashier who was familiar with the workings of the City of London proposed the creation of a bank clearing house based on the London model. The suggestion was enthusiastically received, and the NYCH came into existence at 14 Wall Street with 52 banks participating. Instead of making settlements in cash, henceforth they were made via clearing-house certificates representing gold on deposit at member banks. Moreover, balances were netted and only the net amount had to be settled. Conditions of membership – weekly audits, minimum reserve levels and daily settlement of balances – enhanced the stability of the New York banks.

The NYCH played a crucial role in mitigating the financial panics that were a regular and devastating feature of Wall Street in the second half of the 19th century and the early 20th century. On ten occasions between 1860 and 1914, the members, acting in concert through the clearing house, fulfilled the lender of last resort function of a central bank. They created credit by making emergency issues of clearing-house certificates, probably illegally, to provide credit to prevent New York banks and businesses from failing. The establishment of the Federal Reserve System in 1913 relieved the NYCH of its unofficial central-banking role. It focused on facilitating the completion of financial transactions by clearing the payments involved. Member banks exchanged cheques or other forms of payment among themselves, after which the NYCH recorded the resulting charges to their accounts. Outstanding balances were settled through the New York Fed.

The NYCH now has three subsidiaries that undertake the clearance of transactions: the Clearing House Inter-Bank Payments System (CHIPS); the Electronic Payments Network (EPN); and the Small Value Payments Company (SPVCO). They are separately managed but share technology and operational resources.

Clearing House Inter-Bank Payments System
Established in 1970, the Clearing House Inter-Bank Payments System (CHIPS) is a computerised payments network for direct transfers of

large-value payments between banks, both members and non-members, eliminating the use of official cheques. Terminals in banks are connected to a central computer at the NYCH which routes the payments between sending and receiving institutions. At the close of business, a bank receives a report on all the messages sent or received by it. Participants are required to settle their net balances through the FRBNY. The value of transactions handled daily by CHIPs has increased from $4m in 1971 to $1.6 billion in 1981, $8.6 billion in 1991 and $1.2 trillion in 2001. There are on average 242,000 transactions per day. CHIPs handles 95% of all cross-border US dollar payments in the world.

Electronic Payments Network

Formed in 1975, the Electronic Payments Network (EPN) is the largest private-sector automatic computer-based clearing and settlement operation for making recurring transactions, such as payroll payments. It provides a national network for domestic consumer and commercial payments. It has 1,200 member financial institutions, comprising 179 commercial banks, 70 savings banks, 592 credit unions and 27 savings and loan associations. In 2001, it processed 1 billion transactions with a total value of $4.1 trillion.

Small Value Payments Company

Set up in 1998, the Small Value Payments Company (SPVCO) focuses on the electronic exchange of cheques to "electronify" small-value payments.

Depository Trust & Clearing Company

The other large privately owned Wall Street clearing corporation is the Depository Trust & Clearing Company (DTCC). Formed in 1999, it is a holding company for two subsidiaries, a depository, the Depository Trust Company (DTC), and a clearing corporation, the National Securities Clearing Corporation (NSCC). In 2002, it acquired four more clearing corporation subsidiaries, the Government Securities Clearing Corporation (GSCC), the Mortgage Backed Securities Clearing Corporation (MBSCC), the Emerging Markets Clearing Corporation (EMCC) and EuroCCO. There is also Omego, a joint venture with Thomson Financial, a financial-information provider, which develops and markets trade-processing software. The DTCC is owned by its principal users – big banks, broker-dealers and other financial-services entities, including the National Association of Securities Dealers (NASD) and the NYSE.

The NYSE had operated a system for the clearance and settlement of securities transactions since 1892, but in the late 1960s, as the volume of trading soared, it almost collapsed under an avalanche of paperwork. The DTC and the NSCC were established to solve different aspects of the "paper crunch" through the application of computer technology and new thinking on clearance and settlement.

The DTC, formed in 1973, is the world's largest securities depository and a clearing house for the settlement of securities trading activity. It provides a wide range of securities-custody, asset and related services for its participants. The DTC's network links more than 11,000 broker-dealers, custodian banks and institutional investors, as well as transfer agents, paying agents and exchange and redemption agents for securities issuers.

As common custodian of some 2m securities issues, the DTC enhances securities industry efficiency. Most of these securities take the form of electronic entries, rather than countless pieces of paper. The issues are worth more than $20 trillion. The DTC processes over 200m institutional trade confirmations per year and $1 trillion in cash dividend, interest and reorganisation payments.

The NSCC, created in 1976, consolidated and streamlined the hitherto separate clearing operations of the NYSE, the American Stock Exchange and the NASD. It is the oldest and much the largest of the DTCC's clearing corporations. It processes virtually all broker-to-broker stock and corporate- and municipal-bond trades in the US. Its principal activities are centralised clearance, settlement and post-trade information services for equities, bonds, mutual-fund and annuity transactions to more than 2,000 brokers, dealers, banks, mutual funds, insurance carriers and other financial intermediaries. It guarantees completion for all trades involving stocks, corporate and municipal bonds, money-market instruments, American depository receipts, exchange-traded funds, unit investment trusts, mutual funds, insurance-industry products and other securities. The NSCC nets trades and payments among participants, reducing the volume of securities and payments that have to be exchanged by an average of 95%. In 2001, it processed around 14m transactions per day.

12 Regulation and regulators

The financial-services industry is one of the most heavily regulated sectors of the US economy. The government regulates financial institutions and the financial markets for three main reasons: to safeguard the soundness and integrity of the financial system; to protect investors and depositors; and to enhance control of monetary policy. To accomplish these ends, the banking sector and the futures and securities markets are regulated by a variety of agencies and institutions.

Banking regulation

The soundness of the banking system is so fundamental to the well-being of the economy that the regulation and supervision of banking is almost as old as the banking system itself. Regulation involves the establishment of regulatory agencies that formulate and issue specific rules and regulations for the conduct of banking. Supervision concerns the soundness of the industry in general and of individual banks in particular. It involves continuous monitoring of the conduct of the industry and of individual banks by regulatory agencies to ensure prudent operation and conformity with laws and regulations.

The aims of bank regulation are to protect depositors and the deposit-insurance fund; to safeguard the economy against the malfunctioning of the banking system; and to guard bank clients from the misuse of power by banks.

The regulation and supervision of the 10,000 banks and numerous other deposit-taking institutions in the United States is conducted by a variety of agencies with overlapping jurisdictions. This bewildering "system" is the outcome of historical developments and the dual state and federal chartering of banks in the United States. The agencies and the depository institutions for which they are responsible are summarised in Figure 12.1.

The regulation and supervision of the US banking system is shared among the following bodies.

Office of the Comptroller of the Currency
The Office of the Comptroller of the Currency (occ) charters, regulates and supervises the 3,000 federally chartered national banks, which own

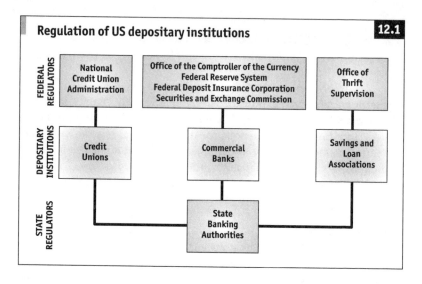

Regulation of US depositary institutions 12.1

more than half the assets in the commercial-banking system. It also supervises the federal branches and agencies of foreign banks. The OCC was established as a bureau of the US Treasury Department in 1863. It is based in Washington DC and has six district offices as well as an office in London to supervise the international activities of US national banks. The comptroller is appointed by the president for a five-year term.

The OCC supervises national banks throughout the country and carries out on-site inspections. It issues rules, legal interpretations and regulations about banking, bank investments, bank community development activities and other aspects of bank operations.

Federal Reserve System

The Federal Reserve System (Fed) is responsible for supervising the 1,000 state chartered banks that are members of the Federal Reserve System (jointly with the state banking authorities), all bank holding companies, the foreign activities of member banks, the US activities of foreign banks, and Edge Act corporations (through which US banks may conduct international banking business). It also has secondary responsibility for the national banks (with the OCC).

The Fed, which comprises the Federal Reserve Board in Washington DC and 12 regional Federal Reserve banks, was established by Congress in 1913 as the central bank of the United States. Some of the regulations issued by the Fed apply to the whole banking industry, but others apply only to member banks: all national banks, which are members by law, and those state banks that have chosen to join. The Federal Reserve Board also issues regulations that implement federal legislation regarding consumer credit protection. The bank supervisory functions are co-ordinated by the Board's Division of Banking Supervision and Regulation.

The Federal Reserve Bank of New York, which is responsible for the Federal Reserve System's Second District that includes Wall Street, conducts on-site and off-site examinations of member banks and branches of foreign banks in its district.

Federal Deposit Insurance Corporation
The Federal Deposit Insurance Corporation (FDIC) and the state banking authorities are jointly responsible for the 6,000 state banks that have FDIC insurance but are not members of the Federal Reserve System. The FDIC is an independent executive agency that was established in 1933 to insure bank deposits. The FDIC is managed by a five-member board that includes the Comptroller of the Currency, the director of the Office of Thrift Supervision and three members appointed by the president.

Securities and Exchange Commission
Banks come under the regulatory and supervisory authority of the Securities and Exchange Commission (SEC) as publicly held companies, and are required to comply with its regulations regarding the disclosure of financial information and file Exchange Act reports. Bank securities offered for sale to the public must be registered with the SEC. It has authority to investigate and take enforcement action regarding securities violations committed by banks and bank holding companies.

State banking authorities
The state banking authorities are jointly responsible for the 1,000 state banks that are members of the Federal Reserve System (with the Fed) and the 6,000 state banks that have FDIC insurance (with the FDIC). They have sole responsibility for the 500 banks that do not have FDIC insurance.

National Credit Union Administration
Established in 1970, the National Credit Union Administration (NCUA) is an independent federal agency that is responsible for chartering, insuring, supervising and examining federal credit unions, and for the

administration of the National Credit Union Share Insurance Fund (NCUSIF). The chartering and supervision of federal credit unions and the insurance of members' accounts through the NCUSIF were provided for by the Federal Credit Union Act of 1934.

Office of Thrift Supervision

The Office of Thrift Supervision (OTS) is a bureau of the Treasury Department, established by Congress in 1989 in the wake of the savings and loans scandals of the 1980s to act as the primary regulator for the approximately 2,000 federal and state thrift institutions belonging to the Savings Association Insurance Fund. The OTS charters federal thrift institutions. It develops regulations governing the savings and loan industry and supervises and examines thrift institutions.

Commodities markets regulation

The Commodity Futures Trading Commission (CFTC) was set up by Congress in 1974 as an independent agency responsible for the regulation and supervision of the US commodities futures and options markets. It protects market participants against manipulation, abusive trade practices and fraud through continuous market surveillance and has powers to order exchanges to take specific action to restore an orderly market. It reviews all proposed new contracts. All individuals working in the futures markets are required to register with the National Futures Association, a self-regulatory organisation approved by the CFTC.

The CFTC has five commissioners, with staggered annual retirements, who are appointed by the president. They develop and implement agency policy and direction. The CFTC is based in Washington DC and has offices in Chicago, Kansas City, Minneapolis and New York (cities with futures exchanges) and Los Angeles (for enforcement purposes).

Securities industry and securities markets regulation

The SEC is responsible for the regulation of the securities industry and securities markets. It is a civil law-enforcement agency, the purpose of which is to enforce federal securities laws to protect investors and maintain fair, honest and efficient markets. For the protection of investors, the SEC requires public companies to make disclosures of financial and other relevant information to enable investors to make informed judgments about a company's securities. To safeguard the integrity of the markets, the SEC oversees the enforcement of federal legislation governing the activities of stock exchanges, options exchanges, broker-dealers, investment advisers, mutual funds, public holding companies and the accountancy profession.

Although it is the primary overseer and regulator of the US securities markets, the SEC works closely with many other institutions, including private-sector organisations, state securities regulators, self-regulatory organisations, principally the stock exchanges, other federal departments and agencies and Congress.

In the wake of the 1929 stockmarket crash, Congress passed the Securities Act 1933 and the Securities Exchange Act 1934. The intention was to restore investor confidence in the integrity of the capital market through government oversight and more formal market structures. The principal purposes of the legislation were to ensure that:

◪ companies publicly offering securities for investment inform the public truthfully about their business, the securities on offer and the risks involved in investing;

◪ securities markets professionals – investment bankers, brokers, dealers and stock exchanges – treat investors fairly and honestly, giving priority to investors' interests.

The SEC was established by the Securities Exchange Act 1934 as a government agency to give effect to these intentions. It has five commissioners appointed by the president who each serve a five-year term with staggered annual retirements. The commissioners determine the interpretation of federal securities laws, the amendment of existing rules and the enforcement of rules and laws. They also propose new legislation to Congress to take account of market developments.

The SEC is based in Washington DC and has 11 regional and district offices. It has 2,900 staff and four divisions:

◪ Division of Corporation Finance. This oversees corporate disclosure of important information to investors. Corporations are required to comply with disclosure regulations when stock is initially sold and afterwards.

◪ Division of Market Regulation. This establishes and maintains standards for fair, orderly and efficient markets by regulating the principal securities market participants: broker-dealer firms; self-regulatory organisations (SROs), including the stock exchanges, the National Association of Securities Dealers (NASD), the Municipal Securities Rulemaking Board (MSRB), and clearing houses; transfer agents (parties that maintain records of stock and bond owners); and securities information processors. SROS are membership organisations that create and enforce rules for their members based on federal securities laws. Those that are overseen by the SEC are at the forefront of the regulation of broker-dealers. The division also oversees the Securities Investor Protection Corporation (SIPC), a private, non-profit organisation established by Congress in 1970. Modelled on the Federal Deposit Insurance Corporation (FDIC), which insures bank deposits, the SIPC protects investors against losses if a brokerage firm is forced to liquidate.

◪ Division of Investment Management. This oversees and regulates the $15 trillion investment-management industry. It also administers the securities laws affecting mutual funds and other investment companies and investment advisers.

◪ Division of Enforcement. This investigates possible violations of securities laws. When appropriate, it recommends SEC action, either in a federal court or before an administrative law judge, and negotiates settlements on behalf of the SEC. Although the SEC has only civil enforcement authority, it works closely with criminal law-enforcement agencies throughout the country to bring criminal cases when appropriate.

The Sarbanes-Oxley Act of 2002 gave the SEC additional responsibilities. It brought the accountancy profession within its oversight by establishing a new Public Company Accounting Oversight Board with members appointed by the SEC. The legislation also required the chief executives and chief financial officers of public companies to certify personally that the reports their companies file with the SEC are accurate and complete. To pay for the additional workload, the agency's budget was nearly doubled to $467m. When he signed the act on July 30th 2002, President George W. Bush hailed its provisions as "the most far-reaching reforms of American business practices since the Great Depression".

13 Global money centre

New York is America's principal domestic money centre. It is also one of the three global money centres, together with London and Tokyo. The global money centres provide a comprehensive range of financial services, especially wholesale financial markets, to a world-wide clientele. Each is the biggest money centre in its time zone.

There are other important money centres, which serve an international clientele and have many ties to the global centres. These regional international money centres supply financial services to a region (such as North America, Europe or Asia) and intermediate financial flows from the global centres, other regional centres and domestic centres. The principal regional international money centres are in North America: Chicago (especially for derivatives), Boston (especially for asset management), San Francisco, Los Angeles, Philadelphia and Toronto; in Europe: Frankfurt, Zurich, Paris, Amsterdam, Milan and Madrid; and in Asia: Hong Kong, Singapore, Sydney and Seoul, with Manila, Shanghai and Taipei growing rapidly. Bahrain, Rio and Johannesburg are also significant regional money centres.

There are additionally a number of offshore money centres. These are financial entrepôts that act as intermediaries for international flows but have little connection with their local financial system. Examples of such financial flags of convenience are the Cayman Islands, the Bahamas, the Netherlands Antilles, Luxembourg and the Channel Islands. At the other end of the spectrum are innumerable main-street money centres, cities that serve the financial requirements of their locality. If they are unable to fulfil the needs of their local clientele, they can supply introductions to specialist providers in money centres higher up the hierarchy.

How does Wall Street stand in relation to the other main money centres? Unfortunately, it is not possible to make direct comparisons between money centres in respect of many relevant criteria because of lack of comparative international data. Moreover, even the data that are available are generally collected by country rather than by money centre. The following tables present a variety of international yardsticks that are of relevance to aspects of Wall Street activities and are indicative of its standing.

Table 13.1 **Domestic stockmarkets, end 2001**

	Market value ($ trillion)	% of market value	Turnover ($bn)
New York	11,027	41	10,489
NASDAQ	2,897	11	10,935
Tokyo	2,265	8	1,661
London	2,150	8	4,551
Euronext	1,844	7	3,180
Deutsche Börse	1,072	4	1,440
Toronto	615	2	460
Italy	527	2	2,269
Switzerland	527	2	594
Others	3,856	14	–
Total	26,780	100	–

Source: International Financial Services, London

Table 13.2 **Markets for foreign equities, 2000**

	Number of foreign corporations listed	% of listings	Turnover ($bn)	% of world turnover
NASDAQ	488	16	844	15
London	448	15	2,669	48
New York	443	14	1,142	21
Euronext	420	14	74	1
Germany	245	8	321	6
Stockholm	19	1	96	2
Others	1,019	33	380	7
Total	3,082		5,526	

Source: London Stock Exchange

Securities

The New York Stock Exchange (NYSE) is much the largest in the world. By market value, it is five times the size of the stockmarkets of Tokyo, London and the Euronext group (Paris, Amsterdam, Brussels and Lisbon) and ten times the size of the Frankfurt market. NASDAQ came second in market value in 2001, although the subsequent substantial depreciation of the value of many NASDAQ-listed stocks may have lowered its ranking. The

Table 13.3 **Banking industry, 2000**

	Number of banks	Number of branches ('000)	Bank deposits ($ trillion)	Return on assets (%)
US	8,315	64.1	4.2	1.9
Japan	3,085	40.5	4.5	0.2
Germany	2,915	43.3	2.4	0.4
France	1,116	25.7	0.9	0.8
UK	411	12.5	2.6	1.4

Source: International Financial Services, London

Table 13.4 **Foreign-exchange trading, 2001**

	Daily average ($bn)	% share
UK	504	31
US	254	16
Japan	147	9
Singapore	101	6
Germany	88	5
Switzerland	71	4
Hong Kong	67	4
France	48	3
Others	338	21
Total	1,618	100

Source: Bank for International Settlements, triennial census of foreign-exchange and derivatives trading

two leading US exchanges had much higher trading volumes than any other exchange, NASDAQ's being fractionally higher than the NYSE.

In recent years many large international corporations have listed on foreign stock exchanges, seeking to tap capital markets around the world. NASDAQ has the largest number of listed foreign corporations, followed by London, New York and Euronext. But London has much the largest volume of trading in foreign equities, followed at some distance by the NYSE.

Banking

The United States has a far greater number of banks than any other country. This is a result of historic banking regulations that inhibited bank mergers and protected local banks. Many US banks are small units with only a few local branches, or even just a lone headquarters. Deposits provide a better indication of the scale of a banking system than banks or bank buildings. In total, US banks have the second-highest level of deposits, a little less than Japan. But in relation to the size of the US economy, the level of bank deposits is significantly lower than in the other major economies, reflecting the importance of the financial markets rather than financial intermediaries in the United States as well as the low level of personal saving. It has the lowest average of deposits per bank and the highest rate of bank profitability as measured by return on assets.

Foreign exchange

Wall Street ranks second as a centre for foreign-exchange trading behind London, which has been the world leader in this activity for many years. Between them, London and New York account for almost half of world foreign-exchange trading, conducting much larger volumes of business than other centres.

Asset management

US money centres occupy six of the top ten positions as locations for fund management in a survey conducted in 2000 by Thomson Financial that ranked cities by institutional equity holdings. The survey revealed a clear division between the global money centres, London, New York, Tokyo, and also Boston, which constitute a top tier of locations for fund management. San Francisco, Los Angeles, Paris, Philadelphia, Zurich and Denver constitute a second echelon with significantly smaller total portfolios.

The United States is much the largest source of financial assets under management, particularly pensions and mutual funds, categories in which US assets constitute more than half the world totals. The level of US financial assets explains why so many US cities are important centres for asset management.

Derivatives

The pioneering roles of the Chicago Mercantile Exchange and the Chicago Board of Trade in the development of financial futures, and the Chicago Board Options Exchange and the American Stock Exchange in the case of exchange-traded options, are reflected in the leading position

Table 13.5 **Asset management, top ten locations, 1999**

City	Country	Assets[a] ($bn)
London	UK	2,461
New York	US	2,363
Tokyo	Japan	2,058
Boston	US	1,871
San Francisco	US	726
Los Angeles	US	569
Paris	France	458
Philadelphia	US	419
Zurich	Switzerland	414
Denver	US	340

a Assets under management ranked by institutional equity holdings.
Source: Thomson Financial, *Target Cities Report 2000*

Table 13.6 **Sources of assets, 1999** ($bn)

	Pensions	Insurance	Mutual funds	Total
US	7,765	3,168	6,843	17,776
Japan	1,544	1,825	464	3,833
UK	1,365	1,333	371	3,069
France	71	714	655	1,440
Germany	139	819	237	1,195
Netherlands	427	242	75	744
Others	1,667	3,399	2,428	7,494
Total	12,978	11,500	11,073	35,551

Source: International Financial Services, London

of the United States in exchange-traded derivatives. However, as other exchanges have developed derivatives trading the US proportion of world exchange-traded derivatives has diminished, falling from 46% in 1995 to 35% in 2001.

The most dynamic expansion in financial derivatives in recent years has been in over-the-counter (OTC) options and swaps developed by banks for clients, an activity in which US securities industry firms play a leading role. Wall Street ranks second in OTC derivatives turnover

Table 13.7 **Exchange-traded derivatives turnover, 2001**

	Annual number of contracts (m)	% share
US	1,577	35
South Korea	867	19
Germany	674	15
France	328	7
UK	302	7
Brazil	192	4
Japan	159	4
Others	405	9
Total	4,504	100

Source: Tradedata

Table 13.8 **Over-the-counter derivatives turnover, 2001[a]**

	$bn	% share
UK	275	36
US	135	18
Germany	97	13
France	67	9
Japan	22	3
Switzerland	15	2
Others	153	20
Total	764	100

a Average daily turnover in April.
Source: Bank for International Settlements, triennial census of foreign-exchange and derivatives trading

behind the City of London, which is the leading booking location by a sizeable margin.

Insurance

The United States is much the largest insurance market in the world, generating more than one-third of total premium income. This provides a strong domestic base for the US insurance industry – the home market is the principal focus of most US insurance firms. Insurance companies are big institutional investors and purchasers of financial instruments.

Table 13.9 **Insurance markets, 2000**[a]

	Total ($bn)	Life (% of total)	Non-life (% of total)	% world share
US	865	51	49	35
Japan	504	80	20	21
UK	237	76	24	10
Germany	124	45	55	5
France	122	70	30	5
Italy	63	59	41	3
South Korea	58	76	24	2
Others	471	58	42	19
World total	2,444	62	38	

a Gross insurance premiums.
Source: International Financial Services, London

Table 13.10 **Employment in leading money centres**

	Employees ('000)
Tokyo (1997)	522
New York City (2001)	378
London (2001)	324
Hong Kong (1996)	158
Frankfurt (2001)	80

Employment

Employment in financial services in money centres seems a straightforward comparative measure of magnitude. But in practice, employment data is fraught with problems arising from discrepancies in city boundaries, job classifications and the frequency of censuses. Table 13.10 presents employment statistics from various official sources of the numbers working in banking and insurance (both retail and wholesale, except for London, which is wholesale only) in five large money centres.

Using employment as a yardstick, Tokyo emerges as the world's leading money centre. But this is at odds with other evidence. Much of Tokyo's workforce is engaged in domestic retail activities and not really comparable to the New York or London workforces, which mostly undertake the wholesale financial activities that make them global money centres. Discounting the Tokyo workforce to take account of this, it appears that employment in wholesale financial services in each of the three global money centres is probably 300,000–350,000 people. This suggests a total workforce of around 1m for the global money centres. The data for Hong Kong and Frankfurt, two of the leading and larger international regional money centres, suggest that maybe a further 1m people work in wholesale financial services in the dozen or so regional centres. Thus the total wholesale international financial-services industry workforce is (a flying guesstimate) around 2m.

14 Wall Street in crisis

Crisis and Wall Street are words that have been linked together many times over the years. Usually the combination has been simply sensationalist, but on two previous occasions it was well warranted: in the early 1930s; and in the mid-1970s. In the early 2000s, once again, the juxtaposition was fully justified.

The Wall Street crises of the early 1930s, mid-1970s and early 2000s have several features in common: a slump in stock prices, that alienated investors; an upsurge of financial scandals, that generated a hostile political reaction; and a downturn in revenues and profits that undermined the profitability and potentially the stability of financial services firms. An additional factor in the early 2000s was terrorism, that threatened death and destruction.

The 90% fall in the Dow between summer 1929 and summer 1932 and the 50% decline between early 1973 and late 1974, led to a widespread loss of investor confidence in the stock market and financial intermediaries. Both declines were followed by the withdrawal of millions of individual investors from the stock market. Investor disenchantment not only blighted the business of brokerage firms and sales of mutual funds, it created a political climate sympathetic to legislative reform.

The revelations of outrageous market practices by the Pecora hearings of 1932–34 galvanised politicians to pass a raft of New Deal reforms of the financial services industry, including the creation of the Securities and Exchange Commission as Wall Street's cop on the corner. By making Wall Street a more honest and more efficient marketplace they contributed to its subsequent expansion and prosperity, though at the time practitioners resented the interference in their money-making activities and the increased costs arising from regulation. Moreover, regulation inevitably introduced market distortions, of which the most drastic was the Glass-Steagall Act's separation of securities, banking and insurance activities, a separation unknown in the rest of the world. Such distortions of market forces have a cost in terms of efficiency and the international competitiveness of the industry.

The falling stock markets of the early 1930s and mid-1970s mirrored the economic recessions in both decades. Depressed stock prices and negative economic growth are bad news for financial services industry firms and financial centres. Every bank and firm was adversely affected, though only a single major firm needed rescue; Kidder Peabody in 1930. But on both occasions there were large-scale lay-offs of staff and shareholders saw little return on their investments. After the crisis of the early 1930s, Wall Street business was stunted and only moderately profitable for a generation. In the mid-1970s, the crisis on Wall Street made a significant contribution to the fiscal crisis that overtook New York City in 1975. Activity was subdued for a decade from 1973, the lack of alternative opportunities leading the major money-centre banks to pursue petro-dollar recycling business with an unbridled enthusiasm that their shareholders had much cause to regret in the 1980s.

Crisis of the early 2000s: investor confidence

After a bull market lasting almost 18 years, investors had become used to the comforting idea that financial markets, despite the occasional bout of turbulence such as the 1987 "market correction", went one way only – up. But after peaking in early 2000 stock prices lurched lower and lower – by summer 2002 the Dow was one-quarter off its peak and the NASDAQ Composite was down by a breath-taking three-quarters. Moreover, individual stocks staged collapses much more spectacular than the stock indexes, some, such as Enron and WorldCom, becoming worthless.

The anguish and anger of stockholders went wider and deeper than before, because there were many more of them – 84 million – and because they had factored the inflated market valuations of their mutual fund and pension plans into their expectations of a prosperous lifestyle or a comfortable retirement. A likely outcome was the withdrawal from the stock market of millions of individual investors, as in the 1930s and 1970s. Among investors locked into retirement and other savings plans more conservative investment strategies became favoured, including the forsaking of actively managed funds for cheaper trackers. Moreover, there was widespread support among investors for attempts at legal redress from financial services firms, and for political retribution upon Wall Street and its ways.

Crisis of the early 2000s: scandals

As stock prices headed south Wall Street scandals soared, generating a vision of rampant greed, sharp practice and downright dishonesty in the financial services industry and in corporate boardrooms generally. "Never", Henry Paulson, chief executive of Goldman Sachs, told the

National Press Club in Washington, had American business "been under such scrutiny, and, to be blunt, much of it is deserved", adding that US corporations were held in a "position of low repute" not seen "in my lifetime".

There were four distinct strands to the Wall Street scandals of the early 21st century: the role of securities industry analysts; the conduct of initial public offerings (IPOs); accountancy firm conflicts of interest; and stock options and executive pay-offs.

Scandals: securities industry analysts

By the late 1990s, as the securities analyst's "sell note" became an endangered species, it was clear that most reports of investment bank analysts did not provide a dispassionate critique of corporate stock performance and prospects. In fact, their services had been co-opted by corporate finance departments, one of the investment banks' prime profit centres (particularly in the boom years), to promote clients' new issues or to cultivate relations with potential clients that might lead to new corporate finance mandates. In fulfilment of these functions, analysts shamelessly pumped up the bubble in Internet and technology stocks that ballooned in 1998–1999 and burst spectacularly in 2000.

The victims of the corruption of the role of the analysts were those who believed their self-serving "analysis" of the value of the stocks they promoted, which was millions of small investors. Not that the latter were blameless, displaying a greedy appetite for get-rich-quick tips. Many analysts and some Wall Street economists also perpetrated a broader deception, a piece of wishful thinking that they may well have come to believe themselves, that of the "new economic paradigm". According to this fairy tale, the trade cycle had been abolished, the e-tech revolution was producing miracles in productivity and prosperity, and conventional measures of stock and market valuations were redundant. Ingenious mathematical formulas were fabricated to justify stratospheric stock prices. New yardsticks of value and performance were developed while measures based on earnings, profits and dividends were felt to be irrelevant in this brave new world. It was thoroughly bogus, but it was what the "day traders" and the professionals too wanted to hear and believe.

In spring 2002, Merrill Lynch paid a $100 million fine to settle accusations of analysts' conflicts of interest, introducing new procedures to eliminate such conflicts. It was no small irony that the Glass-Steagall restrictions were being laid to rest by the Gramm-Leach-Bliley Act 1999 at the very moment that a new set of abuses, similar in essence if different in detail to those that brought about its introduction in 1933, were being perpetrated. The revelations about what Merrill Lynch's stock analysts had truly thought about some of the Internet stocks they were peddling (Henry Blodget: "crap") led to calls for the introduction of a new Glass-Steagall-style separation of securities analysis and corporate finance. Whether this meant the establishment of a legal fire-break between firms undertaking these activities, or the strengthening of internal "Chinese walls", remained to be seen. But the invocation of Glass-Steagall was symptomatic of a revived political will in Washington to set Wall Street's house in order.

Scandals: conduct of IPOs

The conduct of IPOs was another controversy that focused on the investment banks. One issue was under-pricing, many new issues doubling in price when trading commenced, prompting some issuers to protest that they had been short-changed in the amount of capital raised. But it was very nice for those who had been allocated stock. Complaints from ordinary investors about being unable to obtain initial public offering allocations were ignored by the investment banks that reserved "hot issues" for favoured customers. More gravely it was alleged that they also reserved them for the senior managers of companies that gave them corporate finance mandates, including the issuing companies themselves, allocations which amounted to kickbacks. In January 2002 Credit Suisse First Boston paid a $100 million fine to settle investigations into its IPO allocation practices. Other firms also came under investigation, particularly Salomon Smith Barney, which had provided IPO allocations to Bernie Ebbers, the former chief executive of WorldCom, who had profited from them to the tune of $11m.

The Ebbers revelation in September 2002 prompted the *Wall Street Journal* to observe that: "The question isn't just how financial firms allocate hot shares: it is why they allocate them. That's what markets are for. Why can't the capitalists embrace capitalism?... Stalin would be proud of the way IPO shares are distributed." The adoption of an auction system of IPO allocations was advocated by critics as a means of achieving better prices for issuers and eliminating favouritism. With the issue under scrutiny by the House Financial Services Committee and the SEC, which had asked the National Association of Securities Dealers and the New York Stock Exchange to come up with solutions, and with New

York State attorney general Eliot Spitzer also on the case, legislation was again on the cards.

Scandals: accounting firms conflicts of interest

During the 1990s the Big Five accountancy firms rapidly developed the consultancy side of their activities, since this part of their business mix, rather than the mature audit side, offered potential for highly profitable growth. But a potential problem arose when both audit and consultancy services were provided to the same corporate client – the danger being that the audit function would be conducted in such a way as not to disrupt the lucrative consultancy relationship, meaning less rigorously.

Just such a dilemma appears to have arisen in the case of accountants Arthur Andersen and Enron, an energy firm. Following Enron's spectacular collapse in December 2001, it emerged that far from showing an accurate picture of the corporation's liabilities the accounts failed to disclose enormous off-balance sheet items and a vast burden of hidden losses. Moreover, the shredding of paperwork relating to Enron in some Andersen offices established that at least some Andersen executives were aware of the shortcomings of its audit, despite having signed off the auditor's report giving Enron's accounts a clean bill of health. For Arthur Andersen the end came in June 2002 when a court found it guilty of obstructing justice during an SEC investigation. But there were plenty more corporate accounting scandals in the pipeline and Andersen was not the only one of the Big Five leading firms of accountants to be caught up in them.

The revelations about false accounting, the cavalier conduct of senior executives, some of whom used the corporations they managed as personal piggy-banks, and the compromised oversight by the accountancy profession, the supposed guardians of the integrity of corporate accounts, fundamentally undermined confidence in the financial markets. Even the best-run and strictly audited companies were blighted by the crisis of confidence in corporate accounts, since if the numbers were not to be believed how could a valuation be put on a corporation? And what was an appropriate stock price? The matter went to the very heart of the market system.

The Enron-Andersen scandal and the threat to the integrity of corporate accounts prompted Congress to pass new legislation, the Sarbanes-Oxley Act of July 2002, which placed a ban on auditors providing nine kinds of non-audit services, established a new board to oversee audits of public companies, itself being overseen by the SEC, and toughened punishments for executives who falsified accounts. This legislation, which was the most radical of several proposals, was widely supported in Congress and rapidly received the assent of the president.

Scandals: stock options and executive pay-offs

In the 1980s and 1990s there was an enormous expansion in the scale of executive stock options. This was justified as providing an incentive for management to maximise a corporation's stock price, which was its overriding objective according to the prevailing theory of shareholder value.

In fact, in some cases far from aligning the interests of management and stockholders the granting of substantial stock options to senior executives prompted them to ramp the stock price, cash in their options and get out. Some pushed up the stock price by fraudulent accounting. Others through a stream of acquisitions, taking advantage of the favourable provisions of acquisition accounting. But whatever the device, the eventual outcome was the same – the collapse of the company. Not that it mattered to those who had already sold their options – an investigation by the *Financial Times* revealed that senior managers and directors of the 25 largest US public companies to go bankrupt between January 2001 and July 2002 walked away with gross payments totalling $3.3 billion – "a stunning pay-off for failure".

The sec responded to the succession of corporate collapses and revelations of accounting irregularities by publishing new rules in June 2002 requiring chief executives to vouch personally for their corporation's financial statements, on pain of possible prosecution if they proved false or misleading. The obligatory certification of the accuracy of corporate accounts by chief executives was also a provision of the Sarbanes-Oxley corporate fraud act, wilful violation of which can be punished with a 20-year prison sentence.

In the 1930s, the revelations of the Pecora hearings and other reminders of Wall Street's misdemeanours had sustained legislative reform for a full seven years. Was Sarbanes-Oxley just the beginning of the early 21st-century political reaction to the Wall Street scandals? With a long and lengthening line of financiers and corporate executives under indictment, whose trials would keep Wall Street in the public eye for years, would there be further regulatory legislation? And what shape would the financial services industry be in at the end of the process?

New century, new crisis

The early 2000s saw a sharp downturn in the level of activity and profitability of most Wall Street firms. Two of their most profitable activities, mergers and acquisitions and corporate capital raising were particularly hard hit, depressing the revenues of the securities industry. Firms adjusted to falling revenues by cutting costs, firing thousands of staff. Nonetheless, many experienced worsening revenue:cost ratios as income fell faster than expenditure.

The deteriorating operating ratios at many Wall Street firms meant an increased risk of financial problems at individual firms and in the sector as a whole. Since the 1970s, securities industry firms have often sought to compensate for revenue falls by attempting to generate profits from proprietary trading. Some have succeeded, others have simply exacerbated their problems. Moreover, the general effect was to increase the risk level of the industry as a whole. A further cause for concern about the sector was that declining profitability leads to the depletion of reserves, rendering individual firms and the industry as a whole more vulnerable to unanticipated external shocks. Yet another threat arose from the pack of impending legal suits by investors seeking compensation for losses. These included the largest ever class action consolidating 300 individual suits against 40 investment banks, which if successful could cost them as much as $6 billion. Overall, the downturn of the early 2000s increased the likelihood that a major Wall Street firm would get into difficulties, though the extent of the threat was uncertain. But the size of the leading firms following the growth and concentration of the 1990s, meant that if one or more of them did get into trouble its problems might well pose a systemic risk to the financial system itself.

After the September 11th attacks terrorism presented a real and potentially lethal threat. But it had not been the first time that Wall Street, the capital of capitalism, had been the target of terrorists. In 1921, a massive bomb exploded in the street outside the J.P. Morgan building at 23 Wall Street, killing 30 passers-by. Apparently it was placed by anti-capitalist anarchists, but the perpetrators were never caught. In 1975, a bomb placed by Puerto Rican nationalists at the Fraunces Tavern, an 18th-century landmark hostelry, killed four. And in 1993, there was a failed attempt to blow up the Twin Towers with a truck bomb in the basement. Further testament to the attraction of financial districts as targets for terrorists are the attacks on London's financial district, the City, by IRA bombers in the 1980s and 1990s. But the total destruction of the

World Trade Centre was of a different order of magnitude, as was the lingering threat posed by terrorism.

It could mark the beginning of the end for high-profile specialist financial services districts such as Wall Street and the City of London. For years technology has permitted financial services firms to locate almost anywhere, but most leading firms have maintained their key front offices in the historic financial districts. The foremost reason is the human factor: physical proximity confers advantages for both individual workers and financial firms. For individuals, it is the stimulus of being surrounded by like-minded colleagues and competitors at the heart of the markets. For firms, it is the breadth and depth of the labour market for highly skilled, specialist staff. The terrorist threat could tilt the balance against concentration and in favour of dispersion.

The demise of Lower Manhattan as a specialist financial district will be gradual – though further terrorist outrages would doubtless accelerate the process. Although many firms displaced by the events of September 11 have returned, others have chosen not to and the likelihood is that over time more firms will chose to remove themselves – or a large part of their operations – from the line of fire by relocating elsewhere in New York City or further afield. Wall Street – the place – will get new tenants who provide a less tempting target for terrorists.

But for the other Wall Street – the US wholesale financial services industry – the damage inflicted by the September 11th attacks and the crisis of the early 2000s should prove no more than temporary setbacks. Indeed, studies suggest that the process of globalisation, with the integration of more and more countries, including perhaps China, India, Indonesia and Brazil, into the international financial system, will provide an unprecedented boost for the international financial services sector. From the ashes of Ground Zero, a yet mightier US wholesale financial services industry will arise, which, most likely, will continue to be known by its traditional shorthand: Wall Street.

Appendix 1: Financial-services industry institutions and organisations

American Bankers Association
1120 Connecticut Avenue NW
Washington, DC 20036
Tel: +1 800 5512572
E-mail: custserv@aba.com
Website: www.aba.com

American Bankers Insurance Association
1120 Connecticut Avenue NW
Washington, DC 20036
Tel: +1 202 6635163
Fax: +1 202 8284546
E-mail: sspires@aba.com
Website: www.theabia.com

American Financial Services Association
919 18th Street NW
Washington, DC 20006
Tel: +1 202 2965544
Fax: +1 202 2230321
E-mail: afsa@afsamail.org
Website: www.americanfinsvcs.com

American Stock Exchange
86 Trinity Place
New York, NY 10006
Tel: +1 212 3061000
Fax: +1 212 3061802
Website: www.amex.com

Bank Administration Institute
One North Franklin, Suite 1000
Chicago, IL 60606
Tel: +1 800 2249889
or +1 312 6832464
Fax: +1 800 3755543
or +1 312 6832373
E-mail: info@bai.org
Website: www.bai.org

Bank for International Settlements
PO Box
CH-4002 Basel
Switzerland
Tel: +41 61 2808080
Fax: +41 61 2809100
E-mail: email@bis.org
Website: www.bis.org

Bank Securities Association
303 West Lancaster Avenue, Suite 1C
Wayne, PA 19087
Tel: +1 610 9899047
Fax: +1 610 9899102
E-mail: bsa@ix.netcom.com.
Website: www.bsanet.org

Bond Market Association
40 Broad Street
New York, NY 10004
Tel: +1 212 4409400
Fax: +1 212 4405260
Website: www.bondmarkets.com

Boston Stock Exchange
100 Franklin Street
Boston, MA 02110
Tel: +1 617 2352000
Fax: +1 617 5236603
Website: www.bostonstock.org

Chicago Board of Trade
141 West Jackson Boulevard
Chicago, IL 60604-2994
Tel: +1 312 4353500
Fax: +1 312 3413306
Website: www.cbot.com

Chicago Board Options Exchange
400 South LaSalle Street
Chicago, IL 60605
Tel: +1 312 7865600
Fax: +1 312 7867409
Website: www.cboe.com

Chicago Mercantile Exchange
30 South Wacker Drive
Chicago, IL 60606
Tel: +1 312 9301000
Fax: +1 312 9303439
Website: www.cme.com

Chicago Stock Exchange
One Financial Place
440 South LaSalle Street
Chicago, IL 60605
Tel: +1 312 6632222
Fax: +1 312 7732396
Website: www.chicagostockex.com

Cincinnati Stock Exchange
400 South LaSalle Street, 26th floor
Chicago, IL 60605
Tel: +1 312 7868803
Fax: +1 312 9397239
Website: www.cincinnatistock.com

Commercial Finance Association
225 West 34th Street, Suite 1815
New York, NY 10122
Tel: +1 212 5943490
Fax: +1 212 5646053
E-mail: postmaster@cfa.com
Website: www.cfa.com

Commodity Futures Trading Commission
Three Lafayette Centre
1155 21st Street NW
Washington, DC 20581
Tel: +1 202 4185000
Fax: +1 202 4185521
Website: www.cftc.gov

Depository Trust & Clearing Company
Tel: +1 212 8551000
Fax: +1 212 9082350
Website: www.dtcc.com

Federal Deposit Insurance Corporation
550 17th Street NW
Washington, DC 20429-9990
Tel: +1 202 7360000
E-mail: publicinfo@fdic.gov
Website: www.fdic.gov

Federal Financial Institutions Examination Council
2000 K Street NW, Suite 310
Washington, DC 20006
Tel: +1 202 8727500
Website: www.ffiec.gov

Federal Reserve Bank of New York
33 Liberty Street
New York, NY 10045
Tel: +1 212 7206130
Website: www.ny.frb.org

Federal Reserve Board
20th Street and Constitution Avenue NW
Washington, DC 20551
Tel: +1 202 4523000
Website: www.federalreserve.gov

Financial Institutions Insurance Association
21 Tamal Vista Blvd, Suite 162
Corte Madera, CA 94925
Tel: +1 415 9248122
Fax: +1 415 9241447
Website: www.fiia.org

Financial Markets Center
PO Box 334
Philomont, VA 20131
Tel: +1 540 3387754
Fax: +1 540 3387757
Website: www.fmcentre.org

Financial Services Co-ordinating Council
101 Constitution Avenue NW, Suite 700
Washington, DC 20001
Tel: +1 202 6242422
Fax: +1 202 6242414
E-mail: info@fsccnews.com
Website: www.fsccnews.com

Financial Services Forum
745 Fifth Avenue, Suite 1602
New York, NY 10151
Tel: +1 212 3083420
Fax: +1 212 3087383

Financial Services Industry Council
2000 Pennsylvania Avenue NW, Suite 6000
Washington, DC 20006
Tel: +1 202 7775000
Fax: +1 202 7775100
Website: www.fsic.executiveboard.com

The Financial Services Roundtable
805 Fifteenth Street NW, Suite 600
Washington, DC 20005
Tel: +1 202 2894322
Fax: +1 202 2891903
Website: www.fsround.org

Futures Industry Association
2001 Pennsylvania Avenue NW, Suite 600
Washington, DC 20006
Tel: +1 202 4665460
Fax: +1 202 2963184
Website: www.futuresindustry.org

International Finance and Commodities Institute
2 Cours de Rive
1204 Geneva
Switzerland
Tel: +41 223 125678
Fax: +41 223 125677
Email: info@riskinstitute.ch
Website: riskinstitute.ch

International Securities Exchange
60 Broad Street
New York, NY 10004
Tel: +1 212 9432400
Fax: +1 212 4254926
Website: www.iseoptions.com

International Swaps and Derivatives Association
360 Madision Avenue, 16th floor
New York, NY 10017
Tel: +1 212 9016000
Fax: +1 212 9016001
Website: www.isda.org

Investment Company Institute
1401 H Street NW
Washington, DC 20005
Tel: +1 202 3265800
Fax: +1 202 3265874
Website: www.ici.org

Mortgage Bankers Association of America
1919 Pennsylvania Avenue NW
Washington, DC 20006-3438
Tel: +1 202 5572700
Fax: +1 202 5572700
Website: www.mbaa.org/

Museum of American Financial History
26 Broadway, Room 947
New York, NY 10004
Tel: +1 87 798 FINANCE
or +1 212 9084519
Fax: +1 212 9084601
Website: www.financialhistory.org

National Association of Insurance and Financial Advisors
2901 Telestar Court
Falls Church, VA 22042-1205
Tel: +1 703 7708100
Fax: +1 703 7708224
Email: akraus@naifa.org
Website: www.naifa.org

National Association of Securities Dealers
1735 K Street NW
Washington, DC 20006
Tel: +1 202 7288000
Fax: +1 301 5906506
Website: www.nasd.com

National Credit Union Administration
1775 Duke Street
Alexandria, VA 22314-3428
Tel: +1 703 5186300
Fax: +1 703 5186671
Website: www.ncua.gov

National Futures Association
200 West Madison Street
Chicago, IL 60606
Tel: +1 800 6213570
Fax: +1 312 7811459
Website: www.nfa.futures.org

New York Board of Trade
Website: www.nybot.com

New York Clearing House
Website: www.nych.org

New York Mercantile Exchange
World Financial Center
One North End Avenue
New York, NY 10282-1101
Tel: +1 212 2992000
Website: www.nymex.com

New York Stock Exchange
11 Wall Street
New York, NY
Tel: +1 212 6563000
Fax: +1 212 6565557
Website: www.nyse.com

Office of Thrift Supervision
1700 G Street NW
Washington, DC 20552
Tel: +1 202 9066000
Fax: +1 202 8980230
Website: www.ots.treas.gov

Options Industry Council
The Options Clearing Corporation
One North Wacker Drive, Suite 500
Chicago, IL 60606
Tel: +1 888 6784667
or +1 312 4636193
Fax: +1 312 9770611
Website: www.optionscentral.com

Pacific Stock Exchange
115 Sansome Street
San Francisco, CA 94104
Tel: +1 415 3934000
Fax: +1 415 3934202
Website: www.pacificex.com

Philadelphia Stock Exchange
1900 Market Street
Philadelphia, PA 19103-3584
Tel: +1 215 4965000
Fax: +1 215 4965653
Website: www.phlx.com

The Risk Management Association
One Liberty Place
1650 Market Street, Suite 2300
Philadelphia, PA 19103-7398
Tel: +1 800 6777621
Fax: +1 215 4464101
Website: www.rmahq.org

Securities and Exchange Commission
450 Fifth Street NW
Washington, DC 20549
Tel: +1 202 9427040
Website: www.sec.gov/

Securities Industry Association
120 Broadway, 35th floor
New York, NY 19271-0080
Tel: +1 212 6081500
Fax: +1 212 9680703
Website: www.sia.com

Society of Financial Service Professionals
270 South Bryn Mawr Avenue
Bryn Mawr, PA 19010-2195
Tel: +1 610 5262500
Website: www.financialpro.org

Appendix 2: **Principal players**

Many thousands of firms are participants in the Wall Street markets. Here are brief profiles of some of the principal Wall Street banks and investment banks. All the data on assets and principal activities is for the end of 2001 or is the latest available.

Bank of New York
One Wall Street,
New York, NY 10286
www.bankofny.com

		Principal activities	% share total revenues
Total assets	$81 billion	Securities servicing and global payments services	47
Shareholders' equity	$6 billion	Financial market services	17
Employees	19,181	Corporate banking	17
		Retail banking	11
		Private client and asset management	8

Established in 1784 by Alexander Hamilton, the Bank of New York is Wall Street's oldest bank. It provided the first loan to George Washington's new government and was the first corporate stock to be traded on the New York Stock Exchange upon its foundation in 1792. In the 19th century it took a leading role in the finance of US canal and railroad construction and the development of industry in the New York region.

During the 20th century the Bank of New York focused on corporate lending and the processing of the daily transactions of Wall Street's securities brokers. It also has a significant retail banking business with 350 branches in the New York metropolitan area and administrative offices in nine other states. In 1988, the Bank of New York absorbed another venerable New York bank, Irving Trust, an acquisition that made it the tenth largest US bank. The establishment of an overseas presence began in 1966 with the opening of an office in London. It has 29 branches and representative offices in 26 countries, plus a network of over 2,300 correspondent banks.

Bear Sterns

383 Madison Avenue,
New York, NY 10179
www.bearstearns.com

		Principal activities	% share total revenues
Total assets	$185 billion	Fixed income	33
Shareholders' equity	$5 billion	Institutional equities	24
Employees	10,452	Investment banking	15
		Global clearing services	17
		Wealth management	11

Bear Stearns was established in 1923 as an equity trading house and prospered in the 1920s bull market. From the outset, it also traded government securities and soon emerged as a leading player in the Treasury market. In the 1960s, it expanded its retail securities operations and began to open regional offices. It developed investment banking activities from 1970s.

Today it is a mid-sized US investment banking, securities trading and brokerage firm. In addition to its headquarters in mid-town Manhattan, it has offices in eight other US cities and 11 locations overseas. US activities generate 89% of net revenues. Employee stock ownership, both directly held and through compensation plans, amounts to 44% of the total outstanding, an unusually high proportion that helps to align employee and stockholder interests.

Citigroup

153 East 53rd Street,
New York, NY 10043
www.citigroup.com

		Principal activities	% share total revenues
Total assets	$1,051 billion	Global consumer	48
Shareholders' equity	$81 billion	Global corporate	38
Employees	268,000	Global investment management and private banking	10
		Investment activities	4

Citigroup is the largest financial services company in the world, with a presence in more than 100 countries. It combines the corporate and retail commercial banking activities of Citibank, the insurance products of Travelers Group, and the investment banking and securities business of Salomon Smith Barney. It is the world's largest credit card issuer.

Citibank traces its origins to the City Bank of New York, which was formed in 1812 to meet the financing needs of a private group of New York merchants. In 1865 at the end of the Civil War, it upgraded its state banking remit under charter to a national remit under charter and took the name National City Bank of New York. This change permitted it to undertake such profitable functions on behalf of the US Treasury as distributing the new national currency and acting as an agent for government bond sales. Upon the opening of the transatlantic cable in 1866, a project in which its chairman was closely involved, National City adopted the wire code address "Citibank".

Focusing on corporate banking, National City expanded steadily preserving a reputation for prudence and soundness that led to its emergence as the biggest bank in the United States in the 1890s. Its lead was consolidated through a series of acquisitions in the opening decades of the 20th century. In the 1920s it pioneered personal banking services and consumer loans. Through an associate, the National City Company, it also developed a thriving securities underwriting and distribution business.

In 1897, National City became the first big American bank to open a foreign department specialising in the finance of overseas trade. In the 1900s it developed ties with foreign correspondent banks all over the world. Beginning in Buenos Aires in 1914, it rapidly built a Latin American branch network. The acquisition of the International Banking Corporation in 1915 brought branches in Europe and Asia. By 1917, National City had an international network of 35 branches, far more than any other US bank.

National City was hard hit by the depression of the early 1930s, slipping to third place. Moreover, it was obliged by the Glass-Steagall Act 1933 to divest the National City Company, which was shut down. During the 1930s and 1940s it pursued a defensive strategy, successfully holding onto its branches and the rest of its business. Rapid growth resumed in the 1950s, but by the end of the decade it was running out of sources of funding. Citibank's solution in 1961 was an ingenious new form of deposit, the negotiable certificate of deposit (CD), which, by eliminating the "funding squeeze", facilitated rapid expansion in the 1960s.

As a top money centre bank, Citibank was a prime recipient of petrodollar balances from the oil producers in the 1970s. It deployed the funds as loans to Less Developed Countries (LDCs), particularly in Latin America. The onset of the LDC debt crisis in August 1982 was bad for Citibank and its shareholders. In 1987, it set aside $3 billion for bad debts, the largest ever corporate write-down. Its problems were compounded by a blizzard of bad debts in the commercial real estate market. The outcome was a $2.6 billion recapitalisation in the early 1990s.

The 1990s saw an uneven recovery in Citibank's fortunes. Although many of its core businesses recovered strongly, it was beset by further real estate losses and new problems such as rising credit card write-offs. In 1998, it agreed a merger with Travelers Group, an insurance company cum investment bank. The deal drove a coach and horses through the Glass-Steagall ban on the combination of commercial banking, investment banking and insurance activities, a hitch that was resolved by the passage of the Financial Modernization Act (Gramm-Leach-Bliley) 1999.

The investment banking dimension of Travelers Group comprised a combination of the large retail brokerage firm Smith Barney, acquired in 1993, plus the leading Wall Street investment bank Salomon Brothers. Salomon began in 1910 in New York as a money broker but soon moved into underwriting. Its big break came in 1917 when the flood of government securities issues to finance participation in the first world war provided an entrée into the lucrative government-bond market. Expansion continued in the 1920s boom, and as a bond house the firm avoided the fallout from the 1929 crash.

In the 1930s, it attracted attention for making the first bond issue under the new New Deal regulatory arrangements. Activity picked up during the war due to government war bond issuance, and continued into the prosperous 1950s. The 1960s saw a huge expansion of business and Salomon's arrival as one of the top tier Wall Street underwriters. Diversification began in the second half of the decade, with an expansion of merger and acquisition activity and the opening of offices in London, Hong Kong and Tokyo in the 1970s. The market turbulence of the 1970s presented problems, but there were opportunities too and the firm entered the 1980s as the largest dealer in US government securities. It was a vigorous participant in the leveraged buy-out boom of the 1980s and expanded the advisory side of its business. The late 1980s and early

1990s saw a variety of set-backs and losses, which resulted in Salomon being overtaken in the league tables by other leading Wall Street firms. In 1997 it was acquired by insurance giant Travelers Group.

Credit Suisse First Boston

FFCC, P.O. Box 900,   11 Madison Avenue,
8070 Zurich, Switzerland   New York, NY 10010
www.csfb.com

		Principal activities
Total assets	$1,023 billion	Investment banking, comprising:
Shareholders' equity	$44 billion	– Securities Division
Employees	27,550	– Investment Banking Division
		Asset management

Credit Suisse First Boston (CSFB) is a global investment bank that provides a range of financial services from 78 locations in 37 countries to corporate, institutional and public sector clients and wealthy individuals. It is a wholly owned subsidiary of Credit Suisse Group (CSG), a Swiss banking and financial services company founded in 1856. CSG comprises CSFB, its investment banking and asset management arm, and Credit Suisse Financial Services, its retail business.

Credit Suisse's participation in international investment banking began in 1970 when it formed a joint venture with White Weld, a dynamic US investment bank that was active in Europe and a leading firm in the eurobond market. In 1974, the joint venture was renamed Credit Suisse White Weld (CSWW) following an injection of capital by Credit Suisse which made it the largest partner. In the mid-1970s, CSWW ranked second only to Deutsche Bank in eurobond underwriting. Problems at White Weld in New York led to a merger with Merrill Lynch in 1978. Being unable to come to an agreement with Merrill about a way forward, Credit Suisse took full control of CSWW.

Credit Suisse had two options for developing the business: internal organic growth; or the formation of a new joint venture with another partner. Wary of the cost and risk of the go-it-alone path, an alliance was negotiated with the leading Wall Street investment bank First Boston Corporation in 1978. Under the terms of this agreement, First Boston acquired an interest in CSWW (renamed CSFB) while Credit Suisse took a 25% shareholding in First Boston.

First Boston originated in the 1920s as the underwriting subsidiary of the First National Bank of Boston (FNBB). In 1934, following the Glass Steagall Act 1933, the spun off securities underwriting subsidiaries of Chase and FNBB combined to form First Boston Corporation (FBC). Inheriting a strong client list and good connections with former commercial banker colleagues, FBC prospered and in the 1960s and 1970s was bracketed as a top tier Wall Street investment bank, along with Goldman Sachs, Merrill Lynch, Morgan Stanley and Salomon Brothers. But it was slow to develop an international dimension to its business, a short-coming that was remedied by its tie-up with Credit Suisse.

CSFB prospered in the 1980s, ranking first in global equity underwriting and amongst the top three in global debt financing. But mounting competition, especially from the Japanese banks, and internal dissension at FBC after the 1987 market crash led to a capital restructuring in 1988. The outcome was that Credit Suisse purchased a controlling interest in First Boston, which was merged with CSFB to form CS First Boston. A further restructuring in 1996 led to a new injection of capital and another name – Credit Suisse First Boston. The acquisition in 2000 of mid-sized Wall Street firm Donaldson, Lufkin & Jenrette, further enhanced its investment banking capabilities.

Deutsche Bank

Taunusanlage 12,
D-60262 Frankfurt am Main, Germany
www.deutsche-bank.com

31 West 52 Street,
New York, NY 10019

		Principal activities	% share total revenues
Total assets	$903 billion	Corporate and investment banking	57
Shareholders' equity	$39 billion	Private clients and asset management	36
Employees	94,782	Corporate investments	7

Deutsche Bank is Germany's foremost bank and the eighth largest bank in the world, ranked by assets. Formed in Berlin in 1870, it has weathered two world wars, three economic depressions and a divided Germany to become one of the world's leading financial institutions. It is a "universal bank", undertaking a full range of financial activities including retail banking, investment banking, asset management and other financial services, as well as having extensive investments in industrial and other companies.

Having lost all its overseas operations as a result of the war, Deutsche Bank began to re-establish an international presence in the 1960s. In 1968, in conjunction with three other European banks, it established a toe-hold in the United States through the formation of the European-American Bank & Trust Company in New York. It opened its own first US branch office in New York in 1979.

The 1980s saw a major expansion of its foreign operations, especially in investment banking with the strategic objective of building a global investment bank. In the wake of the stock market crash in October 1987, when other firms were laying off staff, its US securities affiliate, Deutsche Bank Capital Corporation, increased its workforce. The following year, at a moment when many foreign firms were leaving, Deutsche Bank entered the US treasury market. In 1990 the Federal Reserve recognised Deutsche Bank Government Securities Inc as a primary dealer in US government securities.

A series of acquisitions accelerated the development of Deutsche Bank's investment banking business: in the US, C.J. Lawrence Inc, in 1986, and ITT Commercial Finance Corporation in 1995; in Canada, McLean McCarthy, in 1988; and the following year, Morgan Grenfell, one of London's leading merchant banks. In 1999, Deutsche Bank purchased Bankers Trust New York Corporation, establishing a major footprint on Wall Street. In 2001, 16% of Deutsche Bank's staff were located in North America.

Bankers Trust was founded in 1903 by a consortium of New York national banks to provide trust services to their customers. It subsequently developed into a major wholesale bank catering to large corporations and wealthy individuals. It also established a significant presence overseas, particularly in London. By the late 1990s, the business comprised four core activities: commercial banking, money and securities markets, corporate financial services, and fiduciary services. In 1997, it acquired retail securities broker Alex. Brown.

Goldman Sachs
85 Broad Street,
New York, NY 10004
www.gs.com

		Principal activities	% share total revenues
Total assets	$312 billion	Trading and principal investments	40
Shareholders' equity	$18 billion	Commissions	19
Employees	22,677	Financial advisory services	13
		Underwriting	11
		Asset management	9
		Securities services	8

Goldman Sachs is perhaps the most highly esteemed and influential Wall Street investment bank.

Founded in 1869 by a German immigrant, its initial business was dealing in promissory notes. Moving into securities trading, in 1896 it became a member of the NYSE. In 1906, it conducted the first of many IPOs. In the next few years it organised issues for a clutch of small companies that grew into large corporations, including Sears Roebuck, F.W. Woolworth, Continental Can and Merck, establishing a continuing relationship.

The firm prospered in the 1920s, but its investment subsidiary Goldman Sachs Trading Corporation suffered severe losses from the 1929 crash. Recovery was achieved in the mid-1930s through the development of trading in commercial-paper and the revival of both primary market and secondary market securities activities. After a lull during the war and immediate post-war years, in the 1950s and 1960s it made further forward strides: in 1956 it co-managed the Ford Motor Company's landmark IPO; and in 1967 it successfully handled the largest block trade ever made, which established its pre-eminence in institutional trading.

Goldman's unsurpassed effectiveness in transactions services such as block trading and arbitrage as well as in equity research, propelled it to the top of the underwriting league tables in the late 1970s and early 1980s. It did not participate in the leveraged buyout and junk bond booms of the mid-1980s, bolstering its status but at a cost in profitability. But the early 1990s saw record profits: in 1993 it was one of the most profitable companies in the world, and as a partnership the bulk of the profits went to the 150 partners.

The following year, 1994, saw a sharp drop in profits due to trading losses in the bond market and other misfortunes. This triggered an exodus of partners that depleted the firm's capital base, which raised the issue of the appropriateness of the partnership form of organisation for a leading Wall Street investment bank in an era of corporate giants – all the other firms had incorporated years earlier. Moreover, impending regulatory changes posed the threat that the firm would be vulnerable to a takeover bid by a commercial bank. After anguished debate amongst the partners, a successful IPO was conducted in 1999.

J.P. Morgan Chase

270 Park Avenue,
New York, NY 10017-2070
www.jpmorganchase.com

		Principal activities	% share total revenues
Total assets	$693 billion	Investment banking	51
Shareholders' equity	$41 billion	Treasury and securities services	12
Employees	90,000	Investment management and private banking	8
		Retail and middle market financial services	29

J.P. Morgan Chase is the name adopted following the acquisition of J.P. Morgan by Chase Manhattan in 2000, a combination of two of the most venerable US banks. It was the culmination of a process of concentration amongst the New York wholesale commercial banks that had been underway since the 1950s, and had accelerated in the 1990s. The outcome is a giant bank whose activities encompassed global commercial banking, investment banking, asset management, private equity, and retail banking and insurance.

On the Chase Manhattan side, the earliest predecessor was the Manhattan Company, which was formed in 1799 as a rival to the Bank of New York with an office at 40 Wall Street. During the 19th century the Bank of Manhattan developed into a substantial regional retail bank with a prosperous New York City client base. Chase National Bank was established in 1877, named after Salmon P. Chase, Secretary of the Treasury under Abraham Lincoln. Focusing on corporate accounts, it grew rapidly, as did its associate Chase Securities Corporation which became a major underwriter and distributor of stocks and bonds in the 1920s bull market. In 1930, following the acquisition of seven other major New York City banks, it emerged as the largest bank in the world.

The merger that created Chase Manhattan in 1955 combined Chase's corporate and international wholesale activities and the Bank of Manhattan's retail operations. Under the direction of David Rockefeller in the 1960s and 1970s, the bank became closely and controversially associated with US foreign policy. In the 1980s it was battered by a run of domestic bad loans and the LDC debt crisis, as well as growing competition from rising regional banks. It responded with a major attack on costs that resulted in a several rounds of redundancies and curtailed operations. In 1995, it was acquired by Chemical Bank, which adopted the more prestigious Chase Manhattan name.

Chemical Bank, founded in 1823, was another New York bank that conducted a mixture of retail and corporate banking activities. In 1991, it merged with Manufacturers Hanover Corporation, at the time the largest bank merger ever. The combination of Chemical Bank and Chase Manhattan in 1995 created the largest bank in the United States. Yet further acquisitions included the investment banks Hambrecht & Quist, in 1999, and Robert Fleming, in 2000. A few weeks after the takeover of Fleming, it was announced that Chase Manhattan was merging with J.P. Morgan.

The origins of J.P. Morgan go back to 1838, though the name was not adopted until 1861. Its senior partner, John Pierpont Morgan was the dominant figure on Wall Street in the late 19th century and early 20th century, playing a key role in the financing of US industrialisation. During the first world war, the firm raised millions of dollars for the Allied governments and it continued to prosper in the 1920s.

Following the passage of the Glass-Steagall Act 1933, J.P. Morgan elected to pursue commercial banking and its investment banking operations were hived off as Morgan Stanley. In 1942, additional capital was raised by a public issue. In need of yet more capital, in 1959 J.P. Morgan merged with Guaranty Trust to form Morgan Guaranty Trust (it reverted to the original name in 1969).

From the 1960s, J.P. Morgan developed investment banking and securities activities outside the United States, especially in London. It was an early beneficiary of the relaxation of the Glass-Steagall restrictions that began in the 1980s, being the first bank to be allowed to underwrite corporate debt securities in 1989 and equities in 1990. In the 1990s, it expanded its US investment banking business, but at a slower pace than did the pure investment banks. Asset management was another growth area, being boosted by the acquisition of a controlling interest in American Century Investments in 1997.

The acquisition of J.P. Morgan by Chase Manhattan at the end of 2000, created the third largest US bank (behind Citigroup and Bank of America). The combined mega-bank retained both brands, using the J.P. Morgan brand for its investment banking, wholesale and international operations, and Chase for its retail activities.

Lehman Brothers

745 Seventh Avenue,
New York, NY 10019
www.lehman.com

		Principal activities	% share total revenues
Total assets	$247 billion	Fixed income	33
Shareholders' equity	$8 billion	Investment banking	29
Employees	13,090	Equities	27
		Client Services	11

Lehman Brothers is a mid-sized international investment bank. Its global headquarters are in mid-town Manhattan, with regional headquarters in London and Tokyo. In 2001, US operations generated 63% of total revenues, Europe 29%, Asia 7% and Latin America 1%.

Founded in 1850 by German immigrants, Lehman Brothers was originally a commodities trading firm. Investment banking business was developed by the second generation and by the beginning of the 20th century the firm was a leading Wall Street underwriter. In 1977 it merged with another venerable "white shoe" investment bank, Kuhn Loeb, and in 1984 it became part of Shearson Lehman American Express, at the time the second largest Wall Street securities industry firm. But the combined entity was torn by cultural problems and in 1994 Lehman Brothers was spun off as an independent firm.

Merrill Lynch

4 World Financial Center,
New York, NY 10080
www.ml.com

		Principal activities	% share total revenues
Total assets	$419 billion	Private client services	46
Shareholders' equity	$20 billion	Global markets and investment banking	45
Employees	57,400	Investment management	9

Merrill Lynch is the largest retail brokerage firm in the United States and a global investment bank. It opened for business as a broker in 1914, but soon diversified into securities underwriting. In 1930, having foreseen and largely avoided damage from the Wall Street crash, the retail broking business was sold and the firm focused on investment banking. But ten years later the businesses were reunited in pursuit of a radical new business model, a "department store of finance" to provide the full range of retail clients' investment requirements. During the 1940s and 1950s, Merrill Lynch vigorously and imaginatively promoted retail investment, establishing itself as a household name. In 1959, it became the first Wall Street firm to incorporate.

During the 1960s, the firm diversified its activities and expanded internationally. Through a series of acquisitions, it entered the government bond market in 1964, real estate in 1968 and asset management and options trading in1970. A London office was opened in 1960, which allowed participation in the growing eurobond market. Over the decade it opened 20 overseas offices, being the first American brokerage house to establish a presence in Tokyo in 1961.

The firm's expansion necessitated greater capital and in 1971 it became the second NYSE member to make a public issue. The launch of its Cash Management Account in 1977, a money market account with chequing and credit card facilities, constituted a successful challenge to the commercial banks. Its acquisition of leading international investment bank White Weld the following year, gave a major boost to its capital markets capabilities; a decade later it was topping the US and global debt and equity underwriting charts for the first time.

International expansion continued in the 1980s and 1990s, notably in Asia. A regional headquarters was established in Hong Kong in 1982 and in 1985 it became the first foreign securities firm to become a full member of the Tokyo Stock Exchange. In 1993, it was the first US securities firm to open an office in the Republic of China. With the acquisition of the UK securities firm Smith New Court, in 1995, Merrill Lynch became the biggest equity firm in the world. Acquisitions in America, Britain and Australia in the late 1990s substantially enhanced its asset management business. By 2001, the firm had 13,900, employees outside America, 24% of its total workforce.

Morgan Stanley

1585 Broadway,
New York NY 10036-8293
www.morganstanley.com

		Principal activities	*% share total revenues*
Total assets	$482 billion	Securities	66
Shareholders' equity	$20 billion	Credit services	19
Employees	61,300	Investment management	15

Morgan Stanley was a creation of the Glass-Steagall Act 1933, which required the separation of commercial and investment banking. J.P. Morgan, Wall Street's foremost firm, chose to continue to conduct business as a commercial bank. The firm's investment banking business was spun-off to the new firm, incorporated in 1933, that was headed by the former J.P. Morgan partners Henry Morgan and Harold Stanley. Thanks to Morgan's prestige and contacts the new firm prospered from the outset; its clients included nearly half the top-50 US corporations and within a couple of years it had emerged as the leading Wall Street underwriter.

In 1941 Morgan Stanley became a member of the NYSE, brokerage commissions forming a crucial source of income during the war. The firm's post-war recovery was blighted by the launch by the Justice Department in 1947 of a suit against Morgan Stanley and 16 other investment banks alleging a conspiracy in restraint of competition. The antitrust suit was eventually thrown out in 1953 and Morgan Stanley reassumed its leadership of the investment banking sector.

The 1950s and 1960s were prosperous decades for the firm. Milestones included its record $300 million bond issue for General Motors in

1954. It established a French subsidiary to broaden international operations in 1967, and in 1969 diversified into real estate. The early 1970s saw dynamic development in a series of directions: in 1972, it created a mergers and acquisitions department; in 1973, it opened a research department and made a forceful entry into the equity markets; and in 1975, it established an asset management division. But the 1970s also saw a shift from "relationship banking" to "bottom line banking", a development that undermined the firm's business advantage.

Although Morgan Stanley's business continued to expand, in the early 1980s it failed to keep abreast of the muscular conduct of some rival firms. The mid-1980s saw the advent of a new and more aggressive management team. The adoption of a more forceful business strategy necessitated an increase in capital and with this objective Morgan Stanley went public in 1986. By the end of the decade, the firm had regained its leading position.

At the same time, the firm was aggressively diversifying, both operationally and geographically. Operationally, the foremost direction was asset management. Geographically, the focus was on Europe, particularly London, and emerging markets. By the mid-1990s, Morgan Stanley was generating more than half its revenues outside the United States. Today, the firm has more than 700 offices in 28 countries.

In 1997, Morgan Stanley merged with Dean Witter, Discover, the fourth largest US retail brokerage firm, which also had a large credit card business. The combined firm was, at the time, the largest asset management company and securities firm in the United States. Morgan Stanley gained access to millions of retail customers through Dean Witter's extensive network of sales offices, which, in turn, saw an increase in stock offerings and investment products as well as access to international markets.

UBS

GHDE CA50-AU
P.O. Box, 8098
Zurich
Switzerland
www.ubs.com

		Principal activities
Total assets	$838 billion	Wealth management and business banking
Shareholders' equity	$29 billion	Global asset management
Employees	69,700	Global investment banking (UBS Warburg)
		US securities and investment banking (UBS PaineWebber)

UBS is a Swiss-based international bank and financial services firm. It was formed in 1998 through the merger of Union Bank of Switzerland and Swiss Bank Corporation. With 1,500 offices in 50 countries, it has a presence in all the major financial centres. Staff are located 41% in Switzerland, 39% in the Americas and 20% in other European countries and elsewhere.

In 2000, UBS established a substantial presence on Wall Street through its acquisition of PaineWebber, a major US broker-dealer and asset management firm. Formed in 1880 as a retail brokerage house, by the 1920s PaineWebber was one of the largest retail brokers on Wall Street with 25 branch offices. During the 1960s and 1970s it expanded nationally, having 229 branches by 1980. It also developed institutional broking and asset management, and went into investment banking through a merger with the well-known firm Blyth Eastman Dillon in 1980. In 1994, it acquired another legendary Wall Street house, Kidder Peabody, making it the fourth largest US broker-dealer firm.

Today UBS PaineWebber, based at 1285 Avenue of the Americas in New York, is one of the top US broker-dealer firms and wealth managers. In 2001 it had 8,718 financial advisors operating from 369 offices across the United States, with 1.9m client relationships and $460 billion of invested assets.

Appendix 3: Key events, 1792–2002

1792	Buttonwood agreement – forerunner of NYSE established
1817	NYSE adopts formal constitution and rents building
1861–65	US Civil War – big government bond issues
1866	Transatlantic telegraph cable links Wall Street with London market
1867	Introduction of the electric stock ticker at NYSE
1873	Stock market crisis
1878	Telephone installed at NYSE
1889	*Wall Street Journal* begins publication
1896	Dow Jones Industrial Average – publication begins
1895–1904	Corporate merger boom
1901	US Steel formed – first $1 billion corporation created by J. P. Morgan
1903	NYSE moves to large new building at 18 Broad Street Stock market panic – J. P. Morgan stabilises the Market
1908	American Stock Exchange created
1912	Pujo hearings into the Wall Street "Money Trust"
1913	Federal Reserve System established
1914–18	First world war
1914	NYSE closed for 4 months due to war
1917	US enters war – Liberty bond sales boom
1920	Charles Ponzi's chain letter style investment scheme in Boston collapses
1921	Anarchist bomb explodes outside J. P. Morgan building at 23 Wall Street, kills 30 passers-by
1920s	National City Bank and other commercial banks conduct substantial securities underwriting business competing with the investment banks
1924–25	Mutual funds begin in Boston
1924–29	1920s NYSE bull market
1929	Stock market crash
1929–33	Great Depression
1932	Insull Utility Investments, a massive utilities combine, collapses
1932	Ivar Kreugar, a failed financier, commits suicide

1932–34	Pecora hearings into Wall Street business practices
1933–40	New Deal banking, securities and investment legislation
1933	Banking Act (Glass-Steagall) – separates conduct of securities underwriting, commercial banking and insurance activities
1934	Securities and Exchange Commission established
1938	NYSE reforms – management made more professional
1939–45	Second world war
1941	US enters war – Pearl Harbor attack – war loans
1944	Bretton Woods agreement on fixed exchange rates
1948–53	Antitrust suit against 17 top investment banks – thrown out in 1953
1950–53	Korean War
1953–59	1950s NYSE bull market
1957	Standard and Poor's 500 index launched
1963	Interest Equalization Act – inadvertently promotes rise of the euromarkets
1963	President Kennedy assassinated – stock prices plunge 3%
1960s	Merger boom associated with the formation of conglomerates
1964–75	Vietnam War
1966	NYSE Composite index launched
late 1960s	Back office "paper crunch" – broker-dealer firms overwhelmed by paperwork
1970	NYSE approves public ownership of member firms
1970–74	Investors Overseas Services scandal
1971	NYSE incorporates
1971	NASDAQ established
1971	Dollar devalued – end of Bretton Woods system of fixed exchange rates
1972	Chicago Mercantile Exchange introduces currency futures contracts – first financial derivative
1972	Money market mutual funds launched
1973	Chicago Board Options Exchange established to trade financial options
1973	Black/Scholes paper on options pricing
1973	Equity Funding Corporation scandal
1973	Depository Trust Company established as central securities depository
1973	Quadrupling of oil price leads to global recession 1973–75
1973–74	Stock market slump

1974	Franklin National Bank fails
1974	Employee Retirement Income Security Act (ERISA) – enhances employee retirement funds protection
1975	"Mayday" – abolition of securities brokerage fixed commissions
1975	Bomb placed by Puerto Rican nationalists at the Fraunces Tavern, a Wall Street landmark, kills four
1977	Merrill Lynch launches its Cash Management Account – competes with banks for retail deposits
1977	First "original issue" junk bond underwritten by Lehman Brothers Kuhn Loeb
1977	"Bought deal" – aggressive new underwriting technique – launched
1979–80	Hunt Brothers silver market corner collapses
1979	Second oil price shock – Federal Reserve raises interest rates to fight inflation
1982	"Shelf registration" (Rule 415) of new securities permitted by SEC
1982	Mexico unable to service foreign debts – start of LDC debt crisis
1982	Garn-St Germain Act – allows savings and loans to diversify their assets
1982–87	1980s bull market
1983	BankAmerica buys discount broker Charles Schwab – marks beginning of banks' re-entry into securities business
1986	Insider trading scandal – Ivan Boesky arrested
1985	Onset of savings and loans crisis – lasts till early 1990s
1987	Citicorp makes $3 billion provision against LDC loans
1987	Stock market crash
1988	RJR Nabisco $32 billion leveraged buyout by KKR (completed 1990) – largest ever takeover
1989	Junk bond market collapses
1990s	Mergers and acquisitions boom
1990	Drexel Burnham Lambert files for bankruptcy
1990	Michael Milken pleads guilty to fraud
1990–91	Gulf War
1991	BCCI fraud
1991	Charles Keating of Lincoln Savings and Loan convicted
1991–2000	1990s bull market – longest ever
1993	World Trade Centre bomb

1995	Netscape IPO marks beginning of the technology stocks boom
1995	Daiwa's New York branch loses $1.1 billion due to rogue trader
1997–98	Asian economic crisis
1997	Morgan Stanley merger with Dean Witter
1998	Long-Term Capital Management – leading hedge fund bailed out
1998–2000	Technology stocks bubble
1998	Citigroup formed by merger of Citicorp and Travelers
1999	Goldman Sachs IPO
1999	Deutsche Bank buys Bankers Trust
1999	Financial Modernization Act (Gramm-Leach-Bliley) – repeals Glass-Steagall restrictions on the combination of financial-services activities
2000	Dow Jones Industrial Average peaks at 11,500, and then declines
2000	NASDAQ Composite index slumps
2000	J. P. Morgan Chase formed by merger of J. P. Morgan and Chase Manhattan
2001	AOL-Time Warner merger – largest ever with combined value of $340 billion
2001	Terrorist attacks on World Trade Centre and Pentagon kill thousands
2001	Enron, large energy trading company, reveals vast losses and files for bankruptcy
2002	Financial and corporate scandals proliferate – Global Crossing, Tyco, Adelphia, QWest etc.
2002	WorldCom, a major telecoms corporation, becomes biggest ever corporate bankrupt
2002	Arthur Andersen, accountants to Enron, collapses
2002	Sarbanes-Oxley Act – brings accountancy profession under the oversight of the SEC and requires corporate chief executives to certify their companies accounts

Further reading

Carosso, V., *Investment Banking in America: A History* (Harvard University Press, London [distributed by OUP], 1970).

Clowes, M.J., *The Money Flood: How Pension Funds Revolutionized Investing* (Wiley, New York, 2000).

Corporation of London, *London – New York Study: The Economies of Two Great Cities at the Millennium*, Final Report, June 2000.

Cross, S.Y., *The Foreign Exchange Market in the United States*, Federal Reserve Bank of New York, 1998.

Economic Report of the President 2002, United States Government Printing Office, Washington DC, 2002.

Chancellor, E., *Devil Take The Hindmost: A History of Financial Speculation* (Macmillan, London, 1999).

Endlich, L, *Goldman Sachs: The Culture of Success* (Little Brown, London, 1999).

Federal Reserve Board Flow of Funds Accounts of the United States, Federal Reserve Board, Washington DC, 2002.

Geisst, C.R., *Wall Street: A History* (OUP, New York, 1997).

Hayes, S.L. III and Hubbard, P., *Investment Banking: A Tale of Three Cities* (Harvard Business School Press, Boston, 1990).

Hayes, S.L. III (ed.), *Wall Street and Regulation* (Harvard Business School Press, Boston, 1987).

Henriques, D.B., *Fidelity's World: The Secret Life and Public Power of the Mutual Fund Giant* (Touchstone, New York, 1995).

Kindleberger, C., *Manias, Panics, and Crashes: A History of Financial Crises* (Macmillan, London, 1978).

Levinson, M., *Guide to Financial Markets* (The Economist/Profile Books, London, 1999).

McGahey, R., Molloy, M., Kazanas K. and Jacobs, M.P., *Financial Services, Financial Centers: Public Policy and the Competition for Markets, Firms, and Jobs* (Westview Press, Boulder, Colorado, 1990).

Miller, N.C., *The Great Salad Oil Swindle* (Coward McCann, New York, 1965)

Mishkin, F.S. and Eakins, S.G., *Financial Markets and Institutions* (Addison Wesley, Harlow, 1998).

Sobel, R., *Inside Wall Street* (W. W. Norton, New York, 1977).

Sobel, R., *Salomon Brothers 1910-1985* (Salomon Brothers, New York, 1986).

Sobel, R., *The Big Board: A History of the New York Stock Market* (Free Press, New York, 1965).

Sobel, R., *The Great Bull Market: Wall Street in the 1920s* (W. W. Norton, New York, 1968).

Index

Figures in italics refer to line graphs, those in bold to Tables. 'NYC' indicates New York City.